D0311143

Praise for UNDERGROUND AMERICA

"Bold and heartbreaking." —John Hood, *Miami SunPost*

"Average news-watchers who think they have a grasp on the immigration debate may well find these stories, speaking for millions of invisible American residents, no less than revelatory." —*Publisher's Weekly*, Starred Review

"The storytellers hold many different jobs, have different reasons for leaving home and different expectations about U.S. life. Decades after arriving, many want desperately to go home and cannot." —Susan Salter Reynolds, *Los Angeles Times*

"Throughout *Underground America*, the mistreatment of illegal immigrants painfully echoes this country's shameful past of slavery. These immigrants are now an invisible force that has helped grow our economy and infrastructure—they've built America, but have nothing to show for it." —Holly Otterbein, *Philadelphia City Paper*

"*Underground America* is an excellent introduction to an ongoing social disaster. It gives a face to people in the country who are one injury, one legal problem, away from ruin." —Oscar Villalon, *The California Report*

"This book is both archive and call to action, a document and a communiqué. These narratives complicate and trouble the mythologies around 'illegal immigrants'; the combination of stark and sometimes brutal concrete description of lived experience and astute analysis on the part of the people recounting those experiences undermines the received notions that 'they are taking our jobs,' or 'they are merely a drain on the system . . .'" —Jen Hofer, *CultureStrike*

"The editors have chosen these tales with an eye for human rights violations and abuse. But they have also found inspiring stories."
—John Freeman, *Houston Chronicle*

"'McSweeney's Voice of Witness Series is dedicated to illuminating human rights crises through oral history,' and this new installment is an enlightening look at the plight of two dozen of the many people living here without legal documentation. You will be inspired to get out there and do something!" —Lisa Sharp, Nightbird Books, Fayetteville, Arkansas (Book Sense/ Indie Notable Book)

"*Underground America* does an excellent job of showing the human side of the underground world of millions people in the United States."
—Susanna Zaraysky, *New America Media*

UNDERGROUND AMERICA

UNDERGROUND AMERICA

NARRATIVES OF UNDOCUMENTED LIVES

EDITED BY
PETER ORNER

ASSOCIATE EDITORS
ANNIE HOLMES · JAYKUMAR MENON

ASSISTANT EDITORS
TOM ANDES · POLLY BRESNIK · CORINNE GORIA
SANDRA HERNANDEZ · DAVID WILLIAM HILL
JOELL HALLOWELL · ALEX GORDON · MIMI LOK
AGUSTIN MAYES · DANTIA MACDONALD
A. NICOLE STEWART · AILEEN S. YOO

Interviews by
TOM ANDES · NEELANJANA BANERJEE
DOUG FORD · CORINNE GORIA · JOELL HALLOWELL
SANDRA HERNANDEZ · DAVID WILLIAM HILL · ANNIE HOLMES
MIMI LOK · MICHELINE MARCOM · ELIZABETH MCGRAIL
EDIE MEDIAV · JAYKUMAR MENON · PETER ORNER
NICK REGGIACORTE · ALBERTO REYES · IRUM SHIEKH
A. NICOLE STEWART · DEBORAH RAE TURNER · CORRIN WILLIAMS
YUMI WILSON · AILEEN S. YOO

VOICE OF WITNESS

Copyright © 2008 Voice of Witness

All rights reserved, including right of
reproduction in whole or part in any form.

For more information about Voice of Witness, see voiceofwitness.org

Verso
UK: 6 Meard Street, London W1F 0EG
US: 20 Jay Street, Suite 1010, Brooklyn, NY 11201
www.versobooks.com

Verso is the imprint of New Left Books

ISBN: 978-1-78663-231-9

Cover photos by Theo Rigby
Printed in the USA

EXPERT CONSULTATION AND ASSISTANCE FOR THIS BOOK

BANAFSHEH AKHLAGHI
*National Legal Sanctuary for
Community Advancement*

CATHY ALBISA
*National Economic and
Social Rights Initiative*

RADHIKA BALAKRISHNAN
Marymount Manhattan College

ELVIS CINTRA
Hispanic Interest and Services

VICKY CINTRA
Hispanic Interest and Services

DOUG FORD
*University of Virginia, School of
Law/Legal Aid Justice Center*

TERESA FOSTER
Immigration Consultant

ADAM JEFFRIES
Farmworker Legal Services

SANDRA HERNANDEZ
Los Angeles Daily Journal

BROOKE HEWSON
*American Immigration
Lawyers Association*

THOMAS KEENAN
*Interdisciplinary Human Rights
Project, Bard College*

DAVID KRAUSE
Dominican University

SIN YEN LING
Asian Law Caucus

JOREN LYONS
Asian Law Caucus

RACHEL MEEROPOL
Center for Constitutional Rights

JAYKUMAR MENON
*Centre for International
Sustainable Development
Law*

LORENZO OROPEZA
*Community Worker,
California Rural
Legal Assistance*

NANCY PALANDATI
*California Rural
Legal Assistance*

ROBERT PRESKILL
Corporate Law Group

CONSUELO SANDOVAL
*United Methodist Mexican-
American Ministries*

RENEE SAUCEDO
La Raza Centro Legal

GREG SCHELL
*Migrant Farmworker
Justice Project*

PAROMITA SHAH
*National Immigration Project
of the National Lawyers Guild*

PENNEY SCHWAB
*United Methodist Mexican-
American Ministries*

JEP STREIT
Cathedral Church of Saint Paul

MATTHEW STRUGAR
Center for Constitutional Rights

DONALD STULL
University of Kansas

MATT THOMPKINS
Day Worker Center

FRED TSAO
*Illinois Coalition for
Immigrant and Refugee Rights*

LEE TUCKER
*National Immigration Project
of the National Lawyers Guild*

DEBORAH RAE TURNER
Dallas Morning News

CORRIN WILLIAMS
*Community Economic
Development Center of
Southeastern Massachusetts*

STEVEN WONG
Lin Ze Xu Foundation

SHELDON ZHANG
San Diego State University

CHRISTIAN ZLOLNISKI
University of Texas at Arlington

ADDITIONAL INTERVIEWERS: Anisse Gross, Will Pritikin, Stacey Tomkins, Andrew Touhy. TRANSCRIBERS: Justin Carder, Matt Carney, Jennifer King, Rachel Meresman, Jeff Porter, Selena Simmons-Dufin, Leanne Vanderbyl, Wyatt Williams, Miranda Yaver. TRANSLATORS: Polly Bresnik, Paulette Chow, Patsy Kng, Angie Kirk, Carmen Letona, Alberto Reyes Morgan, Miguel Trelles. PROOFREADERS: Elisa Bonesteel, John Farley, Drew Gilmour, Adam Krefman. COPY EDITOR: Georgia Cool. RESEARCH: Chris Benz, Alexandra Brown, Darren Franich. FACT CHECKER: Alex Carp. OTHER: Jordan Bass, Eli Horowitz. LEGAL ADVISOR: Doug Ford. DEVELOPMENT ADVISOR: Dantia MacDonald. MANAGING EDITOR: Chris Ying. FOUNDING EDITORS: Dave Eggers, Lola Vollen.

CONTENTS

VOICE OF WITNESS

Voice of Witness (VOW) is a non-profit dedicated to fostering a more nuanced, empathy-based understanding of contemporary human rights crises. We do this by amplifying the voices of men and women most closely affected by injustice in our oral history book series, and by providing curricular and training support to educators and invested communities. Visit www.voiceofwitness.org for more information.

EXECUTIVE DIRECTOR & EXECUTIVE EDITOR: Mimi Lok
EDITOR: Dave Eggers
MANAGING EDITOR: Luke Gerwe
EDUCATION PROGRAM DIRECTOR: Cliff Mayotte
EDUCATION PROGRAM ASSOCIATE: Claire Kiefer
RESOURCE DEVELOPMENT ASSOCIATE: Natalie Catasús

CO-FOUNDERS

DAVE EGGERS
Founding editor, Voice of Witness; co-founder of 826 National; founder of McSweeney's Publishing

LOLA VOLLEN
Founding editor, Voice of Witness; founder & Executive Director, The Life After Exoneration Program

MIMI LOK
Co-founder, Executive Director & Executive Editor, Voice of Witness

VOICE OF WITNESS BOARD OF DIRECTORS

IPEK S. BURNETT
Author; depth psychologist

MIMI LOK
Co-founder, Executive Director & Executive Editor, Voice of Witness

CHARLES AUTHEMAN
Co-founder, Labo des Histoires

KRISTINE LEJA
Senior Development Director, Habitat for Humanity, Greater San Francisco

NICOLE JANISIEWICZ
Attorney, United States Court of Appeals for the Ninth Circuit

JILL STAUFFER
Associate Professor of Philosophy; Director of Peace, Justice, and Human Rights Concentration, Haverford College

TREVOR STORDAHL
Senior Counsel, VIZ Media; intellectual property attorney

ALL STORIES ARE REFUGEES FROM DANGEROUS LANDS

by Luis Alberto Urrea

Undocumented immigrants have no way to tell you what they have experienced, or why, or who they are, or what they think. They are, by the very nature of their experience, invisible. Most of us pass them by—some of us might say a prayer for them, some of us wish they would return to their countries of origin. But nobody asks them what they think. Nobody stops and simply asks.

Let me tell you a brief story.

Outside of Chicago, there is a pancake house. The busboys are all undocumented. Nothing particularly unusual about this. Yet one of them is particularly worthy of notice: I'll call him Alex. Alex is short and fierce—he looks like an Aztec warrior. He has a ponytail. His arms are covered with tattoos. He is a death-metal guitarist.

He's also straight-edge: no drugs, no cigarettes, no alcohol. He lives six miles from the restaurant, rooming with an undocumented single mother. They are not romantically involved.

Alex helps his hostess keep house; he pays rent; he cooks for her; and he helps the children with their schoolwork. They show him how to use the computer. He rides to and from work every day on a bicycle donated to him by a Republican businessman who eats breakfast at the pancake house several days a week and noticed that Alex worked faster and harder than the waitresses. He chose to reward Alex's excellent work ethic.

That the benefactor is a Republican is not really shocking. After all, the suburb where Alex works is overwhelmingly conservative: Bush/Cheney bumper stickers still, though tattered, proudly adorn many SUVs. The businessman, of course, is legal. It is always important to point this out. Legal aliens always do.

It is also not surprising, for those who know much about the squalid border situation, to hear that Alex has parents back in Mexico who, betrayed by Mexico's chaos and corruption, are old and infirm and have no money with which to survive. Alex sends the majority of his money home to help his parents and, more importantly, his kid brother. Alex doesn't want this brother to come north. Alex isn't proud to be here. He's working so hard he can't afford to return home to see his brother get married—but he is managing to help pay for that wedding and that family's sad homestead in the Motherland.

Here's the part that you might find surprising.

After one of the busboys from the pancake house hanged himself in his closet, unable to take the pressure of the illegal life, Alex discovered a lump in his own throat. The owners of the restaurant got him to a clinic. The biopsy cost five hundred dollars. It was cancer. There was no way Alex could afford the surgery—he couldn't even afford the biopsy.

Alex was going to die.

But the American businessman of the American pancake house had another idea. He didn't want Alex to die. The old-timers who ate their oatmeal and waffles every day, the moms stopping by after dropping their kids off at school, the cops, the store clerks from the strip-mall, they didn't want Alex to die either. Not like that. Not alone and forgotten.

They took up a collection and paid for the entire thing. They covered the medical costs and the surgery. Right there in the pancake house, they took up collections and set up donation jugs, and they saved Alex's life. And this, too, is a reason why he doesn't think he can go home yet. He feels he owes his service as thanks.

There will be people outraged by this story. Why is Alex our problem?

Maybe it's a human story.

* * *

In listening lies wisdom. Decide whatever you want to decide. Put on your WHAT WOULD JESUS DO bracelet and carry water around Arizona for the parched souls wandering in the desert, or put on your night vision goggles and get your lawn chair out on the Devil's Highway and hunt down some illegals. But first, inform yourself. I have been struggling to silence my own prejudices on this issue for years. I am trying to pay attention.

It should serve as an indication of how truly lacking understanding is on this issue that those who suggest we stop and educate ourselves are often vilified as apologists for the invasion. If one were to, oh, let's say edit a book of oral histories of the immigration experience, that editor would be amazed at how quickly claims of America-hating follow. It might be interesting to note here that looking at the stories of these immigrants does not, perforce, dictate that the looker is against our sovereign nation's well-being. The old cliché, knowledge is power, is true. Perhaps we should recall that the first great American anti-immigration political movement of times past was called the Know-Nothing Party.

I am telling you this not as a traitor, but as a patriot. I love my country, and so do the editors of this book. Real patriots are not afraid of the truth, and they are not afraid to love the stranger. How can we understand the problem if we don't listen? How can we fix it if we don't understand it?

—LAU, 2007

PERMANENT ANXIETY

by Peter Orner

In the fall of 2005, I represented an asylum-seeker in a case before the Immigration Court in San Francisco. It was my first case since I left the law to write fiction. My client, Eduardo, was from Guatemala. In the 1980s, the Guatemalan army carried out a campaign of systematic murder against indigenous people like Eduardo. His father was killed, but Eduardo, his mother, and sister were spared death. Instead, they were held captive and terrorized for nearly a decade in the home of a paramilitary officer. It was in this house in a slum far from his native village that Eduardo and his sister grew up.

In Eduardo's own words:

> We stayed in his house. Even when the man was gone, we didn't leave the house. We didn't play with other children in the area. When I was about five years old, I pastured cows with my sister. Sometimes we would lose one and stay out until five or six in the evening to try and find it. If we couldn't find it we'd tell the man, shaking with fear. He'd take out a whip and

beat us, leaving our backs bloody. Or he'd use an extension cord or television antenna. When my mother tried to defend us, he would shove her and threaten her with a machete. Anytime there was a problem, that man would hit my mother and tell her he was going to torture her, quarter her. One day I asked my mother what "quarter" meant. She told me, "It's when they remove pieces of a person's body when they're still alive."

When he was fourteen, Eduardo managed to escape to Guatemala City, where, for the first time, he went to school. Seven years later, his mother and sister also escaped. It was then that his former captor made it known through his network of paramilitary contacts that he was looking for Eduardo. So, at twenty-two, Eduardo fled Guatemala, making his way north through Mexico to the U.S. border. There he swam across the Rio Grande into southwestern Texas, where he was arrested on the north bank. Eduardo requested asylum and was placed in temporary detention, a place he later said was a lot like jail. Later, with the help of lawyers and relatives, he was released and eventually made his way to California, where I took on his case.[1]

Given the details of his story and the fact that being granted asylum rests primarily on a few basic principles—including whether the asylum seeker has been persecuted in the past on the basis of at least one of several factors, among them ethnicity, and whether he reasonably fears that such persecution might happen again in the future—I went into the hearing with confidence. Call me naïve. That day in October 2005, the judge rushed through the case, comporting herself with an air of *I've heard all this before.*

---

[1] I was working as a volunteer with the Immigration Unit of the Lawyers' Committee for Civil Rights, a national organization with an office in San Francisco. The Lawyers' Committee matches lawyers with people in need of assistance with their asylum cases. I was assisted on Eduardo's case by Leticia Pavon.

Asylum denied.

Afterward, as Eduardo and I sat there dumbfounded, staring at the empty judge's chair (in my memory, it keeps spinning after she departed), the opposing government counsel came over and said, not without sympathy, that Eduardo had been credible and that our case had been a strong one. She suggested that the judge might have just simply seen one too many Guatemalans that day.

One too many Guatemalans. Over the next few months those words rattled around my head. Eduardo had survived a horrific experience only to be considered one of too many. Maybe Eduardo's essential problem was his very existence. His presence alone seemed to have pushed the judge over some imaginary line.

Even so, I thought, the courts acknowledge asylum-seekers like Eduardo. His story was heard, if not quite listened to. Afterward, I began to think about all those other people out there implied in the phrase *one too many Guatemalans,* which seemed to me another way of saying *one too many stories.*

Of course, not everyone who enters this country illegally has a good case under U.S. asylum law. Poverty, for instance, no matter how severe or degrading, is not considered a cause for asylum. Still, I couldn't help thinking how many stories—legally tenable or not—go untold. The truth is that many millions of immigrants in this country, the so-called undocumented, are here to work—for themselves and for their families. We hear a lot about these people in the media. We hear they are responsible for crime. We hear they take our jobs, our benefits. We hear they refuse to speak English. But how often do we hear *from* them?

I may have lost Eduardo's case,[2] but as a writer I believe strongly in the power of stories to render absurd certain distinctions drawn by

---

[2] The good news for Eduardo is that it wasn't lost for good. On appeal, his case was overturned and he was granted asylum, in a rare reversal by the Board of Immigration Appeals. He is now living and working in California.

our laws.[3] I also have faith that a reader willing to walk in someone else's shoes for a while will take more time than a hurried judge to listen to a life story.

So with the help of a dedicated team of graduate students in the Creative Writing Program at San Francisco State University, as well as a group of volunteer lawyers, writers, and independent filmmakers, I began searching for stories. These stories became a part of Voice of Witness, a book series devoted to publishing the oral histories of people around the world who have had their human and civil rights violated.

Our interviewers spread out across the country to listen and collect the stories of more than sixty people.[4] We went to New York City and Washington, D.C. and Chicago and Houston. We traveled to Dodge City, Kansas; New Bedford, Massachusetts; Biloxi, Mississippi; and Mount Vernon, Washington. We talked to people in living rooms, on the street, in public libraries, in nursing homes, and once in the parking lot of a putt-putt golf course. We received valuable assistance from generous individuals we met along the way, including an endlessly resourceful Roman Catholic sister in western Kansas, an airport shuttle-bus driver in Washington, D.C., and a poet in Galesburg, Illinois, among many others.

There were also times when we did not have to go looking very hard to find stories. A number of our direct connections were made through friends and family. Consider your own life: what is the degree of separation between you and someone who lacks documents that allow them to stay in this country legally?

---

[3] There may be a legal difference between an asylum-seeker trying to prove persecution and what one might call an economic refugee, but I contend that in the face of a desperate human being, the difference can become almost meaningless. In addition, often people do not even apply for asylum out of fear of deportation should they lose, choosing instead to risk living here as an undocumented person.

[4] Twenty-four of which were chosen for this book.

Our process was hardly systematic, and this book is not a comprehensive examination of the life of undocumented immigrants in the United States in 2007. Yet I'm not even sure such a thing is possible. We are, after all, talking about a diverse population that is estimated to total somewhere between twelve and fifteen million people.[5]

Although statistics show that a significant proportion of the undocumented come from Latin America, we cannot begin to talk honestly about this population without recognizing that they hail from across the globe. What follows in this book are the accounts of individuals from more than a dozen countries, including Mexico, China, South Africa, Colombia, Peru, Pakistan, Guatemala, and Cameroon. As we gathered these stories, recurrent patterns began to emerge, the most predominant being that many of our narrators cannot depend on the basic legal protections most of us take for granted. In story after story, the law is most often something to fear, not something to call upon for help.

Further, the law forces undocumented people to live in a state of permanent anxiety. The sheer number of undocumented immigrants makes it impossible for the government to enforce immigration laws uniformly. Because we lack the resources, political will, and social consensus to uniformly enforce, meaning deport twelve to fifteen million people, we choose to penalize the few, and allow the majority to live in fear. But the undocumented are not, to use a term I must have picked up in law school, per se criminals no matter how much we treat them as such. Needless to say, arbitrary enforcement leads to incredible paradoxes. Some of the narrators in this book are in college

---

[5] No reliable figures exist because the undocumented have not been counted. Congress has estimated the number to be about twelve million people, while other estimates, including one released by Bear, Stearns & Co., place the number at twenty million. See: *Christian Science Monitor,* "Illegal Immigrants in the U.S.: How many are there?" May 16, 2006.

and live more or less openly; others toil on farms and in factories for fifteen hours a day and hide away at night. One narrator owns various businesses, employs many *legal* workers, and has assets worth almost a million dollars. Another is a cleaning lady whose daughter died in federal custody while chained to a bed.

The lack of legal protection afforded to undocumented immigrants—as well as the capricious enforcement of laws—has led to serious human rights abuses, both by the government and by those private individuals who would exploit the vulnerability of undocumented people. It is not that undocumented people do not have human rights.[6] It is that exercising these rights in the real world is another matter entirely.

The culture of anxiety that is every day life in America for the undocumented all too often precludes people from seeking protection, even when that protection may in fact be available. The fear of deportation, of being separated from one's family, of losing one's job, frequently overrides any wish to go to authorities. Examples in this book abound where the law—in the form of immigration agents, police officers, the county sheriff—is far more interested in whether a person is here illegally than other, and perhaps more egregious, violations of the law.

Yet we are a country that prides itself on our human rights record, so much so that we—to our credit—monitor violations committed by and in other countries throughout the world. At home, however, undocumented people experience significant human rights abuses that include, to name only a few here: unsafe working conditions, separation of families, arbitrary detention, forced labor, harassment, working for less than minimum wage,[7]

---

[6] Including those enshrined in the Universal Declaration of Human Rights and the International Covenant on Civil and Political Rights, as well as certain Constitutional rights, among these the right to free speech.

[7] In violation of state and federal law. For example, see California labor code §1171.5,

and violence.[8]

Given the dangers they face, we were surprised by the willingness of undocumented people to talk to us. One academic expert on labor and immigration issues told us we were wasting our time, saying that the undocumented would never put their stories on record. Yet we discovered that most people we approached were not only willing to talk, they welcomed the invitation be heard. For many of them, it was the first time anybody had ever asked them to really talk about themselves and their families.

Lately, there have been cases in which the government has appeared to retaliate against undocumented people who have dared to speak up,[9] to say, as Adela does toward the end of this book, *Here I am. See me.* The individuals you are about to meet took a risk in talking to us and allowing their stories to be shared with the public. They did it because they wanted you to read them.

In the beginning, we thought of organizing the book by occupation. The table of contents would look something like: 1. Migrant Farmworker 2. Meatpacker 3. Construction worker 4. Day Laborer 5. Nanny.

---

which states: "All protections, rights, and remedies available under state law, except any reinstatement remedy prohibited by federal law, are available to all individuals regardless of immigration status who have applied for employment, or who are or who have been employed, in this state."

[8] Undocumented people are often reluctant to report crimes to the police. For a discussion of this particular issue, see the Republican Debate in November 2007 when Mitt Romney took Rudy Giuliani to task for allowing undocumented immigrants to report crimes in New York City without disclosing their immigration status. (*Washington Post,* November 29, 2007, "In Debate, Romney and Giuliani Clash on Immigration Issues")

[9] A prominent recent case of possible government retaliation involves Elvira Arellano, 32, mother of an American-born son. See the *New York Times,* August 21, 2007, "Illegal Immigrant Advocate for Families is Deported." In another case, one involving an undocumented Vietnamese student, the legally present parents and siblings were jailed temporarily after their daughter commented publicly on the DREAM Act, a pending bill in Congress that would open a path to citizenship to undocumented children who came to the U.S. with their undocumented parents. See *USA Today,* "Immigrant's Family Detained After Daughter Speaks Out," October 16, 2007.

We abandoned this idea after one of our narrators, the man who calls himself El Mojado, put it this way: "One job? Last year I worked in a dairy. Now I lay carpeting. I used to work in a body shop. Before that I was a meatpacker... I've sold chickens." Or take Inez, who told us, "I've lived here for three years. The Hudson Valley, New York. At first I picked cherries. I got to be as dark as this chocolate brown sofa. So much sun. After a while a girl asked me to work with her on housecleaning. You see how all my life is work? I'm in a restaurant now. I wash dishes for however many hours they need me. I don't stop washing until my hands are rubbed raw."

These men and women cannot be summed up by the jobs they do, no matter how hard or how many hours a day they work. In fact, the only thing that truly links them together is their lack of federal immigration status—in other words, certain pieces of paper. An undocumented person is not undocumented at all. Of course they have documents: family photos, diplomas, driver's licenses,[10] love letters, emails, credit card bills, tax forms, homework, child's drawings...

That the people in this book are an integral part of this society and this economy is indisputable. This is not a partisan position; it's reality. Among the first American combat casualties in Iraq was a young Guatemalan marine who entered illegally into the United States as a teenager in 1997; his name was José Gutiérrez. Two weeks after his death, the United States granted Lance Corporal Gutiérrez posthumous citizenship in honor of the ultimate sacrifice he made for his country.[11]

* * *

We cannot begin to understand the situation facing undocumented people in this country unless we start listening to them directly.

Although there is much pain in these stories, *Underground America*

---

[10] In Hawaii, Maine, Maryland, New Mexico, Oregon, Utah, and Washington.

[11] CBS News, *60 Minutes II*, August 20, 2003.

is not a compendium of suffering. This is a collection of voices. These narrators are neither uniformly saints nor sinners. When they are not being detained or deported, when they are not hiding from ICE agents, the border patrol, or Minutemen—when they are not being abused on the job, when they are not being preyed upon by those who take advantage of their lack of status—the people in this book are struggling the best they can to get through the day, to keep their families safe, to make a little money, maybe even to save some. Is there anything more American than this? It's only that they must keep silent. And there's nothing very American about not being able to speak up.

—Peter Orner, 2007

EDITOR'S NOTE

The narratives in this book are the result of extensive interviews with men and women from around the United States who risk imprisonment and deportation by being in this country without documentation. A small corps of dedicated volunteers transcribed and translated hundreds of hours of recordings. Then, with the guidance of the interviewees, the editors of this book shaped those raw transcripts into first-person narratives. The sixteen core narratives and eight shorter accounts featured in this book are the end result.

In almost all the cases, the names of the narrators and their families have been changed to protect their identities. In some of the more sensitive cases, we also changed locales and company names. However, the stories themselves remain faithful to the speakers' words, and have been carefully verified to the best of our abilities.

Most of the narratives were chosen because they demonstrate gross human rights violations. Others are more subtle, reflecting the dehumanizing lack of dignity afforded to undocumented people.

Various appendices and a glossary are included in the back of the book to provide context for the narratives and some explanation of the complex machinery of U.S. immigration law. Please note that immigration law is extremely complex and regulations are subject to frequent change. The information in the appendix and glossary is advisory and not meant to be comprehensive. Additional interviews, excerpts from raw transcripts, and news articles are also available on the Voice of Witness website: voiceofwitness.org.

In the nearly five years since *Underground America* was first published, a great deal has changed, and yet much remains the same for the estimated 11 million undocumented immigrants who call this country home.

The vast majority of those men and women continue to live and work in a country that relies on their labor but largely fails to recognize their presence or contributions. The vast majority of undocumented people living in the United States continues, in spite of some signs of progress, to live in a legal netherworld. They are, of course, on a day-to-day basis, as American as any other American. Yet without the basic protections that most Americans take for granted, undocumented people remain, in many ways, both here and not here. Hence, most continue to exist with a sense of fear and mounting anxiety. And who can blame them. Life has become that much harder for many of them in recent years.

In 2012, more than 400,000 people were detained and deported under massive immigration dragnets. At the same time, some states, including Arizona and Alabama, attempted to enact their own punitive measures. The goal of these local laws was simple: make life so hard, so unbearably difficult for the undocumented, that immigrants would abandon their lives here and return to their homelands. In Alabama, lawmakers sought to require schools to look into the legal status of students. In Arizona, state officials came up with a laundry lists of laws that made it legal to harass and target Latinos—or anyone else who appeared to be foreign born—in the name of public safety. In the end, federal courts stepped in to restore some common sense and fairness. But as many of the voices in this book repeatedly explained, those who come here without documents are already forced to tolerate unspeakable hardships and abuse. They persevere because they have no choice. Like previous waves of emigrants, Diana, Elisabeth, and other narrators in this book have come here in search of a better life, or a chance to help those they left behind.

Who are the deported? They are mostly ordinary men and women: the mother who is sent back to Mexico, and leaves behind a son; the father who dies in the desert attempting to make the journey back to his family; the parents who are detained and sent packing, leaving their U.S.-born children to be placed in foster care. These are people whose lives are forever changed.

And yet, as bad as the past five years have been for those without papers, something has changed. Some immigrants refuse to remain silent, to stay in the shadows. They are the so-called DREAMers, young immigrants like Lorena and Estrella, who were brought to this country illegally as children. They are speaking out, leading marches modeled after earlier civil rights movements. And in return, they have won an opportunity to live without fear for two years under a special program that provides them work permits and a temporary reprieve from deportation.

At the same time, shifting demographics have also spurred significant changes. Federal lawmakers are currently considering the most sweeping overhaul to our nation's immigration laws in decades. Whether such legislation can survive through Congress remains unclear. But what is clear is that the voices in this book and their stories won't go away. Nor will the abuses they suffer and the tragedies they endure, unless something fundamental changes in the way we talk about those who care for our children, help harvest our food, and, above all, live right alongside us.

—Sandra Hernandez
Editor of the Spanish edition of *Underground America*
June, 2013

DIANA

AGE: *44*
COUNTRY OF ORIGIN: *Peru*
OCCUPATION: *Entrepreneur, housekeeper*
HOME: *Biloxi, Mississippi*

POLISHING THE SLOT
MACHINES BEFORE KATRINA

In Peru, Diana was running a retail store in the central highlands of the Andes when the economy soured. She came to the United States, where she found work as a cleaner on the night shift at a floating casino in Biloxi, Mississippi. On August 28, 2005, the day before Hurricane Katrina hit, management required her to work extra hours, telling her that there was going to be an inspection the next day. As the storm bore down, Diana took refuge in a church. Afterward, Diana was part of the reconstruction effort, helping to rebuild the Gulf Coast with other Latino workers. When the bulk of the construction was over, Diana was arrested for not having the appropriate documentation. She is currently free on bail. We met her over dinner at her friend's house in Biloxi, a city still recovering from the storm. She was reluctant to talk at first. After the table was cleared and our hosts had retreated to the living room to watch television, she spoke quickly in Spanish, in a low voice. "My story is very crude," she said.

I didn't really know what a hurricane was. I thought hurricanes were simply hard rain. The day before Katrina hit the Gulf Coast, everyone was leaving. But we went on cleaning: vacuuming, polishing the slot machines. They made us work extra hard that day. I said to myself, I wonder what Katrina is? What did I know? I was used to mountain thunderstorms like those in my hometown of Huancayo.

Huancayo is in the central highlands of Peru, in the Andes. I worked in the garment industry there as a retailer. I owned a store that sold clothing and shoes. During the time of Fujimori, we were doing very well. There was a lot of work, a lot of money. There was no reason to come here. Then, a recession and a loss of stability led to a change of government, and the whole economy declined. The factories were closed. There was no purchasing power. People just stopped buying. My store had no sales. In 2003, seeing very little hope, I decided to come to the United States.

I'd been to the U.S. once before, to visit my son who had immigrated about six years earlier. He'd made a long journey to cross the border into the U.S. and I hadn't seen him since he'd left. I asked God many times to help me to see my son, and made the effort to try and obtain a travel visa. That's what made it possible to visit him. I stayed with my son and worked at a poultry processing plant in Carthage, Mississippi. I was there for about five months. But when I returned to Peru, I saw a lot of poverty, saw that the economy wasn't getting any better. And so I made the decision to go back to the U.S., this time for good.

A KIND OF SOLITUDE

I'd made a lot of acquaintances working in Mississippi the first time around, so even though my son had moved to New York, I decided to go back to the south. But when I arrived in Carthage I learned that the poultry plant was no longer offering jobs to undocumented workers, only those with papers. I had no job. But then in a store run by Hispanics, I saw an ad in a Spanish-language newspaper. It was for a job at a hotel three hours away, in Biloxi. I traveled there, saying to myself, "I'm going off to a place I don't know." I was alone and had heard that hotel jobs were sometimes traps where women were captured and made to do who-knows-what. I was fearful, but I went.

There's a small Peruvian community in Biloxi. That's what made it possible for me to find a place to live. I rented a room from a Peruvian man for $250 a month, living there with a friend I'd made, a woman named Marisol. The room was very hot. We had no fans or anything. I couldn't bear it for very long. I left and moved into another Peruvian lady's apartment. She worked at the hotel and helped me get a job there. We were coworkers. I had never held that kind of job before. It was very hard work and the conditions weren't fair. The management exploited us. I only stayed at that hotel for about two months and then got a job at a place called the Grand Casino Biloxi. It was a floating casino off the Gulf shore. There I worked shifts from midnight until seven a.m.

I made $6.50 an hour as part of a cleaning crew. That came out to a little over $200 per week before taxes. Wages in Mississippi are very low. Much of our shift was spent cleaning slot machines, polishing the fingerprints off them so they would shine. It was hard work; all jobs here are hard. Life became monotonous: work and then home, and then back to work again. It was terrible to have to come home to a room of four walls, without your family by your side. Not your children, sister, mom, dad, none of your loved ones. And by this time I was living in a one-bedroom apartment with five or six others. It was the only way any of us could afford the rent and our other expenses. It is difficult to explain, but one comes to live in a kind of solitude, even though you see your coworkers and the people you live with every day.

EVERYONE ELSE WAS LEAVING

The day before the hurricane arrived, I went to work at the casino as usual. That day the management made us work like never before.

We cleaned absolutely everything, working extra hours. People were saying that Katrina was coming but I wasn't sure what it was. Where I'm from we'd never heard of hurricanes.

Everyone on the overnight cleaning crew was Hispanic. There were Americans who worked the night shift, too, but my American coworkers didn't clean. They did other jobs, like security and food service. That day, some of them said to me, "Diana, what are you still doing here cleaning? Let's go! Katrina's coming!" But everyone on cleaning crew had been told by the supervisor to stay longer than our usual hours that night, that there was going to be an inspection the next day. Everyone else was leaving. They left us there to go on working: cleaning and cleaning.

My American coworkers knew the hurricane was going to be a disaster; that's why they left. Why we were made to stay and work I don't understand because all our work turned out to be for nothing. The next day there was no casino. The hurricane had washed it away.

IN THIS RICH COUNTRY

One of my roommates was from Honduras. She had a car. The day of the hurricane, I knew it was going to be bad, so I told her, "We've got to get out of here! This is going to be terrible!" We lived only a half-block from the Gulf, but my roommate said, "I'm not going anywhere." "You'll die," I told her. "The roof will fall in on you." But she wouldn't leave and I don't know how to drive. Inside I was saying to myself, Oh my God, I don't want to die. Where could I go?

Then my friend Marisol called me. It was like a call from God. She asked me where I was going to go to get shelter from the hurricane. When I told her I didn't know, she said she'd come by to pick me up. We drove to a church—a black church. That's where we waited for the storm to pass, thank God. We watched out the window, the trees falling, the cars being blown around, and finally it was just a cloud—we didn't see anything. And then some men told us that there was a message that the worst was coming, and that the roof might be lifted from the church, and that we should all go into the kitchen where the roof was supposedly more secure. Everyone started to sing Christian music in English. That night we slept on the floor and on the pews. We were there for about twenty-four hours.

When the hurricane was over I returned to my apartment. It was in ruins. The windows were destroyed. Gone. And trees had fallen on the apartment building. Before the storm came, I'd told a girl in the building to leave. I guess she took my advice because I later learned that she had gone to a shelter at the very last minute. Good thing she did because a tree had fallen right on her apartment. Katrina was an incredible thing.

We spent fifteen days without water or electricity. And there was a shortage of food. Even the church where we had gone for shelter to wait out the hurricane was without anything. They weren't prepared to have us stay there; they couldn't help us. Later on, that church and some other churches got food and began to try and help people. We stayed at one of the churches because there was no way we could stay at our apartment. But we had nothing: no electricity, no water, nothing. And the heat in August and September was suffocating. It was so hot I don't know how we were able to endure it. We'd go looking for water at the big hotels on the waterfront, rummaging through the trash for water bottles with water still in them. It was horrible. There was no water to drink or to bathe with. There was nothing. A lot of people got sick from the flies.

After Katrina, we lived in far worse conditions than those in the places we'd left to come to the U.S. In this rich country! There was no aid. It was about a month before any help came. Until then we suffered a terrible time. Garbage was all over the street, as though there'd been an explosion. I'd never lived in such bad conditions, even in Peru. In Peru, when there's a catastrophe, aid begins to come right away. Not here. Not then.

THEY NEEDED US TO REBUILD BILOXI

After Katrina, not that many Hispanics were still in Biloxi. Many of them had left before the hurricane. The majority of people were American, white and black. When cleanup and reconstruction began there were a lot of jobs available and everyone went to work: removing mud and rocks and fallen trees and things washed in from the ocean. It was hard, dirty work and by the end of that first week most of the whites and blacks had quit. They couldn't take it.

The construction people who'd offered us our jobs began to ask for more Hispanics to work on their crews: more Hispanics, more Hispanics, more Hispanics. They asked us to call people we knew to come and work, and we did.

Laborers began coming to Biloxi, so many that there was a shortage of housing. There was no place to live. Twenty or more people slept in one house, like a hotel. And there was nowhere to eat. It was awful. We exposed ourselves to diseases working those construction jobs. The mosquitoes would bite us and leave enormous wounds. I still have spots on my legs from those bites and from the chemicals and insulation that came off the walls at those jobsites.

When the police passed by our construction sites they never stopped or said anything. The immigrant workers were necessary to get the work done. It couldn't have been done without us because American workers had quit those jobs after only a little while. They needed us to rebuild Biloxi. Now people are returning. The casinos are open again.

Most of the construction ended last year, in 2006. There were suddenly a lot less jobs. Even though the casinos had reopened there was a shortage of jobs. I was out of work. But then I was offered a job an hour away in Bay St. Louis. There aren't many Hispanics around that area. Employers have offices in Biloxi to hire Hispanics for jobs elsewhere, like in Bay St. Louis. I was hired by a service that brought people to hotels and casinos to do the cleaning, or what they call "housekeeping." I worked at a place called Hollywood Casino, from midnight until eight a.m., driven there and back in a van with my coworkers.

One day, toward the end of January, I was in the van on the I-10 with the other members of my crew. It was morning and we had just gotten through with our shift. We were in our uniforms. I was sleeping, but when I felt the van stop, I woke up. I heard my coworkers saying things like, "We've lost!" Two cruisers sat behind us, ICE agents.[1] The driver told us to stay calm.

The agents had stopped us as part of a dragnet. There was nothing suspicious about the van we were in. It belonged to the company we worked for and was all white; there weren't any marks or writing on it at all. I'm sure that the ICE agents knew well beforehand that they were going to stop us. We'd heard they were doing dragnets all over the place, especially in the part of the Gulf Coast where we were—I don't know, maybe because of the ports where ships come in from Russia and other countries.

I had been attending meetings of a group that helps immigrants, learning about what to do if I was ever in this kind of situation with immigration authorities. There I was, going through the very thing I had been learning about at those meetings. So the first thing I did was call the group on my cell phone. The woman from the office answered and I told her what was happening, asking her what I should do. She told me to stay calm, that I had my rights and knew what to say, to be strong and think about what I was going to say before I said it.

---

[1] Immigration and Customs Enforcement, a branch of the U.S. Department of Homeland Security. See the Glossary for more information.

The ICE agents asked us for our permits. Of course, none of us had any. They asked us where we worked. Some of my coworkers told them that we worked at Hollywood Casino. The agents told us to show them identification. Of course we didn't have any so they took us in to an office.

At the office they took our fingerprints, asking each person where they were from and how they got to the U.S. They wanted everyone's story. But I knew my rights from the meetings; I knew I didn't have to tell them. Then came the moment of truth. The agents put my fingerprints into a machine and asked me where I was from. I felt calm, more or less, and said, "No, I need my lawyer. I have a right to a lawyer, I have the right to make a phone call." They told me I'd get a lawyer and my phone call later and asked me again where I was from. But I refused to tell them. "Cooperate with us," they said. "Why are you making this so hard?" But I insisted on the rights I knew I had.

They detained me for a long time, repeating themselves, trying to get me to tell them what they wanted. They were really big men, muscular. They all spoke Spanish. One of them had a nasty face. He grabbed me and shook me and yelled, "Tell me the truth!" He was getting red in the face. But I kept telling them that I had a right to a lawyer and a phone call. "You'll have your lawyer when you appear in court, ma'am," they said. They kept on asking me where I was from until the man with the evil face said, "Give her the phone call." I got through to the immigrant group's office and she got a lawyer on the phone for me. But the lawyer was in Jackson and I was in Gulfport so she wasn't able to come to the ICE office. One of the agents spoke with the lawyer. I'm not sure what they talked about.

Most of my coworkers were Mexican. We had all worked the entire night and were tired and everyone began criticizing me for being stubborn. But they were ignorant of their rights. They had never gone to the meetings I had. I told them, "Don't be afraid, don't tell them where you're from, don't say anything. Just tell the agents you need a lawyer and have a right to a telephone call." The women were crying and the men were nervous. They were scared and gave the agents all the information they wanted and signed the papers the agents told them to sign. And the ICE agents learned where I was from after my coworkers said, "Look, Diana, we've lost. Just tell them you're from Peru." So the agents were able to get that information. If my coworkers had done what I did, if they had insisted on their rights, none of us would have wound up going to jail.

THOSE ARE JUST STORIES

The ICE agents told us we were going to be detained. I was treated worse than any of my coworkers, grabbed and pushed around like a criminal. It really bothered the agents that I wouldn't tell them what they wanted. They put shackles around our arms and legs and took us to a jail in New Orleans—an hour away. We were chained together at the waist, one after the other in a single file.

At New Orleans there were prisoners who were American women. We were separated from each other: the immigrants in one group, American citizens in the other. They treated us horribly. My lawyer had come to look for me at the jail in New Orleans but she never found me. I think that's because the ICE agents were retaliating against me for not cooperating with them. It was terrible there. But it was better than the place they sent us next.

We were transferred to another jail in Tensas Parish.[2] I think that prison was strictly for men. I don't know why they put women there. In the jail in Tensas we were treated the same way they treated terrorists in Peru, terrorists who had killed people. On the ride from New

---

[2] Tensas Parish is a county in northeast Louisiana, adjacent to the Mississippi River and the Mississippi border.

Orleans, we were chained up. We traveled for five hours with those shackles on our hands and feet, unable to move. If you had an itch you couldn't do anything about it.

At Tensas we were issued prison clothes. They were so torn and worn-out they looked like they should have been made into mops. My pants were old and kept falling off, so I had to tie them with a string. Then I was put in a cell with three others. It was very small, with four beds made of concrete and a toilet and a little light bulb that was on all the time, twenty-four hours a day. The beds were hard concrete with vinyl mattresses atop them and really thin blankets. We ate there, slept there, everything; four women in that tiny room, seeing each other's faces day and night.

The cell door had a slot in it for when we were brought food and water. We got breakfast at four a.m., then lunch at eleven, and dinner at six in the evening. That cell was so cold. And it smelled. We weren't able to bathe regularly. They only let us out every two days to wash, one of us at a time because there was only a single shower. Once they didn't let us bathe for a week. We were so dirty. And when we were let out of the cell to shower we went wearing shackles, dragging our chains.

A few times I told the others that we have to report this. They told me to be quiet. "But we're here in this country where human rights are respected," I said. One woman said, "Who told you that? Those are just stories."

The town mayor's wife visited us one time. She was a Christian woman and took us outside one Sunday to get some sun. Since we spent day and night in our cell with the electric light burning all the time, seeing the sky and grass and birds was a relief. We sang Christian songs with her. She gave us candy and shampoo to use during our showers. But I left that place traumatized because it was so horrible. There was one woman who was going insane from being cooped up, from not knowing where to move.

Finally, after fifteen days at the jail in Tensas we were transferred again, this time to Memphis. It was an eight-hour journey from Louisiana to a much larger prison in Tennessee where we had a little more freedom. Our bathroom areas were larger and we were locked in our rooms only during certain hours, not all the time. And there was a small outdoor patio where we could sit. But it was still very hard. I was there for a month.

I prayed to God many times because at my first hearing I had been denied bail by the judge. I was told that because I had resisted signing the papers the ICE agents wanted me to sign I was defiant and so would not be offered bail. But I have great faith in God and so I prayed to be released.

I was able to make telephone calls from the prison in Memphis. Prisoners were allowed to make calls to phones with direct lines, but they had to be collect calls and the person you were calling had to accept the charges. Thank God I had the woman from the office behind me, fighting to get me out. I kept in touch with her and she eventually was able to help me get bail as my guarantor. She drove eight hours to come pick me up.

MY ONLY CRIME WAS WORKING HARD

I'm out of jail but my troubles aren't over. I'm still going to court. If I'd known how tough the immigration laws were, I might have thought more about coming here. But even though the laws are hard on immigrants, there are chances here that don't exist in my home country. In Peru, an older person like me can't find many kinds of work. Here in the U.S. one can work at companies like casinos, hotels, factories—you're not denied work because of your race or age or sex. There's opportunity. Here—even with Katrina—there's not the kind of poverty that there is in Peru, the economic conditions that cause people to leave.

Immigrants shouldn't be treated so harshly. I know that by coming here illegally they break the law. But they don't come to the U.S. to steal or kill or cheat anyone. I invested my whole self in the jobs I worked. Home to work and back home and then back to work again: that was my life. After the hurricane came and destroyed everything I worked men's jobs, doing construction. Who else but immigrants would do such hard, constant work? We worked day and night so that Biloxi could be brought back to life.

When I left Peru I never thought I'd be treated the way I have been in the U.S. In Peru there was a lot of terrorism and war but I had always heard that this country was concerned with human rights. That's how so many people talk about the United States, especially Americans. But there were no rights for us in jail, or anywhere. Our rights aren't respected. I'm resentful of that. What angers me is that there are so many people here who live on the edge of the law. What they do goes unpunished. But I was treated like a criminal. My only crime was working hard.

There was a guard at the jail in Memphis who spoke Spanish. As I was leaving the prison he said, "Behave."

I asked him, "Why should I behave?" When I said that, the guard wanted to know why I was imprisoned.

"For working too much," I told him.

MR. LAI

AGE: *40*
COUNTRY OF ORIGIN: *China*
OCCUPATION: *Cook*
HOME: *New York, New York*

AT THE OTHER END OF
THE CORNFIELD IS AMERICA

Born in the southeastern Chinese province of Fujian, Mr. Lai ran into problems when his family violated the one-child policy.[1] He paid smugglers to provide passage out of China and arrived in the U.S. as an EWI[2] after a year-long journey, which took him through Thailand, Cuba, and Mexico. Mr. Lai has since traveled around much of the U.S. working as a cook to pay off the huge debt he owes his smugglers. He also sends money when he can to his wife and two sons back in Fujian. We first met in the Chinatown offices of a nonprofit serving the local New York Fujianese community. It was there that the polite, reserved Mr. Lai showed us the extent of a recent injury, unwrapping his bandages to reveal a reddened, swollen hand with a deep v-shaped scar. Over several more meetings held in a nearby Korean restaurant, Mr. Lai, now forty, speaks slowly in Mandarin, explaining more about his life and the events that brought him here.

---

[1] China's one-child family policy, first announced in 1979, generally restricts couples from having more than one child. The policy emerged from the belief that economic and social development would be compromised by rapid population growth.

[2] Entry without inspection. Refers to immigrants who enter the U.S. by avoiding official scrutiny.

The place I grew up was called *Cheung Lok*—Long Happiness. It was a very small farming village. People grew rice and sweet potatoes. There were only about three hundred families, a population of about a thousand. My whole family were rice farmers. I have five siblings—two older sisters, two older brothers, a younger sister. I'm the fifth child.

I was a simple kid. Nothing really bothered me. As long as I had food to eat I was fine. I didn't think about whether I was happy or not, whether my parents were rich or poor, if I had good clothes or not; those things didn't concern me. I went to school until third grade, and then I had to quit. My parents said, "Don't study anymore. We don't have the money." So I left school and started looking for work. There were too many people, and not enough food and work to go around. Everyone was a farmer, but nobody had more than a small piece of land to work. It wasn't enough. My siblings weren't going to school, either. My older sister went to school for five years but had to quit for the same reason.

So I went in search of work—herding cattle, making bricks. I was about ten years old when I started looking after cattle. I'd take them up to the mountains, herd them so they could graze on the mountainside. Thinking back to it now, it was kind of fun, always being up in the mountains, running around with the cattle. As I got older I found work making bricks. I was seventeen years old then. After that I worked various jobs in construction, which I continued to do until I came here.

Of all my siblings, I'm the only one who came over. By this time, I was married, with my own family. We were still very poor. There still wasn't enough money coming in, and I wanted to find a way to make more. Also I thought that America would be more free. You can say whatever you want in this country, but China is so strict in so many ways.

The one-child policy, for example. When I was a kid, there wasn't such a thing. People could have as many children as they wanted. But later, population control was very strictly enforced. Officials would go to homes and check up on people, put them under surveillance if they suspected them of "illegal pregnancies."[3] They came to the house one day and warned me about having more than one child. Luckily my wife wasn't at home, as she was heavily pregnant with our second son at the time. We wondered if they already knew, if someone had told them. We'd heard a lot of stories about bribery, forced abortions, forced sterilizations. This seemed to happen more in rural places—I don't know if it was because more people in these areas broke the law, or if it was easier to get away with those kinds of methods there.

People found ways around it, like not registering the birth of their first child, quickly having a second one and then registering them as twins, which are allowed. We couldn't do that, as we'd left it too long—our first son was already five. We were scared they would come back. There weren't too many roads open to us. We decided we had to run. My older sister took us in. She has an old house with an upstairs; my wife and I just hid up there all day, too scared to go outside. If her neighbors found out, they would have reported us and officials would have come for us. We were in hiding for a little over two months. My wife had the baby at my sister's house. Later I found that officials knew about our second pregnancy and had come looking for us. When they couldn't find us, they went to our house and destroyed it, just tore the place down.

I was really angry about this, but I couldn't do anything, couldn't say anything. The whole family would have been in trouble. You had to be careful. You couldn't offend the party. You just can't criticize

---

[3] Varying provincial laws determine what constitutes a legal pregnancy. Generally, population authorities determine legality based on family history—if the family's first child was a girl or disabled, the family is allowed to have a second child—and whether or not the area's yearly child quota has been reached.

the government there. If you do, you'll get thrown in jail. There was also the six thousand RMB fine,[4] for having a second child. We were poor—we couldn't pay it. It was during this time that I first started having ideas about going to America. I'd been hearing people talk about how democratic America was, that there was freedom of speech. At the time I thought I could go over, and then send for my wife and my sons, and then we could have two or three more children! I love kids, I really do. But after I left, the government forced her to have a hysterectomy. If you refuse to do what they say, they'll throw you in jail, or demote you at work. Or if they can't find you they'll destroy your house.[5] That's what they do. That's what they did to us.

The feeling that I had to find a way out for myself and my family grew stronger and stronger over the next few years. We just couldn't go on like this. This was no way to live. And I had so much anger toward the government that I really got to thinking, if I didn't get out then I'd probably just end up in jail. I just had no faith in China. I didn't know how I was going to do it, but I knew I had to go to America.

I'D JUST EAT, SLEEP, EAT, SLEEP

I can't remember much about the journey. I started in Fujian. I was given a Thai passport. The person in the photo is me, but the name is not mine. This was all arranged by the snakeheads.[6] I was intro-

---

[4] RMB (short for Renminbi) is the official currency of China. Six thousand RMB was approximately $725 U.S. in 2000.

[5] In May 2007, riots broke out in Bobai, Guangxi, in the wake of a new crackdown by the provincial government on families that break birth-control regulations. Financial penalties increased and, at the behest of Beijing, parents who failed to pay were punished by having their property confiscated or destroyed.

[6] Snakeheads are human smugglers, generally from China. The term has also been used to describe anyone involved in any aspect of a human smuggling operation, either locally or overseas. See Appendix B for more information on Chinese immigration.

duced to them by some people from my town. I didn't really know who these people were, the ones who introduced me. Just people you come into contact with, when you go out, to a bar or something, they'll say, "You have this problem? Why don't you contact so-and-so?" They were just people who were like me, in a similar position. We'd get to talking and they'd say, "I know someone."

The snakehead I met said he would take care of everything, but that it would cost me thirty thousand dollars. The deal was payment upon delivery—I would arrange to borrow this amount from loan sharks in China, then pay off the big snakehead when I got to the States. The money would go to collectors back in China, who would then give the money to the big snakehead.

It didn't matter if I trusted these people or not. I just had to try it. I agreed to everything. I got my Thai passport, and went to the airport with this guy. We stood in line together at the border control and I was supposed to follow him. I was nervous, but nobody stopped us, they just let us through.[7] We got on the plane to Thailand. I traveled with this guy, just the two of us. The whole flight I was very excited, very happy to be making the journey. Somebody came to fetch me from the airport in Thailand. I was a little scared at that point—what was I going to do if I got caught and put in jail? But the guy said I wasn't going to get caught, that everything would be fine. I was happy to believe him—my mind was set on getting to the States, the sooner the better.

I spent about three months in Thailand. I was locked in someone's house, I don't know where. I was told it was Bangkok. Everything was provided for. I'd just eat, sleep, eat, sleep. There were about twenty of us. There were about two, three people who kept order—the enforcers. All men, Chinese; they spoke Putonghua.

---

[7] Law enforcement authorities in China and many transit countries are often paid to aid illegal immigrants entering and exiting their countries.

They were average-sized, young, about twenty-seven, twenty-eight. Very fierce. They told us we couldn't go out, it was too dangerous, we might get discovered. They kept saying, "You'd better stay in line, or you'll be beaten."

They treated us fine, as long as you kept quiet, as long as you didn't say anything. If you started saying the wrong things or started getting jumpy, they might come and beat you. I saw this happen to some guys who talked too much or said the wrong thing. They beat them right in front of you. If you fought or argued, they beat you. They treated the women the same as the men.

We slept on the bare floor. Just a blanket, one underneath, on the ground, and one on top. There were about two bedrooms and one lounge, about ten people sleeping in each room. We could go anywhere within the house, but not outside. It wasn't that big, about twenty square feet. There was no furniture, nothing in the house. There was a kitchen. There were two people in there who cooked; we weren't allowed to make our own meals. Whenever it was time to eat they'd shout, "Food's ready!" We ate quietly. The food was Chinese style: rice congee. It was okay. As long as we had something, we didn't complain.

The others in the house were all from the same province, Fujian. Many from Fuzhou.[8] We would talk about what we used to do when we were back home, what we were going to do when we got to the States. It was mostly men. Some of them grew up in cities, some were from farms like me. Some were older, some were younger. But mostly men. They were all single people there. Nobody was with their family. There were a few women, but I didn't really get to know them. The women were all by themselves, too; they didn't come with their families. The women were grouped together, the men were grouped together. The men would spend the

---

[8] The capital city of Fujian.

days playing Chinese chess, poker, chatting with each other. We were really bored, but there was nothing we could do.

I didn't know I was going to be there for such a long time. I didn't know it was going to be like this. I was thinking, I wanted to go to America to be free, but here I am, locked up like a prisoner. It didn't make any sense to me. Whenever I asked the enforcers how much longer we'd have to stay, they always said, "In a few days. We'll let you go in a few days." I got tired of asking. I felt helpless. Eventually I became numb.

It was difficult to think clearly about anything. I wondered how my wife and children were. Once or twice I was able to call them, but I didn't get to talk with them for long—the enforcers didn't let us make long phone calls. And I didn't have money to make too many calls. When I spoke to my wife I just told her to take care of herself, the kids. That I was in Thailand, everything was fine. Even if things were bad I would always tell her I was fine. I didn't want her to worry. I didn't want her to think this was a mistake. I knew she was very worried about me, but I kept telling her, "Everything's fine, everything's good. I'm doing well. I have food to eat, I have a roof over my head, so don't worry about me."

When I spoke to my sons, I told them, "Your dad really misses you."

They asked me, "When are you coming back?"

And I said, "Dad isn't coming back. He's going to America, and in the future you'll come too."

BE QUIET AND WAIT

One morning in September, the enforcers woke us up and told us to go. They didn't even give us time to get our things together, just told us to leave with the clothes on our backs, but I was quick, and managed to take a small bag with me. Five of us were flown to Cuba on fake visas. The other people, some had already left here and there. You could say I made some friends there, but I haven't seen them or stayed in touch with any of them since I got to America.

It was bad in Cuba because there was still more waiting. Just as in Thailand, we couldn't leave the house. The Cuban enforcers said it was even more risky here, because we were more obviously foreign. They weren't as fierce as the enforcers in Thailand; they didn't beat us, just told us to be quiet.

Including the five from the Thailand house, there were a couple more Chinese people, so in total there were six or seven people in the house. We stayed on the second story of the house and slept on the floor. It was a bit better than in Thailand because there was carpeting. In general the place was okay, reasonably clean. At least here we could make our own meals, since none of the enforcers could cook. We ate chicken, rice, things like that. We requested the enforcers buy groceries for us. We told them what we wanted, gave them some money, and they went out and bought the food. But since they were Cuban, we couldn't really communicate all that well. A lot of hand gestures and miming, "We're hungry, we want to eat," and they'd say "Okay" by nodding their heads.

We were told to be quiet and wait; there was another snakehead in Cuba who was arranging the next step of our journey. We were there for three months, until one day we were told to pack our things—we were being taken to the airport to go to Mexico.

So this was already six months of traveling, stopping, traveling. I really had no idea it would take so long, and still I hadn't reached America. Back in Fujian, the snakehead told me it would take ten or so days to get to America. Maybe I would have reconsidered if they'd told me the truth about how long it was going to take. Maybe I still would have done it. I don't know.

AS SOON AS I GET TO AMERICA, I'LL BE AMERICAN

We got to Mexico by plane. All of us were really happy. I kept telling myself, "I just have to keep going. It's my last hurdle. And as soon I get to America, I'll be American." We spent four months in Mexico. The same kind of thing, locked in a house. But this place was really big. Outside there were pigs, chickens, sort of like a farm. There was corn growing in the middle of the land. There was so much that you could just go in there and pick it. The whole place was fenced in. We could wander around, but not beyond the fence.

So it was a bit better than before—at least you could walk outside in the fresh air—but it was very quiet. Very dull. There wasn't much to do at all. The same as before: sitting around, chatting, playing chess. We were prisoners still. By this time, though, I had become used to this kind of situation. I had become used to the waiting. I wasn't frustrated in the same way.

Sometimes I was quite happy; other times I felt that my heart was far from being at peace. I felt that I was getting closer to America, but until I actually got there, I couldn't be at peace. Sometimes I thought, I can't believe I've been gone for so long. But I had a lot of faith in myself. I had no regrets. I knew I would get there in the end.

One morning we were told to get in this big truck with about a hundred other people. There were only about ten or so Chinese; the rest were Mexican, Guatemalan, Salvadoran. As soon as we got on, we were moving. We spent sixteen or so hours in the truck. It was very difficult, very uncomfortable. We were standing or leaning the whole time. There were no windows, except for a small one above us in the roof. It was very, very hot. Very crowded. We didn't make any stops, not once during the sixteen-hour journey. We were given plastic bags to go to the bathroom with. The smell was really bad. I thought, This is just too much. This is too harsh. This is not how you treat human beings. But I also thought, If this is the only way to get to the States in one piece, I have no choice but to tolerate it. At some point it will be over.

Eventually, we arrived somewhere with a lot of cornfields. It was about one in the morning, very dark. We were told, "At the other end of the cornfield is America." Then we were told to get out and go into the corn and follow some people. The corn was very tall, taller than me. All I could see was a railroad track running alongside us, about one hundred meters away, so whenever a train came by we would squat down. Next to the railroad track was a road. There were police cars driving back and forth, patrolling the border, so you didn't dare make yourself seen. We were just walking and hiding the whole time, following the leaders. We spent about five hours walking. I didn't get tired, though. All I was thinking of was, "America, America." I could see it at the other end. Eventually we got to a wire fence. One of the leaders cut a hole in it. He pointed to the cornfields and said, "This is Mexico." Then he pointed to the other side of the hole in the fence and said, "This is America."

I crawled through that fence and got to the other side. I can't tell you how happy I felt at that moment. The first thing I saw on the other side was a railroad, and a police post. So we had to hurry up and stay down, especially since the sun was starting to come up. Further along the railroad there were three cars—before we went through, we Chinese were told the cars would be waiting for us. We ran to the cars, got in, and were driven away.

We were traveling for five, six hours with two Chinese guys—the driver and another guy. They didn't tell us where they were taking us. They just said, "This is America. But we're going to go farther." Somebody said New Mexico, but I didn't know for sure. We stopped at a motel on the way. It was good to have a break—get showered, brush our teeth, change our clothes. The second night, I was driven to L.A. When we got there the guy with the driver said, "You're really in America now. Give me the money."

What the snakehead told me back in Fujian—he was a liar. He lied about the time it would take. He also lied about the fee. He told me it was going to cost thirty thousand dollars. But when I finally got here I was told that I owed sixty thousand dollars. He said it was more because it took a lot longer than it was supposed to. I thought this was really unfair. But they wouldn't let me go until I gave them what they wanted.

I had only been prepared to borrow thirty thousand dollars from the loan sharks in China, so there was no way I could come up with the extra money just like that. Those snakeheads, they just tell lies, they never tell the truth. But one thing is true: if you don't pay up, you're not going to live.

At the time, I was staying with three others in an apartment near a Hawaiian supermarket. One woman and two men. They hadn't paid the snakeheads yet, either. The people guarding us were young men; one of them was younger than me by five or six years. They were Chinese. If these enforcers went out, sometimes they would take us out with them. If they didn't go out, we didn't go out. We were never allowed to leave the apartment by ourselves. It was better than being locked up before, because they took me out a few times. I didn't see much though, as I was only allowed short trips to the supermarket to buy fruit, vegetables, that kind of thing. Most of the time we were indoors, watching TV and videos all day.

It was the three of us men in one room, and the woman in her own room. The enforcers stayed in another room downstairs. We slept on the floor. They gave us blankets, but we still had to sleep on the floor. We couldn't really talk. If you spoke loudly, the enforcers would hit you. They kept saying, "Hurry up and get the money. If you don't get the money, we'll beat you to death."

I was constantly phoning home to try and raise more money. I called family, friends, whoever, to get them to help me. I was desperate to pay off the snakeheads and start my life in the U.S. After a month or so I managed to borrow forty thousand dollars, but it still wasn't enough. By that time the others had all left; they'd found the money and paid up. Eventually my older sister was able to get hold of some different loan sharks who lent me the extra money. After two months in L.A., I had the sixty thousand dollars to pay off the snakeheads. When the L.A. snakeheads had received confirmation from the China snakeheads that the fee had been paid, I was free to go.

I DIDN'T KNOW WHERE SOUTH CAROLINA WAS

I was given a plane ticket for New York under someone else's name. It didn't even match the fake Thai passport I was carrying, but nobody checked when I came in. I knew nobody when I arrived in New York, nobody. Nobody came to pick me up when I arrived. I was all by myself. I just got in a cab. I'd been told to just say, "Chinatown." And so I did. The driver said, "Okay." When I started seeing Chinese letters on shop fronts and street signs, I told the driver, "Stop here."

I had no idea where I was going to live. I asked some people in Chinatown where I could find a hotel. The people there said there were several hotels nearby. That's how I found the Wu Shing Hotel, which had rooms for fifteen dollars a night. I stayed in my own room, but it was tiny, with a very small bed. You pretty much just walked in, took your shoes off and lay down.

At the hotel there were a lot of people staying there who had also come from Fujian. I got to talking to one guy who said he said he was from Wang Tau. I told him, "I've only just got here. I want to look for work tomorrow. Where should I go, what should I do?" He told me not to worry, there were recruitment agencies nearby; he'd take me to one in the morning. So that's what happened.

The agent there said I could start working right away, in a Chinese restaurant. I didn't have to sign anything, but I had to pay them thirty dollars for finding the job for me. I was given a phone number for the job, area code 803. They said it wasn't in New York, that I had to take a bus there. They told me how to get to the bus station on 42nd Street. When you get there, they said, buy a ticket on a Greyhound bus to South Carolina.

I didn't know where South Carolina was, but after buying the ticket I had only two dollars left in my wallet, so I thought, Okay, it must be pretty far. Still, I didn't expect to be traveling for hours and hours and hours. In the end it took about seventeen hours, almost a day, to get there. But I didn't mind. I was excited about getting my first job in the States, excited about getting my first wage and sending money back to my family. I wanted them to see I was doing all right, and that it was the right decision to come here.

PEOPLE IN MY SITUATION

It didn't work out well in South Carolina. Straightaway the restaurant boss said, "You don't know how to cook!" And it was true. At the time I didn't know anything, I had no experience. I thought I would be given the chance to learn. Instead he got me to do basic kitchen work like cutting meat, vegetables, that kind of thing. He just kept me on for three days and then told me to go back to New York. I was really upset. I'd gone all the way down there and only managed to earn $180. I had to spend half of that to get back to New York. I felt unhappy, really defeated.

Then the recruitment agency found me another job, at another restaurant. This one had a 914 area code: Westchester, New York. Thirteen days at this place, doing more menial kitchen jobs. Philadelphia after that. The longest job I had was in Florida. I spent two years there. I'd been fired five or six times before I ended up in Florida. I also worked in Virginia, Queens, North Carolina. A few days here and there, generally menial kitchen work. Also a few days in Ohio. Texas. Alabama. Massachusetts. New Hampshire. Indiana.

A lot of places! Seattle was the farthest. I don't know why the bosses fired me after such a short time. I worked hard, did my best. But maybe they got impatient with my lack of experience. Maybe they thought there were plenty more people like me.

Some places were okay, in terms of living standards. The owner of the restaurant would say, "Sleep in the basement," or "Sleep in the lounge." I don't remember a lot about the places. It was all pretty much the same to me. I spent all my time working—a kitchen is a kitchen, that's what you see, what you do. Queens had a lot of black people. North Carolina was very clean, not a lot going on. I felt very comfortable in Houston; it had a Chinatown, with Hong Kong supermarkets, Vietnamese restaurants, a lot of Asians. I was there a little over a month. In Kentucky, I lived up on a mountain with the other restaurant workers. Every morning we would get picked up and be driven down the hill to go to work. We lived in a very old house, about one hundred years old. The wood was rotting, the whole place was unhygienic; it wasn't comfortable at all.

When I worked longer at jobs I would make about $1,600 a month. The recruitment agency would tell us beforehand how much we'd be earning. So, $1,600 sounds good, but you're working very long hours. I'd work about twelve to thirteen hours a day, six days a week. You're on your feet the whole time and have to work really fast, otherwise the bosses yell at you. The money I sent home would go to my family. I'd send the money in U.S. dollars. My wife would change the money into RMB and put most of that toward paying off the loan sharks.

There wasn't a definite time that I would send money home, because I wasn't always working regularly. When I had a job, when I had money, I'd send money back. If I didn't have a job, I wouldn't send money back. I'd usually send about a thousand, two thousand dollars home each time. The loan sharks charge very high interest. For the sixty thousand I borrowed, every month I have to pay over a thousand in interest. So even though I've been in the U.S. for a long time, I still have no money. And I have no job now, so... I hear the interest has been getting lower as people get wealthier in China. So if I borrowed sixty thousand dollars now instead of five years ago, the interest would only be about six hundred a month. A lot of people in my situation have killed themselves because they couldn't pay back the money. They couldn't even pay the interest. I've always thought I just have to keep going; I have to keep working and pay off this debt.

In between the jobs I always came back to New York. Whenever I got fired I'd come back, because it's easy to find work from here. Sure, I got tired of working in so many places, but I had no choice, with so much debt to the loan sharks in China. I had to borrow from them to pay off the people who got me here—the snakeheads. So I was tired, really tired. But as I say, I had no choice.

Most every boss I had was bad. Out of every ten bosses, eight were bad. They were horrible to everybody who worked for them, but especially to people without documentation. They would keep saying, "If you want to keep this job, do your work properly. Otherwise, leave!" Or, even if you were dead on your feet from exhaustion they said, "Work faster! Don't laze about!" Last year, in Indiana, there was an incident. There were two cooks. One of the cooks accidentally sprayed the other one's face with oil while he was cooking. So the manager told the cook who sprayed the oil that he had to compensate the other. He had to pay. But the manager took the money and kept it for himself. It was $3,500. He took it out of the cook's salary. Two months' salary. And he told him, "Get out. We don't want you here." Both the cooks were undocumented. The manager said "I'll go and get Immigration. I have documents, you don't." So the cook had to leave. He didn't dare try and stay or fight for his pay.

MAYBE THIS IS JUST THE WAY IT IS

I'd been working at this Chinese restaurant in Kentucky for about two months. I was one of five, six kitchen staff. I worked as a cook, a wok handler. It was a typical job—long days, twelve to thirteen hours in front of a hot stove. I kept to myself most of the time. I didn't really socialize with the other kitchen staff. I'm pretty quiet with people I don't know well; I don't know how to drink or tell jokes. The boss was Cantonese-speaking, so we didn't communicate well. Myself, I speak Putonghua. Sometimes he got impatient when I didn't understand what he was saying, then another worker would translate and I would get it. But apart from that, things were generally fine.

It was a typical morning. There were several workers going in and out of the kitchen to the alley. The kitchen was small and cramped so we'd use the alley for things like peeling vegetables, washing dishes and pots, that kind of thing. I went out there a few times to throw out some hot water. There was another worker nearby, a woman, who was washing dishes. I didn't really take much notice of her at the time, but I remember that at one point she left the tub of dishes. I wasn't paying attention. She must have gone inside the kitchen or restaurant to get something. After throwing some water out, I went back inside the kitchen to my stove. Suddenly everyone heard screaming—the woman came inside the kitchen, holding her hands up and screaming that her hands were burning with pain.

Then she ran inside the restaurant and came back with the manager. He had a really angry look on his face. He started talking to the workers. I could understand, "Bleach... water." So I guessed he was saying that somebody had put bleach in the woman's bucket of dish water and he wanted to know who'd done it. Nobody said anything. Several times he pointed to me, saying "Was it you?" I could understand that much.

Of course I just kept saying, "It wasn't me" and "I don't know anything." But he kept pointing and asking and I knew then he'd decided it was me. I didn't understand why, I hadn't done anything—but I noticed the woman had her eyes to the floor. The manager saw me looking at her and he waved his hands about and said what I thought was, "No, she wasn't the one who accused you."

Still, he kept pointing at me and asking, "Was it you, was it you?" Maybe he thought if he kept on at me, I'd eventually admit it. But I kept saying no, which made him angrier and angrier. He starting pushing me around, but I didn't fight back. I just turned away and went back to my stove. I just wanted to get back to work.

The next thing I knew I was getting struck from behind—at first I didn't know what was happening, but then I turned around and it was the manager hitting my back, my arms. I tried to defend myself, push him away, but it was difficult—the kitchen was so cramped, I had no space to move. I couldn't get out. I was scared. It seemed like a long time that he was hitting me. There were five or six other workers in the kitchen—some of them stood and watched. Others were carrying on with their work as if nothing was happening. I think they wanted to help me, but were too afraid. Even when you see something bad happening, you have to think of yourself. These are just people you work with; you get along just so you can work. All you really care about is keeping your job.

Then the manager grabbed a cleaver and started attacking me with it. I couldn't believe what was happening. It seemed like he really wanted to hurt me, but when he actually cut my hand open and saw all the blood, he just looked really scared and ran away.

Maybe I passed out, because I can't remember exactly what happened next, except that the police arrived, and then an ambulance, and then I was in a hospital bed. Everything after that is pretty vague, even now, months later. I just know that the whole time I was in the hospital I was afraid that I'd lose the use of my hand. At the same time, I was hopeful that the law would help me. I thought, The police, they'll do something.

The people at the Kentucky hospital were very kind. They didn't ask me to pay any medical bills. They said it was a terrible thing that happened. The doctor there cut my hand open and reconnected something, maybe the bone. He warned me, "If you're not careful, you could lose the use of your hand. And when it gets better, it's still not going to be 100 percent normal."

While I was in the hospital, someone, maybe the police, arranged for a Putonghua-speaking lawyer to come and see me. This lawyer said that the police had gone back to the restaurant and couldn't find the manager. He also said the manager had a previous record, for assault, and that the police were still looking for him. I wondered if I wasn't the first worker he had attacked. The lawyer said that for now, there was nothing else that could be done.

After about two weeks my hand was stabilized, but I still couldn't move any of my fingers. I was in a bad situation. I had no job, and the police still couldn't find the manager. This made me feel hopeless about getting any kind of compensation; it also made me feel unsafe. I didn't know what the manager was thinking, if he wanted to get revenge or something. So I had no choice but to get my things together and buy a bus ticket for New York.

Back in Chinatown, the first thing I did was go and see a man called Mr. Chen. He works for a foundation that's known for helping Fujianese people a lot. I told him about my problem and he said he'd try and do what he could. Hopefully he can help me somehow. Since the attack happened, three months ago, I've been out of work. I can't handle a wok; I can't do anything.

I can't move my thumb. My whole hand is reddened and very swollen, very stiff. The scar goes down the wrist like a V. Two big cuts. That's where the tendons are severed. I can't tighten my fist. I use this brown stuff on the skin—Chinese ointment. I've been seeing a local Chinese doctor for this. He says I'll only regain 50 percent of the use of my hand.

We're all upset about the situation. My wife wants to be here. My sons are already eleven and fifteen years old, and don't know when they'll see their dad again. I still want to get them over here, but how can I afford it, how can I arrange it? All I wanted was to make a better life for my family, but instead I've missed my sons growing up, and I've been apart from my wife for five, six years already. But even with my hand like this, even if I have to do the worst kind of work for the worst pay, my chances of paying off my debts are still better from here than in China. And even if I did want to go back, it would be impossible—I have no money to get out of the States. So you see, I have to stay.

I've heard no news about the manager in Kentucky. I have no idea what's happened. My lawyer, the one in Kentucky, has told me nothing new. I don't even know if he's helping me anymore. When he found out the restaurant wasn't covered for liability, he said, "We'll just talk about this later." I don't know what's going on in his mind. Maybe he thinks he's not going to get paid because the restaurant doesn't have money, doesn't have insurance. I don't have any news about it. I don't know if the manager was ever found, or if he was charged or not. I admit I still have some anger toward him. I don't understand how you can treat another human being like this. I have thought about finding my own lawyer here in New York. So maybe I'll ask Mr. Chen. Or maybe this is just the way it is. Maybe you just have to accept things and get on with your life.

DESPITE EVERYTHING THAT'S HAPPENED

My life now is very hard. Now that I'm not working, I stay at home, in a hotel. I share the room with five others. They're also workers, immigrants, people in similar situations. Sure, you're friendly, you all come into contact, get to know each other, but then you leave. Nobody really stays anywhere for long, so it's hard to make real friends. I can't think of the future right now. My head's full of troubles, full of worries. I can't sleep. I owe the loan sharks a lot of money. I'm separated from my family. But despite everything that's happened, I still don't regret coming over. I really don't. I still think it's better being here, trying to sort out my problems from here, than going back to life in China.

My wife and I don't talk very often. I don't have a lot of money to call her. She knows what happened, but she doesn't have all the details, how bad things have gotten. I don't want her to see the state I'm in. It'll only make her worried and feel helpless. Sometimes we'll call each other if something's happened, here or back home with the kids or someone in the family, if something's going on. If nothing's going on we won't call each other. But when we do talk, no matter what the situation is, we always end up saying the same thing to each other anyway, even if it's not true: "Don't worry, everything's all right. I'm doing well. I have food to eat, I have a roof over my head, so don't worry about me."

SALEEM, 54
Sialkot, Pakistan

Saleem grew up in a working-class family in Sialkot, a two-thousand-year-old city in Pakistan's Punjab province, famous for exporting surgical equipment and sporting goods. In his twenties, he moved to the United Arab Emirates and worked as a carpenter. After developing diabetes, he quit his job and returned to Pakistan. Unable to support his family and educate his young children, he paid a smuggler to get him to the U.S. in 1993, where he found work in Medford, NY. In December 2001, FBI and INS agents arrested him and questioned him about 9/11. Several months later, Saleem was deported to Pakistan, where he now makes ends meet by selling his wife's jewelry. He spoke Punjabi when we met with him in person in Sialkot.

On December 28, 2001, I returned from work around nine p.m. My roommate and I had just finished eating and we were watching television when I heard the bell. About eight to ten FBI and INS officers came in to the apartment. They handed me a paper and started to search the apartment. They pulled out ceiling tiles, looked through the drawing room, bathrooms, inside the washing machine, everywhere. At the end, they told me that they were arresting me for staying in the U.S. illegally. During this processing, they asked me a lot of questions about 9/11.

First they asked, "What do you think about this explosion that happened? Do you think it was good or bad?"

"It was not a good thing," I told them.

"Why wasn't it a good thing?"

"It was not a good thing because a lot of people lost their lives and whoever did it was wrong. I was having my breakfast when it happened. It should not have happened. I mean, so many people died because of that."

"Do you know Osama bin Laden?" they asked me.

"I know as much as they tell us on television," I said. They wanted me to admit that I knew something. But I didn't know anything. My routine was going to work and then returning home.

The next day they took me to the Metropolitan Detention Center (MDC) in Brooklyn, New York. All of my life, I have never showed my body to anyone. They made me strip completely. They put me in maximum security. That place is for dangerous criminals and I didn't belong there. My case was only an immigration violation. It should have been resolved in three or four days.

I never thought that it could happen to me. Neither my father nor grandfather has ever been in such a situation. We are not that kind of people. I didn't speak English and I didn't have a cellmate who could help translate for me. I was completely confused. My biggest concern was my children. Who would support my children if something happened to me?

I stayed in the high security jail for one and a half months. After I got to the general population unit at the MDC, I was able to call my wife in Pakistan. She just cried. My kids did not have the courage to talk to me. I appeared in court in February 2002 and told the judge that I want to leave. A few months later, I was deported to Pakistan. If they were going to deport me, why they did not deport me in the beginning?

After staying in jail, my back muscles have stopped working. I have the sugar disease. The tension elevated my sugar levels. When I came back to Pakistan, I checked my sugar, and it was 429 points. It should be about 120 to 130 points.

If this explosion did not happen, I would not have been arrested. They arrested primarily Muslims. In the television and everywhere else, they were making a huge fuss and saying that Muslims did it and so the enforcement officers came to arrest me. They thought that maybe we knew someone and that they would be able to get the information from us step by step. By God, we did not know anything or anyone.

ROBERTO

AGE: *43*
COUNTRY OF ORIGIN: *Mexico*
OCCUPATION: *Factory worker, cook*
HOME: *San Francisco, California*

THOSE WHO HAVEN'T FALLEN
DON'T KNOW HOW TO WALK

Roberto is a cook in a restaurant in San Francisco. He came to the United States when he was fourteen, working for fruit harvests, tortilla factories, and restaurants in California for nearly thirty years before he was granted a green card. Roberto's wife and daughter, however, were deported to Mexico in the same court proceedings. They left the U.S. three years ago. Roberto showed up to our first interview with a cake he'd made from leftover batter at the restaurant, and a chocolate Easter bunny. Unwrapping the chocolate, he cursed his fingers—they were swollen, scored with white from years of kitchen work, and had cramped up. The last interview was in Spanish, via cell phone. Roberto had left his studio apartment to give his brother's family, who've been staying with him the last year, some time to themselves. He stood on the street outside a Korean pool hall in the Tenderloin. He said he would watch the games from the window as he talked.

I was born in '64 on a small ranch outside of Purépero, in southern Mexico. At thirteen, I left the ranch and went to Mexico City. I'd stopped going to school after fourth grade and had stayed around to help my old man and my mom on the ranch, but after a while,

I needed to leave—I'd started having problems with my old man. Plus, I wanted to go earn some money for myself, see what was out there beyond our ranch.

In Mexico,[1] I got hired to work for an American company named Donald Clean. Even though I was still practically a baby they sent me up to wash windows on the tallest skyscrapers in the city: the Latin American Tower, the Continental Hotel. Up we went, three boys— none of us older than thirteen—on a plank of wood, lassos around our waists, buckets and rags, eighty stories up! We were swinging with the moon, we used to say. I remember looking down at the people in the *zócalo,* the town center, and I couldn't see even their faces— they were just little ants. I was scared to be dangling so high off the ground, but I forced myself to do it because it was my first job. They paid us a thousand pesos[2] each *quincena*[3]—not much. But I'll never forget the job because that was the first money I ever earned myself. I felt independent.

After some time in Mexico, though, I started to dislike the city. There was a lot of crime, a lot of robberies. And my father'd gotten sick. So I left Mexico and went back to Purépero.

But once there, I had even more problems with my old man. He used to hit me before but this time he beat me real bad for staying away such a long time. I got angry. After being on my own, taking care of myself, it seemed impossible for me to live with him anymore. At that point I decided to leave home for good. I decided to come to the United States.

I made my way north to the border with some others I'd heard were going. We got to Tijuana, and from there crossed through the hills in east San Diego with a coyote. That first try, I was caught

---

[1] Mexico City is often referred to as "Mexico."

[2] About sixty U.S. dollars today.

[3] Fifteen days.

by Immigration and sent back to Mexicali in a truck. We all were. I wasn't discouraged, though—I was too young to be. I stayed on the other side of the border for a week, two weeks, maybe a month, working in the fields and earning money to try and make the jump again with the coyote.

When I'd gathered enough, I jumped the border again, and this time I landed in Dulzura, California.[4] I met a guy there who bought and sold fruit from the border all the way up to Bakersfield. So he gave a couple of us who'd just crossed a lift to Bakersfield in the back of his fruit truck.

THERE ARE PLENTY OF PEOPLE OUT THERE

In Bakersfield, we met some gentlemen who invited us to harvest grapes over in Mendota. So we went to work over in that area: in Madera, Sanger, Costa Mesa; we worked all those fields. We worked there for three months and then moved on to other areas when the work dried up. We went wherever they needed workers. They would tell us show up tomorrow at such an hour, on such and such street. So you go stand there at the corner and the trucks show up. The *raiteros*[5] get out of their trucks and say, "We need five for grapes, four for cucumbers, twelve for strawberries," and so on. You offer to go and pick whatever fruit or vegetable you want to pick. The next day, same thing: such and such a street, this many people for this crop. They might say today there are no peaches, only nectarines, so they take forty over there.

With the tree fruit, they give you buckets and you secure those around your waist and you go on up the ladder, cut the fruit, put

---

[4] Dulzura is a small town twenty-five miles east of San Diego, and ten miles north of the Mexico-U.S. border.

[5] Drivers responsible for transporting day laborers.

them in the bucket, fill up the bucket and then go down. They give you a box the size of a small table, with an open top, and you dump the fruit inside. When you dump the fruit, they give you something like a coin, which you keep in your pocket. Then you do the same: go up, fill your buckets, go down, and get another coin.

For each coin, they give you a certain amount of points, depending on what you're cutting. Some of the fruit is labeled first-class and some is second-class. The first-class ones go to canneries, where they make baby food, like for Gerber. For the first-class fruit, you get ten points for each coin. For the second-class, those sold at the market, you get only five points. When you accumulate a lot of coins, you go to get paid. And it's there where they try to trick you; they steal from you. They count the coins and give you whatever count they feel like, they pay you whatever they want. They tell you the rate per coin ahead of time, but when it comes time to pay, they break their words all the time. It's how they make their money, and you can't argue with them. If you argue, they won't allow you to work again. And there are plenty of people out there looking for the same thing, looking for work.

At that time, I would offer to do anything except pick strawberries or radishes. With the strawberries, you have to crawl around, bent over, placing all the berries very carefully, right side up. The radishes are terrible because you have to be on your knees in the mud all day long. They soak the ground to make it easier to unearth them. So, from all the mud and dirt, you come out of there filthier than a pig. You're under the sun, and it gets above a hundred degrees in the middle of the day. The little onions, the chives, you pick wet too. For cilantro you have a little knife, like a hook, and you grab the bunch, you carry the rubber bands in your pocket, and you pull each bunch into the box. You have to put them all in place. But there's times when the cilantro is tiny. And that's when it's harder on the waist and back when you're cutting.

The day after cutting chives or cilantro, you don't want to get up. Your body doesn't want to. Your back is aching because you slept on the floor, too. The ranchers don't buy beds for the people that come. A bed over there is a piece of cardboard on a table. They have big corrals where you can go find a spot to sleep. There are guys that bring their family, their wives, daughters, and sons, and all these people are mixed in together. About a hundred, two hundred people in one field house, all crammed together, for as long as the picking is done. Two, three months. It's difficult there. You learn: anyone who doesn't like to share with people, they will learn to share there in the fields.

That's how we ate, too—all of us together. With ten, fifteen dollars, twenty people can eat for the week. If you don't share, you'll pay the same: ten or fifteen dollars for only one of you to eat for the week. So we would get together and agree to share, and say, here's two dollars for tortillas, and the other two dollars for a piece of meat, and, like that, you gather it all together, cook it up. When we ate after finishing in the fields, we didn't serve ourselves on plates. We'd just put the food in the middle of the table, gave everyone tortillas, and ate everything taco style—tortillas and food, nothing else. And then we went to sleep at eight in the evening, because tomorrow is a long day.

Every day before dinner we would have to wash our clothes by hand. Right there in the fields, you tip a table over and scrub your clothes on its top. The grapes ooze a lot of sugar. Nectarines are covered in this dust that makes your skin itch. Radishes ooze a lot of stuff that also makes you very itchy, gives you sores—I think it's from the chemicals they spray on them. Cilantro is the same, onions are the same. You wear gloves when you're working but, because of the sweat, your skin absorbs everything, right into the pores. A lot of people got used to showering with all their clothes on, instead of washing their clothes separately, and then they would take off their clothes and take another proper shower. You make the showers yourself, too. You have a hose you hang from a post or something and shower right there. Only, put up a cover so that people don't look at you.

There were mostly men there, but there were also some women and children—the men's families. There are families in Mexico that are very poor, and they come over here and have to set even their kids to working in the fields. So I would see eight-, nine-year-old kids working out there, in the sun, all day long. You see it, and it makes you want to cry. I didn't like to see the kids so young out there.

I was still young myself when I started working in the fields— only fifteen years old or so—but I wasn't with my family; I was alone. I was lonely and scared, but you have to keep going—with no money, no one to count on for support, you have to just keep going. You make yourself appear strong, but at the same time you're scared. You never show what you carry with you: all the time you're scared.

After a few years there, though, I knew I didn't like the field-work. So when I was in Sanger once again, I met a guy who worked on people's gardens. He worked for a man in Chico, also a gardener, and I went with him to get work there. I worked there in the gardens of private houses and condominiums. My job was to cut figures into the bushes—birds, elephants, bears, ducks. They paid me ten dollars an hour but I didn't like the work that much. It took a lot of patience, and I didn't have patience at that age. You had to keep the figure in your mind—if you didn't keep the figure in mind while cutting, you would destroy the trees. And these people with money were very strict. So after just a few months working in the gardens, I left and went down to San Jose.

$150 FOR ALL THREE

In San Jose, I got a job in a tortilla factory. They never asked us for papers or a Social Security card. All we had to do was show up, work, and then wait to see if they told us to show up the next day. It was good work, it was easy work: you would place a two-ounce ball of dough on a belt and it goes into the machine, gets pressed. You evened it out, flattened it a bit more, and then put it on the belt to go on to the oven to cook. When it comes off the belt, it's a tortilla. Up ahead there are four people. Two are counting each dozen by hand and the other two are packing them into plastic bags and putting them in boxes as they are: a dozen tortillas or four dozen or whatever it may be. The schedule was from midnight to noon, or from two in the morning to two in the afternoon. The problem was they paid us too little for all of those hours, only $4.50 an hour.

So I got another job. I went to work as a garbage collector. To get the job as driver, though, I had to have a license. So I went to the street where they sold them. There someone just asked me if I needed papers—a social, a *mica*,[6] a license. I said yes, I wanted the whole package. In those days it cost about $150 for all three. So I gave him the money, and the gentleman took me to a pharmacy to get my photo taken. He told the lady at the counter how many pictures I needed, and then told me to pay her whatever the cost was. I paid and he told me it'd be ready in an hour. So, I went home and came back an hour later and the package was ready.

With papers, I was able to get the job as a driver for the garbage collectors. That was the first time I began to work with a false social and *mica*. I still have my fake social, but not the other documents. I threw the *mica* out when I started to put my proper immigration papers in. The driver's license was taken away from me when I left the garbage collection company. That's why I lost my job, actually, because of the fake license.

I had been working there two years and then one day my boss asked for everyone's licenses, to make copies of them. When he took mine he noticed my license looked very different from my coworkers'.

---

[6] Green card.

He asked what had I done to obtain it, and that he wanted me to tell him the truth. I told him the truth: that I wanted to keep my job, that I was happy in my job and, well, I hoped he wasn't going to fire me over this thing that I was doing wrong, but that I bought the fake license. He fired me that day.

So I went to another tortilla factory, and here they did ask me for a social, and they asked for lots of tests to get the job. They gave me a ninety-day trial period, to test me out, and at the end they had the results. They gave me a letter, telling me that they were happy to work with me and they gave me insurance, they gave me a wage— I got paid $8.50 an hour, plus overtime. They even paid for your sick days, what they called 'holidays.'

I worked there for three years, quite content, until 1988. Then I had some bad luck.

TEN YEARS IS A LONG TIME

I worked from two in the morning to two in the afternoon. One day after work, I think I was tired, I don't know. Who knows? You work that many hours a day, you get used to it. Well, I was driving home and I came up to an intersection and I had a green light. Out of the corner of my eye, though, I saw another car coming but I thought it would stop, because it had a red light. But it didn't. We crashed into each other in the middle of the intersection; I hit the other car hard. When I did, I saw a child—a little girl—fly through the window and land on the street.

Even though I felt it wasn't my fault—I had the green light!— I got scared seeing that girl fly out the window like that. I saw her lying on the street and I saw people start to gather around, and I just panicked. I drove off. I didn't even get out of my car until I got home.

When I got to my apartment, though, the police were already

there, waiting. They said that since I left the scene of the accident, I got all of the blame. They took me to jail and then a few days later I had a trial. The judge gave me six months in prison and I had to pay a fine. Back then things were different—they had all my real information, but for some reason Immigration didn't find out about me. I don't know what would happen to someone with that kind of conviction now. But back then, my punishment was only prison.

But prison was enough. Prison was a terrible, ugly place. It's difficult for me to talk about it. My first night there, the "powerful ones"—those who had been there a long time—they beat me up. Just like they did to everyone else, just to show you who they are, show you they're dominant. But after that, I didn't get beaten. Other terrible things happen in there, though. The guards mess with the food—they urinate in it, they put ketchup in the oatmeal just to spoil it, they pour milk all over your dinner. Other things. No, it was an awful experience. I can't talk much about it.

While I was in prison, I continued working in the same tortilla factory. They gave me a timecard when I left the prison and when I returned—so I'd check in and out of prison and in and out of my job. All time accounted for.[7] Another guy who was in there had a truck; he would drive and drop me off at the factory and then go to his job at Chevy's. Then he'd pick me up and take me back to prison. If you worked while you were in there they counted one day as two days served. I worked every day so I only had to stay three months, not six. Even those three months, though, they were some of the worst days of my life. I am not proud of having gone to prison. But

---

[7] Roberto was given a combination sentence for his accident. He was given prison time and fined several thousand dollars—he does not remember the exact amount. Since Roberto was a first-time offender and his was not a serious offense, he was given the option of paying the fine through work outside of the prison. The police van which would transport other more serious offenders to monitored community service jobs would also take Roberto to his job at the tortilla factory, and pick him up after his shift. The money he earned went directly to paying the fine.

I tell myself, those who haven't fallen don't know how to walk. I guess I've fallen so many times now, I should be able to walk forever.

I was still in prison, in 1988, when they gave me the news that my grandfather wanted to see me. Well, I had the bad luck of not being able to go, not just because of where I was but because I didn't have the money at that point anyway. I was very sad, though, because I knew my grandfather was dying—we had a special friendship, and it hurt me that I couldn't be there.

So when I got out of prison a few months later, I started thinking. I'd been away from my home, my family, for nearly ten years. That's a long time for a person not to see his family. I decided to go back to Mexico to see my mother.

Throughout that whole decade, though, I had never written letters or sent any news other than a few words because I was still angry at my father. I would send money to my mother whenever I could with friends going back over the border. I would send fifty, a hundred, two hundred, sometimes whatever I had in my pockets when I was told that so and so is going back to Purépero. Money and just a few words: "I'm okay."

I made my parents suffer a lot during that time—ten years without knowing anything about me. But when I went back, I was actually afraid. I was afraid my father would be upset with me, that he would assault me in the same way as before. I bought an airline ticket from San Jose to Guadalajara and then made the long ride to Purépero, hours and hours outside of the main city. When I got to the house, though, I got a surprise. My father came out as I was greeting the others, and he welcomed me to the house. We both apologized: me for being the mischievous child that I was for a while, and him, well, he apologized for what he did to me. We forgave each other that same day I returned.

Since that day, we have become great friends. Whenever I go visit them, and then have to say it's time for me to return to San Francisco, my father starts crying. He says he's afraid every time I go back that I won't ever return. In the beginning, I was worried, too: I still was undocumented, so I had to keep returning illegally—with a coyote. That first time, the cost of the crossing was six hundred dollars. Now I know it is more than three thousand.

EVERYONE IN THE PLACE WAS UNDOCUMENTED

When I got back, after everything that had happened in San Jose, I decided I didn't want to go back there. I wanted a new life. So I went to San Francisco. I moved to a studio on the corner of O'Farrell and Larkin, right at the bus stop where they sell drugs. There were three of us guys living there together because even though it was a studio, it was big—it had two big closets for beds. But in '89, just a couple of months before the big earthquake, we decided to move into a house in Daly City. I guess we felt more comfortable there. It was me and four of my brothers at that point, all of them had come over to California after me. We lived in the house with a cousin and his wife and three other cousins.

During that time, I was working at a ceramics factory in Sausalito. I started cleaning out the ovens. Then the owner moved me on to painting tiles. She gave us books with all different kinds of designs and told us to just pick which ones we liked and paint those on the tiles, the plates. The work wasn't bad, but tedious—we painted the plates one by one and then put them in the oven to set.

After I'd worked there for about a year, maybe two, we were raided. I'd heard of immigration raids before, but never lived through one. We were all in the back, some painting, some packing up boxes. I remember I'd just put a batch of plates in the oven.

The agents arrived and they yelled, "Immigration!" And everyone started to run for the exits—everyone in the place was undocumented. Most people ran for the emergency doors but Immigration had parked a van right outside the emergency doors and just grabbed everyone as they ran out.

There was a big clay mixer—huge, for eight hundred pounds of clay, with big metal mixing paddles—in the part of the factory where I was. So I jumped in to hide. As I was going in, I unplugged the power cord from the wall above and pulled it inside with me so that the agents wouldn't somehow turn it on with me in there. It had a top, too, and I pulled it down and stayed there, waiting. It had a small opening where they pour the water in, and I looked out through the opening at the Immigration agents as they went around the machines, searching. After hiding in there for about forty-five minutes, I saw the factory owner come out and she started screaming because, since everyone had run out or been taken away, the plates had been left to burn in the oven. All the plates were ruined. The lady was yelling and running around to get the plates out of the oven. And I was there, still inside the mixer, scared, looking at everything through the opening. I saw that the customers from the store started running to help the lady. At that time I still didn't understand much English, but I think she was yelling to stop the machines, to stop the machines because the ovens were burning the plates.

In the end, only three of the workers weren't taken away. Three out of fifty. The other two who remained had climbed up inside the ceiling and hidden inside the air conditioning vents. At the end of the day we were all still scared to go home, to even leave the factory, for fear Immigration would still be waiting for us. The owner—she knew we were undocumented, too—said we could stay. So we slept in a storage closet, with all the heavy tools for the machines.

I worked at the ceramics factory until the owner hired more workers and then at that point, she asked for our papers. She had an inspector come and he asked for my Social Security card. When I gave it to him, he said that it was useless, fake. I was out of another job.

But at that time Stonestown mall was just opening. I saw that a Mexican restaurant was hiring so I went and applied. They asked if I knew how to cook. I said, I don't know the first thing about the kitchen, but I would like to learn. I went in on Monday, and they showed me how to make burritos. And from there, I went to prep, then some cooking, then back to burritos; I started just doing the whole rotation. And it was fine—the work was good. I had no complaints.

Then one day a guy named Wallid, a Jordanian guy, came to the Mexican restaurant and saw me making burritos. He saw how hard I worked, how quickly, and he offered me a job working for him. He told me he would pay me a dollar more than what I was making an hour—he would pay me 290 dollars a week, rather than the 250 I was making at the Mexican restaurant. He said he would pay me in cash, too.

So it wasn't a difficult decision—this guy offered me more money, so I went to work for him. When I first got to the restaurant, I met Jaime. Jaime was an experienced chef who'd been working for Wallid—managing his kitchens, creating recipes—for a few years. He asked me if I wanted to cook there, not just do prep. I said yes, sure, I was willing to do anything. He said, "Let's see"—he tossed a potato at me—"cut it quickly." And I cut it. He tossed a bell pepper at me— "cut the pepper julienne style. Do you know what a julienne-style cut is?" And I did know. I'd learned at the Mexican place. I also knew how to cut chicken breast, how to cut steak, how to butterfly, how to make soups. I kept all of that in my head. So when Jaime tested me on all of these techniques, I already kind of knew how to do them.

So Jaime told me, "You're ready to be a chef!" He put me to making sauces, muffins, bread, cornbread—I was in charge of many things. I started to make more money, as I worked more, and I realized I liked cooking. The hours were long, the pay could have been better, but it was all right. At least I was making a salary.

I THINK I WORKED TOO MUCH

After I'd been working in San Francisco a few years, I returned to Purèpero again. There I met Monica. She was a friend of one of my grammar school friends. We dated a little and very quickly decided to get married. So we did, one day while I was still there in Purépero. I had to go back to work, back to California, but she stayed home and a while later gave birth to our daughter, Jennifer. I came back a month or two later and made the crossing once more, this time with my wife and daughter.

We moved into a studio very close to where I used to live, on O'Farrell and Hyde. It was me, Monica, Jennifer—our new baby—and my brother. My brother slept in the bedroom closet for a while, but when Jennifer got older, and when my son, Junior, was born, we made up the closet for Jennifer, and my brother moved in with another relative.

Up until Monica joined me, I was still working with my fake Social Security number and green card. But, after talking to a few people, I heard that if you have so many years in the United States, you could apply for some kind of amnesty. So one day, when I heard an advertisement on the radio for a lawyer who said she was inexpensive, I decided to call her. There weren't many options for us at the time with the money we had. We met with her and she said that I should apply for asylum and I would become legal that way. She submitted the asylum application for me, Monica, and Jennifer. I didn't know at the time that we didn't really have an asylum case—there's no economic asylum from Mexico. But the lawyer submitted our applications anyway in 1993. And she said we had to just wait and see.

I kept working with Wallid and Jaime. I worked even more because I had to support my family—from seven in the morning until midnight, or from four in the morning until six in the evening. I would come home only to shower and sleep. We never got paid overtime.

The only thing I regret now is not having spent more time with my kids. By that time, Junior was born. I was trying to do the right thing, working to feed my family, to keep them in good clothes. But during those years, I think I worked too much.

I started working shifts from five in the morning until three or four in the afternoon. I would leave work and go to meet Jennifer and Junior at their school in the Tenderloin. Then we'd walk together to the after-school program, where Jennifer took violin and Junior played soccer and basketball. They got help with their homework there, too. While they were studying or playing, I would help out at the center. They would give food to the kids who didn't have lunches, so sometimes I would help them prepare the food, or get sodas, or do anything they needed. It was a good program, and it was free, so I wanted to help.

My children really grew here in San Francisco. They spent their whole lives here. They learned to speak English, and they did very well in school. They did better than their papa—they got past the fourth grade. Jennifer especially—since she had spent nearly ten years here, she had become very accustomed to things here.

I HAD TO PROVE I HAD EXISTED

A little while after our lawyer submitted our asylum applications, we were called to court. I found out there what had happened. The lawyer had lied about the date Monica came into the U.S., and she'd changed Jennifer's birth date to show that she was born in the U.S., not in Mexico. Even though I had the real birth certificate from Mexico with me, she ignored it. She didn't tell me she was doing any of this in my name, and when the government found out, it was a disaster. The judge charged the lawyer with fraud and took her law license away. And for us—she gave us time to find a new lawyer, because the government had already charged us and wanted to deport us.

I found another lawyer, and this one was good. She fought very hard for my case, and she did so with only the facts. She said I needed to collect proof of my life in the United States. I found pay stubs, tax returns, phone bills, even bus tickets I used every day to get to work. I had to go around collecting letters from people that knew me, letters from places where I worked, letters from church. I had to prove that I helped as a volunteer at church. I had to prove I had existed here for ten years.

During this whole time, we were in and out of court, fighting a long time. Fighting to show that it wasn't our intention to submit fraudulent applications; fighting to clear my record of the car accident; to prove my presence here for the last decade. I even had to fight to clear my identity because a long time ago someone had taken my bank account number and my old driver's license and when he got caught by the police, he said he was me.

Finally, when my lawyer submitted my application for suspension of deportation,[8] she thought it was best if my wife Monica and my daughter Jennifer were included in the application. I didn't completely understand how it worked, but the lawyer said that if I won my case then my wife and daughter would get to become legal here with me. If I lost, we all would lose.

It turned out differently. In 2003, the trial finally concluded and the judge gave her order. She agreed that I could stay—she granted cancellation and I got my green card. But Monica and Jennifer, the judge said, must return to Mexico. Since they had crossed illegally,

---

[8] Prior to 1997, certain individuals could apply for "suspension of deportation"—since replaced by "cancellation of removal"—which required an individual to have seven years of continuous presence in the United States, good moral character, and a showing of extreme hardship for the applicant's U.S.-citizen spouse, parent, or child, or to the applicant himself, if the applicant were deported. The remedy was changed by Congress in 1997 to a much stricter standard with the intention of narrowing the scope of persons eligible for relief from deportation. See "cancellation of removal" in Glossary for more information.

and they had been here less than ten years—just barely, though—they didn't qualify for cancellation. They would have to go. They could leave voluntarily, the judge said, and be able to come back in three years, or they could be officially deported and not be able to come back for another ten. Well, we decided they should leave voluntarily.

But it was very hard. My children did not want to leave. Jennifer was in the middle of her sixth-grade year, she was doing very well in school and had good friends here. At that age, your friends are so important. It was hard on Junior, too; Even though he was an American citizen and didn't legally have to leave, we felt it was best if he stayed together with his mother and sister. He was eight then, maybe too young really to understand the reasons for all of it, but he was very sad. I think my kids didn't want to leave me, either.

Monica and I were also worried. We agreed that I would stay in the United States to keep making money for our family. But being separated for so long… she was worried she would have to take care of the kids all alone in Mexico, that we would be apart for too long. I said I would send her money, I would visit as often as my job let me, I would try to do everything I could to get them back here sooner. We were all very upset at what was happening, but it was happening so quickly.

I DON'T RESEMBLE ANYONE

One morning soon after the hearing, I went with them to Guadalajara. When we landed there, I accompanied them to the consulate to have them stamp their documents. Show that they'd actually left the United States. Then they got on a bus for Purépero, and I had to fly back to San Francisco—I had to work the next day. When I got back to our studio, I was all alone.

Some days I sing to myself. "The woman I saw was sad as you can see… Because I no longer want to not know… If you gave to me, the higher part…What's the use of being sad?" I sing. Sometimes I laugh by myself, at myself. Sometimes I talk to myself. Sometimes I cry by myself. Sometimes I scream by myself. Who am I? I'm nobody. A very old saying in Mexico goes, "I am. I don't resemble anyone."

With my green card, it's been easier to cross back and forth. I go to visit them at Christmas and I try to go in the summer, too. I fill these two big suitcases and I bring two big boxes, too—shoes, clothes, toys, Jennifer's asthma medicine, books from their schools. I have to pay extra because I always go over the weight limit for luggage.

When I see my kids, though, I get even sadder. Now, it has been four years that they've been gone. I turn around and they're adults already. I feel I've missed out on their lives. Jennifer is going to turn fifteen soon, but we can't have her *quinceñera*[9] here because she still cannot come back. I'm saving up, though, so we can have a very nice celebration for her in Purèpero. And Junior is growing every day. He talks to me now like an adult—he asks me about my work, he asks me what I do during the day, and sends me messages on my phone about his school and his life there. He never smiles, though. He is very serious.

I miss them both very much. Too much. Sometimes when I'm lonely, I'll get out their old toys from when they were younger. The ones they left here. I'll play with Jennifer's speak-and-spell or Junior's racing track. I just play by myself, though, and sometimes it makes me miss them even more.

Things between Monica and me have been difficult. We both feel very alone. I think she gets angry sometimes that I was able to stay—even though all I do now is work—and she had to go. And we both were very frustrated with what happened last year.

As it was approaching three years since they'd had to leave,

---

[9] A girl's fifteenth birthday, traditionally held as a special event. Analogous to a "sweet sixteen" celebration in the U.S.

I called my lawyer to ask her what the process was for bringing my family back. My lawyer had given my case to another lawyer, though, so I had to go meet with someone new. The second lawyer looked at my papers and said it was very strange that the judge gave my wife and kids only three years outside the country, because normally it's five before they can be petitioned in. And even then, she said, for people from Mexico, even if it's your closest family, they will still have to wait for visas to become available. They might have to wait years for that.

Well, I had the order from the judge that said three years, and I couldn't believe that after waiting for so long they would have me wait even longer to be with my family again. So I went myself, directly to the American consulate in Guadalajara again, and I showed them the order. They looked at it but said, "There's nothing we can do with that. The judge or the agency made a mistake telling you they could come back in three years. They were given voluntary departure; that means they can't apply for another visa for five years. They have to wait."

So we wait still.

I don't know what else to say. I work, I send them money, I wait. I am getting older, too. I'm becoming an old man. I was jumped the other night right outside my apartment. These two guys asked me for a cigarette, then, when I said I don't smoke and turned away, they hit me from behind on my head, my shoulders. They took my watch and broke the bracelet I was wearing for good luck. But that's all. They didn't get my wallet. But I don't do well with that sort of thing anymore. So, I am thinking now I need to change horizons. I have a dream for my family and me. When they come back, I want to buy a house here in the United States, maybe in Richmond, or in Tiburon. Somewhere quiet. I want to be here in California, after living so much of my life here, but I want us to be together. I hope to build a life here with my family. God willing.

LISO

AGE: *38*
COUNTRY OF ORIGIN: *South Africa*
OCCUPATION: *Teacher, nanny*
HOME: *Portland, Oregon*

IF I AM ANYONE'S
SLAVE, I'M CHRIST'S

When an American church contacted a South African pastor to recruit volunteer missionaries in 2005, a thirty-seven-year-old Xhosa[1] woman named Liso quit her teaching job to join the cause. She entered the U.S. on a four-month "R" visa for religious workers, but her host family in Houston turned out to be more interested in her labor than in her faith and good works. A few months on, Liso escaped with only her Bibles and, having overstayed her visa, has ended up as a live-in nanny in Portland, Oregon. Despite her difficulties, Liso leans back in her chair and smiles as we speak in English. She supports her family back home—a husband, twin twenty-one-year-old daughters, and her HIV-positive mother and sister—on a wage of less than five dollars per hour. Although she buys little for herself besides calling cards, Liso calculates that it will be 2010 before she can afford a flight home.

It wasn't long after I got married the second time that a church from Houston sent a letter to my pastor in the Eastern Cape. The American church was asking our church for missionaries to volunteer. My

---

[1] Speakers of one of eleven official language groups in South Africa.

pastor's wife called me that Saturday. She said, "There's a church in the USA that needs a missionary. Are you still interested in going to America?" I said yes right away because—to tell the truth—I have a lot of debt at home. And, you know, we have the idea that everything in America is perfect because that's what we see on TV and in the movies. In America, you find dollars lying in the grass, every leaf on a tree is a dollar. Right now, if you call somebody in South Africa and say, "Do you want to come to America, even if it's to wash my pig?" I promise you that that person will say, "Oh yes, please let me come and wash your pig!" People will do anything to get here, to make money to send home. So, even though missionaries don't get paid, I was sure people in America would help me.

I was a teacher at home and I knew that if I gave up my job I would not get another teaching position—lots of South African teachers are unemployed. But I felt it was God's will for me to become a missionary, the right way to serve Him.

When I first told my husband, he said, "Ah, no! We've been married just five months and then you leave me again?" We had been married before, from 1994 to 1998, when I divorced him. Then, in May 2005, I remarried the same guy! Life's funny that way. Being divorced was not good for me at all. I came to realize that my husband was the best, that there was nobody like him. What helped me to change my mind is that I accepted Jesus Christ as my savior. I went back to my husband and said "I'm sorry," and everything was fine. He didn't even ask me any questions. He just said, "It's okay."

He didn't agree with my decision to go to the U.S.—not at all. He said, "Why leave your job here? At least you have a chance to pay off all the debt after some years." But my salary as a teacher was never enough. Most of the teachers I know are in debt. And not only teachers: every professional in South Africa is in debt. You see, after democracy in 1994, the end of apartheid, everyone could get loans. For example, I borrowed money for my aunt and for building materials for my home. But it was so difficult to repay that loan with the money I was earning as a teacher. I was not making enough money and I had many people to support. I couldn't even buy cigarettes for my husband. He used to work at a dry cleaner and he also did some welding on the side, but then the dry cleaner closed down and the welding workshop got very few jobs. So I was the only one who was working.

I didn't tell him any more about the trip to America. It was difficult for me to explain to him because he is not a born-again Christian, but I knew that if I followed God's will, I would find the right way to get out of debt as well. So I made an appointment in Cape Town to get the visa and I started connecting with the people in the Houston church, calling them without my husband knowing anything. I sent them all the papers they needed, they sent me the letter of invitation, and they bought the ticket. Then the visa arrived in the post. Everything went smoothly. And then I showed my husband: "Here's the ticket." He lay on the bed. He was sick, he was so unhappy. As for me, I was excited to come to America. I thought my husband would come, too, that he would follow after me.

So that's how I entered the country, on a special visa for missionaries. And now you see me here in Oregon—I have no legal papers, I work for one family, and I live in their house. It's not what I imagined. But I am gaining wisdom. I trust God. God knows why I'm here. God knows why I'm illegal. He wanted me to come to the United States for a reason and now I understand what he wants me to learn here.

READY TO WORK FOR GOD

I left my twin girls at home, Thembakazi (Big Hope) and Thembisa (Promise). They're twenty-one now. I myself was a great hope for my parents but I disappointed them when I became pregnant so young, only seventeen years old. I had more education than anyone else in my family, more than my brother, more than my five sisters. My parents were not teachers or anything like that—they can't even write their names. They used to work on the farms in the Orange Free State[2] and they really struggled to educate me. So I was a promising person when I was growing up. Then, when I told them I was pregnant, my father cried tears.

Our family had moved from the farms in 1975, when I was still a child, seven years old, to live in a very small town near Queenstown in the East Cape.[3] After I left school to have my babies, I worked as a cashier in a garage for two years. In 1988, I went back to school to finish my matric[4] and then I studied in college for three years to get my teacher's diploma. In the town where I grew up, there are no jobs. I mean none. There are even a lot of teachers who had been teaching for ten, fifteen years who are now unemployed. Luckily for me, a principal in Queenstown, a lady, got me a job in a rural village three hours' drive from my home. I left my children living with my parents and moved to the village.

I am a Xhosa and this was a Xhosa village. We're still living under the chiefs there, so the governing body or the chief allocates you a place to live. People carry water in buckets on their heads because the only running water is in the river. Cows drink from that water, people wash in it. There's no electricity. People live in round houses with thatched roofs. There's no toilet. These days, in Oregon, I am taking care of a small boy and I try to explain to him what life is like in that village. He says, "No toilet?" I say, "That's right, no toilet." If

---

[2] A former South African province, and the precursor to the modern-day Free State province.

[3] A South African province, home to a majority of Xhosa people.

[4] Short for matriculation. In South Africa, it commonly refers to the final year of high school and the qualification one receives upon graduating.

you have newspaper you use newspaper to wipe yourself. Or stones. He says, "No!" He can't imagine life without a toilet. I say, "Yes, baby, that's what it's like."

The hardest thing about teaching was the lack of books and equipment. Sometimes we just taught out of a book about things that even we as teachers didn't know or understand. Computers, for example. I taught my students about computers, but the first time I touched one was here in America. In South Africa, I only ever saw a computer at the bank.

But there's another big difference between South Africa and here—respect for teachers. When you are a teacher in South Africa arriving at school with your bags and books, kids run to help you. I'm not talking about small kids—big boys come to carry your books. They call us "Miss" or "Teacher." "Yes, yes, Miss." "Yes, Teacher." They have that respect. Even the parents respect teachers. I am talking mainly about the rural areas. In the towns in South Africa, it is different. You hear about kids beating their teachers in town. But in the rural areas, there is still respect.

All the same, after twelve years of teaching, I was ready to leave and to work for God and the church. I packed only my clothes and my Bible to come to the U.S. I carried a small suitcase and a bag, with my special visa for missionaries.

THEY WANTED SOMETHING ELSE FROM ME

I was shocked when I arrived at the place where I was going to stay. In the movies, I never saw people asking for money on the street, I never saw homeless people. Everything in America seemed perfect. According to TV, there are only smart well-dressed people in America. You don't see places like where I went to live in Houston. I expected it to be a city like Johannesburg, but my street was more like a township back home—poor people living crowded in small houses. Street kids.

I went to live in the pastor's daughter's house, just across the road from the church and the school. She was divorced with two children. Two other women lived there who also came as missionaries—one from South Africa and the other from Swaziland. The pastor and his wife lived about ten minutes' drive away.

I started working the very next day, in the school that belongs to the church, teaching classes. But after a few days they said, "Your pronunciation's not good enough to do teaching. The children can't understand you." I was surprised because I taught English at home. I think they wanted something else from me all along.

They did give me a lot of other work after that. With the lady from Swaziland, I cleaned the church, helped with the young children, cleaned their houses. I remember I cleaned the dirtiest garage in the world—I have photographs of that! But this was not right. This was not why I came to this country. When they say you are a missionary, and you come over here, you are coming to help people, to teach the children and to show them the Christian way to live. But we were not doing the missionary work that we'd agreed to do here; we were really working for the pastor's daughter, the three of us, cleaning the house, taking care of the kids when she was out.

There was always something, some more work. The pastor's daughter travels to church conferences all over the world and she sells special neckties at these events. We would pack those ties for her—all kinds of work like that. The pastor's family owns a big farm out of town, so they drove us out there to dig holes and plant trees. We worked fast—I don't even know where we got the strength. Within a few hours, we would be done with our task and they would be shocked. Another pastor came over and said, "I also want a missionary from South Africa from the same church." I laughed because they'll never get somebody like me. I don't have a duplicate.

The pastor's wife and daughter didn't want us to talk to other people, even other church members. If they saw us talking with anyone, they would ask, "What was she saying to you?" People at church felt sorry for us. "Were you a teacher?" "Yes, I was." "So why did you come over here? Why are you working like a slave?" It was a black church and a black family, so they are very aware of slavery.

I said, "I don't know anything about slavery. I know apartheid. If I am anyone's slave, I'm Christ's."

My visa was extendable for one year from January 2006. The first expiration date in my passport said April 24, so I needed to extend it. I kept asking the pastor's family to get it extended. They would say, "Okay, don't worry. We're going to do it for you." But they never did and they never explained why. So my visa expired and I have overstayed. And I know that it was intentional. They didn't want us to go because we were working for them. That's why they wanted us—for cheap labor. If we were legal, we might tell someone how we were treated, we might ask for help or go and work somewhere else. So they kept our papers and held up our extensions because they were afraid that they'd lose us.

The only time I left the house and the church was to buy calling cards so I could call home. One time, they took us into the city center and we walked around the big buildings and shops downtown. Otherwise, they never took us out. The family were not unkind in the way of shouting or anything, but they smiled in a way that we are not used to. They weren't really smiling—I'm sorry to say this—it was a fake smile. They saw us but not really, not with their spiritual eyes. Church here was different, too. As Africans, we do things differently. I asked the Holy Spirit to help me not to look at these people with my eyes, no matter how they treated me or how they lived, but instead to help me to look at them with my spiritual eyes. That way, with God helping me, whatever they were preaching I was hearing the word of God. Whatever they were singing, I was hearing the voice of God.

So this was my position. Instead of being a missionary, I had some kind of job. But every day the work changed—I never knew what I was supposed to be doing. We were paid three hundred dollars every two weeks, six hundred per month. They said they paid us so little because they fed us and gave us clothes, so we didn't need any more money. But those clothes they gave us were so big that they didn't fit me at all. The pastor's daughter was always eating out and her kids ate meals that you take from the freezer to the microwave. The three of us ladies from Africa used to make rice for ourselves if there was food in the house to cook. Most days, they gave us pork neck bones. As a Christian at home, we don't eat pork. But in America we were forced to eat pork because we had no alternative. Then for two months, there was no food for us at all, even though the pastor gave his daughter money to feed us. She said, "You eat too much."

At the church, they served bread and peanut butter after the service every Sunday. When we were so hungry, when we had no food, the lady from Swaziland would go to the school very early in the morning and take some of this bread so we had something to eat. Was she taking the bread or stealing it? I don't know the answer to that.

This is what I did with the $600 every month. First, they took $60 of it for tithing to the church. Then I would pay $20 for a calling card and $20 for cosmetics. (I cut my hair very short because I could not afford hair products.) And then I paid $40 in charges each time I wired money home. That left $460 to send home each month, to pay for my house and to support my parents and my daughters at school. It was not even half of the salary I used to earn at home.

My mother is HIV-positive and so is my sister, so the money also had to pay for their medicine. My father was HIV-positive too, but he passed away in 2004. Only rich people and those with medical insurance can afford to pay for HIV medication. The medication that my mom is using is 366.28 rands[5] every month. On top of that, there are certain things that she must eat, like 100 per-

---

[5] Approximately fifty U.S. dollars.

cent pure juice, and those things are expensive for me. Some who are infected get the medicine from the government hospital, but sometimes the government runs short of medicines. Many who are infected with the AIDS virus, even if they get medicine from the government hospital, they may not have food, or people to give them moral support, no one to take care of them. For example, my sister's CD4 count[6] dropped so low that the doctor told her to go and choose her coffin—he was quite sure she was going to die soon. But because of the love I gave her—and please get me right, I'm not trying to brag—because of the way I supported her morally and spiritually, she is fine and her CD4 count is up. We have to give people with AIDS spiritual drugs as well; it's not enough to heal only the physical body. Even the way the doctors talk to them can be upsetting. One doctor told my mom to go back home, there was nothing she could do, "Just go home and wait for your day to die." I told my mom and my sister that the doctors *cure,* but God *heals.*

Before I came, the pastor's family said that in March, my second month here, they were going to invite my husband to join me. But when I was here in the U.S., they didn't even want to discuss that plan. They asked me why he doesn't find some way to get money himself, like selling bottles to recycling centers. I said, "At home we don't do those things." It made me sick, when they talked like that about my husband, asking me why I support him. It's not their business. That is what I do. I support him.

Now what could I do? I had resigned my position back home. With so many teachers unemployed in South Africa, I knew I would not get another teaching job. So I was not even thinking about going home. Not at all. I just said to myself, "Okay, these are my tests, I must go through them. These are my tribulations. I must face them."

---

[6] A CD4 (or T4) count measures the amount of certain white blood cells. It acts as an indicator of immune system strength.

YOU DON'T TRUST ANYBODY

Everything changed one day in April because one of the church members happened to see my paperwork in the church office. She came to me and asked, "Are you happy here?" I said, "Yes," because I did not trust anybody. I thought she would report me to the pastor's daughter. So I said, "Yes, I'm happy." She said, "Tell me the honest truth: are you happy here?" I could feel she was sympathetic, she was really asking from her heart. So I told her everything. I explained that I couldn't think of leaving—I didn't know anybody, I didn't have anywhere to go. And I would be illegal soon. Everywhere you go in the U.S., they want to see your Social Security number and of course I don't have one.

She told me she and her husband had been worried about me ever since I arrived here. She said, "It was worse when I saw what you were paid at home." That was on Sunday. Then on the Tuesday, she came to see me again. She asked if I would come with them if they got me a ticket. I asked where to, but they did not want me to know. I still did not know if she was serious, but she told me to be ready at eleven o'clock on Wednesday morning. I thought, If this is God's will, I must do it. So I escaped with her and her husband. I took only my Bibles. I left all my clothes there, everything. My teaching certificates are there. I just walked out of the house as if I was coming back. A secret mission. We left Houston the same day and flew here to Oregon. This was just before my visa expired so I was still able to use my passport for picture ID.

That young couple, also a black family, they took a big risk in order to help me. The church in Houston is still looking for them. They want them to repay the cost of my ticket to fly here from South Africa. But in fact it is the church that will suffer if Immigration finds out that they have been making false promises to bring people here to provide cheap labor for them, paying us in cash so there are no records. They lied to the government, saying that I was coming here as a missionary, but then keeping me to clean for them.

I called the South African embassy to find out if they could help with my status. The lady there said, "Ah, you've overstayed. The only thing you can do is apply for a student visa." I told her the schools are so expensive. I've looked on the internet and I can't afford four hundred dollars to pay fees. Others tell me, "You'd better get married." I say, "I'm married in South Africa." Even if I was not married, would I marry just for papers? I don't think that would work for me. One day when I was walking to Barnes & Noble, a car stopped next to me and a Mexican man asked me, "Do you need a ride?" I said, "Okay." He said, "Are you from Africa?" I said, "Yes." Then he said, "I know you don't have any papers. If you have sex with me, I'm going to try to make everything okay." I said, "Look at me. I'm a Christian." Even if I was not married, I was not going to do that. And then, when he was dropping me off, we saw a police car. The Mexican guy immediately ducked down under the dashboard, out of sight. I said, "And you think you can fix my situation for me? While you're hiding from police yourself?"

I don't want to be deported because, if I leave that way, I can never come back again. And one day I do want to come back to America, not to work, but to go to church conferences. If I leave without being deported, I can come back again in ten years' time. So that's my biggest worry now—being deported. If you're illegal here, you're not free at all. Even at church, when somebody asks questions, you think, "Ah, maybe he's working for the INS."[7] You don't trust anybody. You don't want to talk to other people. You're always quiet. You don't want people to know your status. Every day I cross my fingers. "Oh God, please don't let me do anything illegal so I get deported."

---

[7] The Immigration and Naturalization Service, now divided into United States Citizenship and Immigration Services (USCIS), and Immigration and Customs Enforcement (ICE).

I'm afraid all the time. I can be outside the house with this little boy that I look after and I start to imagine what will happen if he tries to run into the road. Say the police are called. They will start asking me questions: "Who are you? How have you been working here?"

PEOPLE HIRE US BECAUSE WE'RE CHEAP

The Houston family who moved here didn't need anybody to work for them, but they helped me by giving me a job when we first arrived. Then I found a job advertised on the internet and I went to work for an Indian family as a nanny. I told them the truth—that I don't have papers. I didn't hide that because it's really dangerous to employ somebody who doesn't have papers. If the government finds out, the employer will be in trouble as well as me. Of course, the reason people hire us is because we're cheap.

I only stayed one week with that family. The second week, I quit because they wanted me to pray to their God. They had vases and money on a small table, like an altar, and when I was feeding their babies, I was supposed to pray there. I said I could not do that. And I quit the job right away.

Actually, the conditions there were not good. I took care of the two children and I cleaned the house. But I didn't do any cooking or shopping—the mother did the cooking. They paid me three hundred dollars per week and I lived with them, downstairs in the garage. There were cars parked on one side, a laundry over there, and then one section was a small office for the husband. I slept on a couch in that office, so there was no privacy. I kept my clothes in this office too, next to the husband's computer. At night, the couch became my bed—I would pull it out. Any time they were leaving the house, they had to come past me. They would call me from upstairs, "Liso, cover yourself! We are coming down!"

The young couple, the ones who helped me escape, asked me,

"Are you happy there? Come back and live with us if you are not happy." I didn't want to bother them, so I said, "Yes, I'm happy." But when my employers said I must pray at their altar, I called the young couple and said, "I'm coming back." I stayed with them again for a while until I found this job, the one I'm doing now.

And this is where I have worked ever since, for over a year. I take care three kids—the twins are nearly a year old, the other one just turned four. I also clean the house and do the laundry, but the wife does the cooking. The babies are up now at seven a.m., and I'm busy all day until eight or nine at night. But they know that I must have Sundays for church. There is no negotiation about that. It's only on Sunday that I don't work at all. I take care of the babies at church in the morning and then in the evening, I attend the service and also Bible study class. My friends in the class are old! One is seventy-two years old, another is ninety-two years old. They're my only friends. We met there in class and they give me a ride to church.

I don't take holidays, I don't take Christmas. Where would I go? What I do is I walk to Barnes & Noble, the bookstore, on Saturdays. I sit and read there for two hours and then I walk back. I have a very strict schedule—at one p.m. on Saturdays, I check my email. After that, I work from four in the afternoon until whatever time the parents come back—it could be midnight or one a.m. I never have a set time for when I finish work.

The couple I work for pays me four hundred dollars a week. I live here for free and they give me food. It made me laugh the other day when I was working out the numbers on the calculator on my cell phone. It comes to not even three dollars an hour, more like two dollars and some cents. They tell me that they don't want to pay more because they give me so many things and they let me use the computer. They said they would raise my pay by 7 percent but they haven't done it.

JUST A SMALL DOOR TO GET INTO AMERICA

I've seen adverts for a thirty-nine-dollar doctor in the newspaper. That's the only doctor I can afford. I think I have to go because my whole side is painful and my muscles are swollen. The pharmacist told me she thinks it is arthritis. It's not easy for me to squeeze wet towels now, or even to open jars. One Saturday, the first time I felt this pain, I told the woman I work for, "I'm not feeling well at all today."

She was really upset. "You were supposed to tell me long ago! Not now!" She's a nice lady, so I was shocked that she would get so upset. But I understand in a way because Saturdays are the only time they go out. I said, "I'm sorry for not telling you." They gave me some tablets, but that Saturday was really hard for me. I was really sick. Then the next morning, she didn't ask me anything. But the husband said, "How are you feeling?" and gave me more tablets.

In South Africa, a nanny is treated as a second-class person. I would never work as a nanny at home. The pay is not even peanuts. But here in America, there is a minimum wage for nannies. Americans can earn a good salary looking after children, because they are paid by the hour. Those who are citizens, they wouldn't accept $400 per week, they wouldn't take even $10 an hour. It's only people like me with no papers who are paid so little.

Out of my $1,600 each month, I send home $1,200. I take off $160 for tithing to my church here and $40 for my calling cards. I don't spend any money here—it's all for my family back home. I never go to a movie. I don't even buy spring water. My family back home are paying off the debts with the money I send. But, like I told you, people believe that in America you can pick up dollars from the grass. Even now, I get text messages on my phone from people at home saying, "Send me money." Oh Jesus, they don't know. "Please, please, please send me five thousand rands."[8] Do they know how much

---

[8] About $750 U.S.

work it takes to make five thousand rands? Do they know what I'm doing? They don't understand a thing.

This couple's friends ask me how I am. I know they worry about me, they feel sorry for me. They see that I'm always working. But I like the kids. I develop something new every day. That's one of the things I've learned: to be happy, you must love your job. And I do, I love my job. I don't even care about privacy, because I've got nothing personal here.

The woman from Swaziland left Houston, too. She found work in another city like I did. But she wrote to tell me her situation was bad, the way they were treating her. She did not eat with the family—she even had to use her own cup and plate. After their dinner, she ate leftovers. If they finished all the food, she would go to bed without eating. This girl grew up in Swaziland so she didn't know anything about apartheid. I told her, "That's apartheid." Because she was wearing a uniform with a white headscarf, washing the dogs. I said to her, "It was not your job, that one. It was not the place for you. It was just a small door to get into America."

I WANT TO PLANT SOMETHING HERE

Sometimes I cry the whole night. I miss my mother and my daughters so much. And my husband. Ah, my husband. The last time I saw him was January 24, 2006. It's as if we have given the devil the keys, me and my husband, because we didn't even stay together all that long and now there is so much distance between us. We don't know what will happen. Every week, I call him. If I have enough money, I call every day, a very short call. "Hi. I love you," I say, then I put down the phone. "Hi. I love you." Until the five-dollar card is used up. "Hi. I love you." Then on Saturdays, I call him as I walk to Barnes & Noble and we talk for thirty minutes. We talk about our debts and we make plans. I also talk with my daughters about how they are doing at school. I tell them they must respect my husband and listen to him, even though he was not around for a long time. I worry about them. They go to church but they are not born-again Christians.

As for me, I try to make sure that whatever I'm doing glorifies the name of God. When the twins in Portland were born, their grandmother was here to help. From the time she left, when the babies were one month old, I would work all day until two a.m., sleep three hours, and be back at work at six a.m. One day, my boss asked me, "How do you manage to do this?" I say, "It's not me. It's God." Truly speaking, it's God. I was glad when my boss's wife once asked me, "Can I go to church with you?" I said, "Praise God." And the boy here, he was so naughty. But God helped me understand how to treat him, how to talk to him. When I started here, he used to hit me, throw things at me, throw things at his parents. But now he's a good boy.

I want to plant something here. I don't go around talking about Jesus. I try to lead by example. The children can feel it. I don't want to leave until I know that I have saved at least one soul here in America. And I have wisdom now. I see how to make money and how to help other people. My eyes are open. Every day in America, I get ideas. I want to learn to swim so I can go home and teach my children to swim. I am taking piano lessons. Someone at my church has promised to teach me to ride a bike. People say, "Is she normal? Why is she doing all those things? Why is she learning piano?" I don't want to waste a minute of my time here. Every second counts. The year 2010 is coming and that's when I will have saved enough money to go home. I love my own country—I see now how good it is. But I need these years in the U.S. to make my plans work.

I've started writing a small book, a pamphlet for people living with HIV. What I learned from my experience with my sister is that the antiretrovirals are not enough. To stay alive, you need the spirit as well as the drugs. So I'm writing about that.

And I'm starting my own business. I'm here in Oregon, but my husband will start the business in South Africa next January—a day-care center and boarding house in our home. I will have computers at my day-care center. People can come to my place and I will teach them how to use computers. I will talk to people who have nannies and tell them the right way to treat their nannies.

You know, I've learned a lot about white people since I came to America. At home, if you're buying a second-hand car, you say, "I want a car that was owned by a white, because they always take care of their cars and have them serviced." But I'm learning that not all whites look after their cars. And some whites eat too much! It's funny. We're no different, nothing special—we're all the same, white and black.

And I've learned about being an illegal worker. I try to explain to people here that South Africa is not like other countries in Africa. Whatever you have in America, you will find it in the big cities in my country, too. And people from other countries in Africa want to come and work in South Africa, just like people want to come and work here in the U.S. And we treat illegals badly, just as illegal workers are treated here. South Africans say, "These illegals!" It's the same in America—here, you hear Americans say, "Our government is wasting lots of money on these people." At home, we call them *amak-were-kwere*[9] and when you want cheap labor you employ them. We don't recognize them as human beings. They're just poor people who come to South Africa to get money. And in America now I'm just like those people. There is one of them who is working on my parents' land at home—a lady from Zimbabwe. She ploughs the whole field using only a spade. And they pay her three hundred rands[10] per month. I say, "Mom, if you can treat that lady nicely, you are going to be treated nicely. If you can raise her salary, God's going to take care

---

[9] A derogatory term for black foreigners.

[10] About forty-five U.S. dollars.

of me here, because I'm in the same position that lady is in." When I go home, I'm going to make sure she gets a South African ID. I don't know how I'm going to do it—I'm going to ask my mom to adopt her or something.

Because I *will* go home. In 2010, after paying my debts back home and paying off the land I bought. My husband and my children, they miss me a lot. We don't know what will happen. At night, I fall asleep thinking 2010, 2010, 2010.

HECTOR, 42
St. Helena, California

Hector has lived and worked in the U.S. for many years, mostly as a field worker in Napa Valley. A serious injury on the job left him unable to work and nearly destitute. A week before giving this interview, he was visited at his home by an Immigration agent. The agent said that he knew Hector and his wife, Isabel, were undocumented, and warned them that if they didn't leave, he would be back to arrest and deport them and their neighbors.

I used to do all kinds of work in the fields around here. I worked for years and years harvesting grapes, removing leaves from tomato bushes, cutting peppers. I'd do everything else they needed, also. One day, about four years ago, I was working on the ridge of a vineyard over in Napa, putting wire up around the perimeter of the field. I got to a point where it was very steep and rocky and I was standing on top of an outcropping and leaning on one of the other wires of the fence for balance. Suddenly the wire broke and I fell ten or fifteen feet onto the rocks below. I couldn't move. It felt like my whole body had cracked like an egg. I was out there alone, so I didn't know if anyone had seen me fall. But there was a small child who came running over to me—he had come with his father to the fields to learn how to do some of the work—and he went running back to tell his dad. He told his dad that I was dead. When his dad came over to where I was laying he was surprised that I was still alive and breathing.

He and another worker started to pick me up by the arms but I asked them to not pull on my right arm—I had to insert the bone back into its socket first. Since I couldn't stand, they had to come back with a tractor to take me back to my own car. We didn't call an ambulance or go to the doctor right away. I didn't want them to. I'd heard that they'll fire you if you have an accident on the job. So I waited and hoped to feel better. But after a few days, I could still barely move. Eventually I went to see the doctor. He said the break was bad, that I'd need surgery, and that I couldn't work for a while. I took the x-rays to show my boss, but he only said that I waited too long to tell him about the fall. I didn't get anything for it.

Last Sunday morning, I was sitting outside our house with my wife, passing time, when a car with green and white stripes slowly pulled up into the street leading to the property. I was afraid. I couldn't tell right away but I thought this guy was either from the Immigration service or was one of the Minutemen who dresses up like they're from the service and tries to hunt down immigrants.

I tried to act very calm and started to walk over to the car—I walk slow since I walk with a cane now. When I got to his window, the man asked if I had papers. I asked, "Why do you ask me that?"

And he said, "Because I am an Immigration agent." And then he began to ask me more questions. "How many people live in this house? How many live in that house? You live here?" And then the agent said, "We're going to come back in seven days and check to see how many of you have papers and how many don't. We're going to take those who don't have documents—we have a warrant."

Me, the only thing I said was, "Okay, thanks a lot!"

As I walked back up the driveway, I told my wife to just stay sitting because I thought if we looked nervous he would come back and take us away right then and there. We waited until he was gone and then we went around to the other houses and told them what had happened. We told them they might think about leaving. We waited until it was dark, and then we packed up all the things we could into my car. We left a lot there but we're too scared to go back.

I receive eight hundred dollars a month from the state disability, and my wife, Isabel, works for the both of us these days. But with her pregnant now, and since we've become homeless, I'm getting worried. Right now we're staying with my cousin. We'll have to find a new place soon.

OLGA

AGE: *39*
COUNTRY OF ORIGIN: *Mexico*
OCCUPATION: *Housekeeper*
HOME: *Oxnard, California*

I'M YOUR MOTHER,
DON'T YOU REMEMBER ME?

Born in Jalisco, Mexico, Olga was a mother by the time she was fifteen. After struggling to provide for her two children, Olga decided to come to California. She and her two children eventually settled in a converted garage in Oxnard, California, a small seaside farming town about seventy miles north of Los Angeles. When her son Victor was in his teens, Olga found out that her son wanted to be a woman. Victor became known as Victoria, or Vica, as she was called by her family. In May 2007, Vica was stopped for a driving violation, and sent to a Los Angeles immigration detention center. By this time, Vica was being treated for AIDS. Her mother and fellow detainees have said that Vica, 23, was repeatedly denied medication while at the federal facility. A petite woman who works cleaning homes, Olga, 39, sat in her modest apartment, surrounded by family photos, and recalled Vica's life in Spanish. She spoke of Victor as a young boy, then as a transgender person, and finally as a detainee who died in federal immigration custody, shackled to a bed.

I clean houses. I'm married. My husband is a house painter. I used to work all the time, six days a week. I'd get up at six in the morning, fix some breakfast for my family, and go to work. Since Vica's death it's been hard to work. The people I work for are very nice and are always hugging me since it happened. One family gave me money to help with the funeral costs. I get home around four and I'm so tired. I'll make myself something to eat, go to the store, or stop by the cemetery.

I had to stop working when Vica died. I couldn't do anything. I was just crying all the time. I started working again because I can't afford not to. When I get up and fix breakfast I think about when Vica was alive. When he was a boy, I worried about him, that he ate well, because I knew he had to take care of his health. Now I just start to cry in the mornings when I make breakfast. I'll sit down to eat and suddenly lose my appetite.

IT TOOK ME A LONG TIME

I was born and grew up in Jalisco, Mexico. When I was fourteen years old, I was raped. That's when Victor was conceived. When my parents found out I was pregnant, my father stopped talking to me. I never told them what happened because I didn't think they would understand. My father wanted to kick me out of the house but my mother convinced him to let me stay. My father was so angry with me. I remember I would sit down to eat, and he would get up from the table. He wouldn't talk to me.

It was very hard because my father remained angry and took it out on my Victor. Victor would crawl over to him, reach out to him, and my father would walk away. Then I got pregnant a second time. I was about eighteen then. I told my boyfriend I was going to have his baby and I never heard from him again. He just disappeared from my life.

After my father found out I was pregnant again, this time he really did run me out of the house. I was completely alone. I remember walking down a long narrow street in the neighborhood. I was holding Victor's hand—he was four—and I was six months pregnant. My father was walking toward me with some friends. He just walked past me as if he didn't know me.

I stayed with a friend and her mother. My daughter Sara was born a few weeks later, she came early, at seven months. She was very fragile, and nearly died one night. I rushed her to the clinic, and the doctor said if I had waited a few more minutes she would have died. Sara was so small. I remember she fit in a cardboard box. I think since I was a little girl, I've always searched for love. I've never really had someone who loved me until my children.

My friend's mother would help watch the kids so I could work. We barely had any money in those days. I worked all day and Victor and Sara would stay with my friend's mother. I just remember working and praying I could scrape enough money together that week to buy a shirt for Victor, or a pair of shoes for Sara.

Victor was five or six when I noticed changes. He walked differently than other boys. He didn't like to play with cars like little boys do. He didn't have little boy friends, only girls. He liked music and to sing. He loved Gloria Trevi.[1] He didn't like to go get his hair cut. He would say, "Mami, why don't you let my hair grow? I like it a little longer." I would tell him it looked better short, like a boy. He would stay quiet after that.

He also played with my daughter's dolls. He did it mostly when I wasn't there. He tried to hide it from me. I think in his mind, he thought I wouldn't accept him.

It took me a long time to accept things. I come from a family that is very reserved. My parents were born on a ranch in Zacatecas. After they were married they moved to Guadalajara. But they were always from the ranch, the kind of people who were always worried about what people might think, what people might say.

---

[1] A Mexican pop singer.

GOD GAVE ME A CHILD TO LOVE

I was always a single mother. The money didn't go far. I worked as a cleaning woman in a clinic. I had several other jobs, too. I also worked in a bakery and worked as a shoemaker.

Since I was little I'd wanted to move to California. When I finally decided I was going to move, it was my father who helped me get the money. We had reconciled. It made me so happy to finally have his support after being estranged for so long. But at the same time I was so sad because I knew the decision to come here meant I would have to leave my kids alone. My mother took care of the children during that year.

I came to Los Angeles because my aunt lived here. I came by bus to Tijuana. We climbed across the hills and down into San Diego. When I arrived in Los Angeles I stayed with my aunt. We got along. She gave me a little money. Then the problems began. Her husband tried to woo me, to make me fall in love. One night, I left for good so my aunt wouldn't have problems. I stayed with a friend of my aunt's. I eventually came to Oxnard, where my older brother lived.

But soon I had problems with my sister-in-law. She didn't really want me living there. One night I went out walking, looking for work. I walked passed a restaurant and saw that they were looking for workers. It was a Mexican seafood restaurant. I started working there and made friends. I didn't need to speak English. Everyone there spoke Spanish, including the customers. The tips helped me survive. I stayed seven years at that job.

I sent all my money back to Mexico. I only kept what I needed for rent and food. I remember my father would tell me, "Don't forget us." I vowed I would never forget them—I would help with what I could.

I came alone because I wanted to find a place, a stable life, before I brought my kids over here. I did the right thing. A year went by before the children saw me. They were still so small, Victor was only seven and Sara was four when they came across. I remember my daughter was playing in the dirt. I spoke to her and she just stared at me. I said, "I'm your mother, don't you remember me?" Her little face turned bright red. I ran over and hugged her. We were inseparable after that. Then Victor came out of the house when he heard my voice. He was a little older and still remembered me. He hugged me and we started our lives together.

When the kids got here I rented another place in Oxnard. It was all I could afford but it was enough. It wasn't much, just a garage behind a house that was divided into two rooms. I bought the kids bunk beds. You could barely walk around in the place because it was so small—the beds, two chairs, and a table took up all the space. But we were happy during the three years we lived in that place.

Victor learned English right away. He told me the kids at school spoke English and Spanish. Both my kids were happy in school. Victor, though, as I said, was a little different. When he was about eleven or so he began putting on makeup. He did it while I was at work, when he was alone with his sister. I have never asked Sara about this, but I think they played dress-up and put on makeup.

I feel guilty about some of the things I did. I was becoming ashamed of my own son. He wore his hair long and plucked his eyebrows. He was older then and I couldn't force him to get his hair cut. I remember that when family would come over, I would tell him to go his room. Can you believe I said that? I can only imagine how that felt. When he would come out of his room I would tell him, "Go to your room." He would never say anything. He would just turn around and go back to his room.

He would save money and buy makeup. I'd walk into Sara's room and I'd see all these lipsticks and other makeup that I knew weren't hers. I never knew where he got it. I don't know how he got the money. Aside from the makeup, he would wear tight jeans and

T-shirts. People were starting to talk about him. My friends, my family, would all tell me they saw Victor. They would tell me he was all dressed up, or all made up. They were making fun of him.

I think I was the last to know, to understand. Victor was in high school the first time I saw him dressed as a woman. He started to make up women's names for himself. We would get calls at home, people asking for Sandra. I would tell them, there is no one here named Sandra. And they would say yes, she gave me this number. I was torn about accepting my child. I would stop and think, I should accept my child. Life is too short. I would stop and think, God gave me a child to love, not to judge. I didn't accept it, at least not initially. Looking back, I should have looked for help, sought out a group or something to avoid some of the really unpleasant things that came later.

Victor began using the name Victoria. I knew he didn't like the name Victor but the name Victoria seemed too long, so I told him, "I'm going to call you Vica." My son was sixteen then. And after that, I did start to think of Victor as a her. She was so happy. Everything was Vica this or that.

You know, my Vica made me realize things. So many people make fun of transgender people. I myself had known transgender people in Guadalajara. I guess I never thought it odd to have transgender friends but I wasn't really ready to have it in my family.

But as I watched how people treated Vica, I began to understand how hard it must have been. People would walk past and point. When I met my husband, the first thing I told him was, I have a transgender daughter. One thing that made me laugh was when he finally started calling her Vica, too. Until the end he called her Vica. For a while we were happy together, all of us. And Vica was always joking, always playing around. We would be in the living room and she'd be in her room singing. I'd tell her stop singing, that she was going to wake up the rats and cockroaches. She'd laugh. Sometimes I don't know what she was doing, but we could always hear her laughing.

She very much wanted to have the surgery. And if she ever had the money she would have done it. If I had the money, I would have supported her in getting it done. She was taking hormones, injecting them. She was very private about it. I only noticed because her breasts were growing and I realized it was the hormones.

Vica never told me about what she did when she left the house. She laughed a lot, played around, but she was also very reserved. We never sat down to really talk. When we did talk it was mostly joking around. I would feel sad and want to share my sadness with her, and Vica would just make a joke.

She started doing drugs in high school. She'd go out and I could smell the marijuana. It got worse when she started doing meth. But she tried to help herself. When the meth got bad, she decided on her own to go to the rehab home. She was out of my house for about two years after that. It was the only time we lived apart. We would talk all the time. I would call her at the rehab house and leave her a message, or she would call me. I would go every week to see her. She was working at the time in Hollywood, as a cashier at Pavilions. But in the end she seemed desperate. I think she got bored with the routine. Finally, things didn't work out. She started up with the drugs again and got kicked out of the rehab center.

She moved into a hotel. She stopped calling me. I thought it was strange. I would call the hotel where she was staying and leave messages and they would tell me she wasn't there. Then I would call her at work and they would tell me she hadn't shown up for work that day. Once, I even went to her work, waiting for her to show up. Then Vica called me one day and asked me to pick her up. She was living in a hotel. She had run out of money. She was in bad shape. I got to the hotel and she just kept saying, "Thank you, Mom. Thank you, Mom."

I asked her what was going on. I told her she was scaring me. When she said she was HIV-positive, I just started to cry. I felt as if I was going crazy. I thought she was going to die. She told me not to worry, that it wasn't an illness that caused you to die right away. She said that if she took care of herself she could live a long time. I really didn't know much about HIV. Sara and Vica looked up information on the internet and gave it to me. I felt a little calmer. I would tell her to take care of herself, to eat well. I would tell her not to do drugs. I would try to give her advice. She moved back home.

Vica never told me how she became HIV-positive but I think it was sexually transmitted. She would get new medication every month. I never saw a month go by without her getting medication.

About two years ago, she realized she had AIDS. It wasn't HIV anymore, but AIDS. She went to get a blood test and the doctor told her. She was working at Vons then, as a cashier. Sometimes she would come home really sad, other times happier. When she came home sad I would ask her what happened, why she was sad. And she would tell me that people didn't treat her well. I'd tell her, "Don't let them hurt you." I would tell her not to get stressed. "Don't let people who are bitter make you feel bad, because it spreads like a cancer."

Oxnard is a small town. We would go out to dinner and I would notice how people would make fun of her. It would make me very upset, really angry. She would laugh and tell me, "Ma, ignore them. Just like you told me."

Sara always accepted her sister, since they were little. There were no secrets between them. Vica had a car but no license. One night I think Vica was drinking, and she was stopped. She called her sister and said she'd been arrested. Sara called to tell me. I was upset because she wasn't taking care of herself, and she was getting into trouble. We stayed in communication. She said she would be there a few days and they would transfer her to Ventura County Jail because she had failed to show up for a court hearing.

I didn't go see her in Ventura. I was working a lot during those days. I'd get home from work and by that time visiting hours were over. I had the hope that she would get out. But at the same time I was scared because I knew in Ventura they have immigration officers.

I remember I got a letter. She wrote, "Guess what, Mom, what I feared most—Immigration has come to see me and they're going to detain me." They moved her to San Pedro Detention Facility about two weeks later.

I told her, "Don't stop calling. Tell me anything. Let me know where you are."

It was a very hard experience to not be able to see her. It was really frustrating. I always sent her money, always. She would tell me to send her cash. When she was detained the first thing she told them was that she had AIDS and that she needed her medication.

When Vica called me, she would tell me they treated her and the other transgender detainees very badly. They would humiliate them, just like other people did. The Immigration and Customs Enforcement people, the security, even the nurses treated them horribly. They would laugh at them, mock them or make comments. And she would call and tell me they wouldn't give her medical care. She was scared because they weren't giving her the medication she needed. She was asking the people inside, the ICE people, to see the doctor.

After a while she was finally taken to the doctor. The doctor told Vica that her T-cell count was low and she needed treatment, medication to help boost her cell count. Vica told him all right, she wanted it. But the doctor told her he would give her some time to think about it because the treatment would be something she couldn't stop taking. She told the doctor okay, I want it, but she never got the medication.

We spoke July 5, and she was feeling well. In fact, that day we said some really beautiful things to each other. I told her to take care of herself. I told her, "Don't stress, you know stress is bad for you."

And I told her to keep insisting and insisting until they gave her the medication. I told her, "You have to insist because you know I love you very much. If you aren't here I don't know what I'll do. I need you to live for me." I told her many things.

She said to me, "You don't know how wonderful it is to hear you say those things. If you could only see the smile on my face right now hearing you talk to me like this." I told her I was glad she was happy, that everything I told her was what was inside my heart. I wanted her to take care of herself. It was the last time we spoke.

The next Sunday came and went and I didn't hear from her. I thought it was very strange. That Monday or Tuesday I got a call from Deanna, a friend of Vica's in detention. Deanna's also transgender. She said, "Señora, your Victoria is very sick. She has a high fever. And they won't pay attention to us and take her to the doctor. They just ignore us. She's lying in bed with a very high temperature. She's vomiting. She has diarrhea. She can't even stand up to go to the bathroom. We have to carry her."

I tried calling around for help, to some organizations that help Latinos with HIV/AIDS. I called six, seven times. I called an attorney, too. I would explain what was happening so they'd realize how urgent this case was, and that I needed help. After I would finish telling them, they would say, "Oh, Señora, we are very sorry but we can't help you. We can't go there and force them to give her the medicine."

Deanna called me again. She said, "Your daughter is very ill, very ill." I felt so desperate. Those were terrible days. I felt impotent at not being able to go see her, to do anything. If I had papers, or a permit, I would have gone the moment I got the call from Deanna. I would have found a way, hired an attorney. I would have done anything.

I got a call on Wednesday, July 17. The phone rang and a person from the Mexican consulate said they were looking for me. The person said, "You know your daughter is detained. Your daughter is very sick. She is in the hospital. And I'm going to give you a permit to go see her. The doctors said she isn't going to live long."

I was alone and just started crying on the phone. They gave me the address of the hospital and I called my daughter Sara and my husband. When I got to the hospital there was an ICE guard. I knew it was ICE because he was wearing a green uniform and it said ICE on the uniform.

When I went in I saw Vica. Her eyes were shut. She was full of drugs. But when I said, "Vica," she immediately opened her eyes. It was hard for her but she looked at me.

She tried to raise her arms to hug me but they fell. She was so pale. She had lost weight. She was too weak. I saw her mouth try to form a kiss, but she couldn't. I could see how hard it was for her to breathe. You could see it in her chest.

And when she tried to move she screamed. I think her lungs were really hurting her because when she moved she would yell, "Oh God." When we arrived, the guards were at the door, but when we came close to her to hold her hand, or speak to her, the guards would immediately come over and hover over the bed. They would watch every movement we made. At first, I didn't notice she was shackled. I only noticed Vica wanted to shift her body because she was tired of being in the same position, but she couldn't move her foot. I thought maybe her foot was stuck in the blanket or something. I lifted the blanket and I saw the chain. My heart was already broken, but to see that... She didn't deserve to die like that. She was already in agony. I told Sara, "She has a chain."

Sara said, "What?" She went and looked and we both started to cry.

I told the guard, "Please, do you think she is going to try and leave like this? She can't even breathe on her own." I said, "Please take the chain off. Let her die in peace." He said he couldn't do that. He asked if I wanted him to lose his job. That was all he said.

We planned to stay with her that night. But there was a shift change around six. We were all told to leave the room. When we tried to go back in, the ICE guards wouldn't let us in. They asked us why were we there and said we couldn't go in without a signed letter or permit.

We returned the next morning and there was a guard standing there. We asked him if we could go in. He said no because we still didn't have a letter.

We went to the car and called the consulate. The official said he would call San Pedro and he would ensure we got in. He called back about twenty-five minutes later and told me everything was taken care of, you can go in now. It was ten a.m. and we spent all of Thursday there. That Thursday night, around two a.m. she couldn't breathe. The doctors had told us that moment would come when she wouldn't be able to breathe on her own.

It was so hard, so hard to decide. Those were some of the hardest moments of my life. When the doctor said she couldn't breathe and I had to put a respirator on her it was so hard for me. The doctor told me she wasn't going to get better. But telling the doctors not to put her on the respirator was like saying I wanted to cut her life short. It was so hard but at the same time I heard the doctor's words: if I *didn't* put her on the respirator she would stop suffering. I think I wanted them to put her on the respirator perhaps to have some hope. But there wasn't even a one percent chance.

My daughter Sara was crying and begging me to put Vica on the respirator. I talked to her a long time, to ask her not to cause me more pain because it was already so hard to make a decision I didn't want to make. But we didn't have a choice. We had to let her rest in peace, to not suffer. And Sara finally understood.

I was exhausted. My husband was there with me. I had told Sara, "Let's go to the waiting room and sleep." And during that hour Vica got very sick. She said, "Mami, Mami." Those were her last words.

When we into the room my child wasn't conscious. She didn't

have any life. She was just lying in bed, but you could see she wasn't breathing.

SOMETHING INSIDE OF ME

My life is so different now. When I wake up in the morning, Vica's death is the first thing I think about. Sometimes I think this is a nightmare and I will wake up. But then I get up and get ready for work.

I'd like to talk to other mothers who have sons that are transgender and tell them to accept them, to love them, to support them. But right now my life is very uncertain. I'm confused. I'm going through such a painful stage. I can only wait for the day when I am reunited with Vica. But right now, I want to make this as public as I can, in English, so the Anglos, the Americans know and people care. This is important so it never happens to another person. It makes me so sad because the people who witnessed what happened to Vica have all been moved to a jail in Texas. One of them called me the other day and said that another detainee in Texas has AIDS and a low cell count, and is starting to get sick like my Vica. They aren't giving this person medical attention either.[2] When I hear this it gives me strength to keep going to do more, to talk. Sometimes I don't want to talk to anyone but something inside of me pushes me to speak out. The pain my daughter went through, all that can't be in vain.

---

[2] These detainees are being held in the South Texas Detention Center in Pearsall, Texas.

ABEL

AGE: *35*
COUNTRY OF ORIGIN: *Guatemala*
OCCUPATION: *Fish factory worker, field hand*
HOME: *New Bedford, Massachusetts*

WE ARE INDIGENOUS,
WE HAVE NO BORDERS

Abel fled his native Guatemala as a child amid the military counterinsurgency campaign targeting the indigenous population during the 1980s. By 1990, he had made his way to New Bedford, where he now lives with his wife and newborn son. A seaport town sixty miles south of Boston, New Bedford has lost twenty thousand manufacturing jobs over the last two decades. Currently, immigrants make up more than 20 percent of the population. Abel has cleaned and packed fish and scallops; stonewashed jeans by hand; and embroidered baseball caps and uniforms for garment finishing companies. Abel, like most of New Bedford's ethnic Mayans, tries to remain as unobtrusive as possible. He spoke Spanish, his second language, during our interview, which took place not long after the roundup of 361 men and women in a March 2007 immigration sweep in New Bedford, one of the largest raids in recent history.

I come from a small town near Quiche, Guatemala. I was born the thirteenth of September, 1972. My native tongue isn't Spanish— I speak K'iche'. I learned most of my Spanish in America. I am a worker here in New Bedford. This story is not invented. It's all things of real life.

My parents were poor. They worked in the fields, harvesting coffee, cane, and cotton. They worked according to the harvest season. They would bring us kids to the fields with them. The workers were given food; but only the workers, not the kids. So, my parents shared their rations with me and my siblings. There were seven of us.

Then came the time of violence. The guerrillas were fighting the army. We were especially worried about General Lucas.[1] He's the one who wanted to kill all the indigenous people. And we were part indigenous. My father was *Catequista*.[2] And my mom is a traditional Mayan. Every time anyone saw us coming they'd say, "Here come the Indians, those *chusmes*."[3]

One day we were detained by the army. It was the most difficult time of my life. It was a Friday. My mom is a midwife. She was taking a course in another town and had to walk four hours across the mountains. On our way home, some soldiers grabbed us. They accused us of being rebels. I was just a kid, barely eight years old. Because my mom was taking courses at the health clinic, for this, they thought we were part of the other side of the fight. But it wasn't true.

They brought me to one spot, my mom to another. They had guns. They put the guns to our heads. And they told me to tell them about my father—where he slept and what he did. When I didn't tell them, they hit me in the head. They threw me on the ground. They dragged my mom by her hair. I saw a soldier put a barrel of his rifle up her *corte*.[4] And they started to shoot their guns. I prayed. I asked God to keep them from doing anything bad to us. I don't know about any miracles from God, but after torturing us for about two

---

[1] General Romeo Lucas Garcia, president of Guatemala from 1978 to 1982.

[2] Catechist. Practitioners of Christianity who take religious instruction through a doctrine of question-and-answer study.

[3] Derogatory slang meaning rabble or vermin.

[4] Skirt.

hours, they put us in their truck in the back with some other people. And then one of the soldiers guarding us fainted—he just fell down. I don't know what the reason was. And so when he fainted, we ran away. Me and my mom. We jumped out of the truck and fled.

When we arrived at the house, and told my dad what happened, he said that we had to leave—that they were going to kill us. But we didn't have the time. The next day the military came and broke into our home. They looked through everything in the house, and only found a flag of the *Acción Católica.*[5] Then the soldiers set fire to our house and left. We were caught in the middle of the flames. My siblings used blankets to put out the fire and so we escaped being burned.

After that we knew no peace. No place was safe. We couldn't work, because the army was so bad, always looking for us. Sometimes I would go to school, but the teacher would only come for two hours. Even the teacher was part of the army. He asked us what our parents did at night. It was said that our teacher killed people.

I CRIED A LOT FOR A LOT OF REASONS

When I was twelve, I left for Mexico with my cousin. I escaped my country and I crossed the border into Mexico. I went through in a bus. I bought a machete so I could get work in the coffee fields, but no one gave me work there because I was so young. At twelve years old, what did I know? I didn't even speak Spanish. In Mexico, I had my first encounter with Immigration. A man grabbed me and said, "You're not Mexican." He took my machete and threw it. Just like that. He threw it far. He took all my money. He took everything I had. He only left me with the pants I was wearing. For food, I only had coffee beans to chew on.

---

[5] An evangelical group of catechists that fled government persecution during the civil war in Guatemala.

I found work picking fruit on a farm estate. There were lots of people there from Guatemala. Maybe five hundred of us. But still I was alone. I missed my siblings, my parents. I cried a lot for a lot of reasons. I cried for my family. I cried because I only had one pair of pants. When I had to wash them, I would stand there naked, waiting for my pants to dry. I was thirteen years old.

I HAVE TO LIVE

I returned home for Christmas. I had grown up a lot in Mexico. I grew up so much that when my mom first saw me, she didn't know who I was. I had to say, "You're my mom." She fainted. She said she thought I had died. She thought that the army had killed me.

When I first got home, I sold eggs. I needed to earn money for my mother and father, who had both fallen ill. All I did was work and eat eggs. After a while, I left again for Mexico, where I knew I could make better money.

I told my mom that I was leaving again. She said, "No, don't ever go! You are my son, and I love you so much." And so she tried to put me in the church to be a priest. But I didn't want that. Eventually, I left home again. I said to myself, "I can't live here. I can't live with these guns and wars and bombs." At that time there were still military problems. There was not peace there yet. It was the time of General Ríos Montt.[6] Montt was worse than Lucas.

I went back to Mexico where I worked for another few years. I felt so much safer. It was so much more peaceful in Mexico. Then some friends said they knew the way from Mexico to the United States. They said it was even better in America. They said we could go by foot from Chiapas to the border. My illusion, my dream, was to come

---

[6] Efraín Ríos Montt succeeded Lucas as President of Guatemala. Widespread, well-documented human rights abuses occurred during his reign.

here because everything would be total peace and calm in the United States. I later found that this was all a sham.

I walked in the desert for eight days. Before then, I didn't even realize that there was a desert there! And I only brought one gallon of water. I finished it after two days, and I had to suffer through days without eating or drinking. It was only three of us traveling together. We didn't come with a coyote. I remember all I kept thinking was, "I have to live, I have to live." We passed the border in Arizona. A friend told me, "You're already in the United States." I didn't know anything—I didn't realize I had crossed the border. All I knew was that I wanted to sleep. The terrain didn't seem any different from one side of the border to the other. It was the same land to me. "You're here," he said. "You made it to the United States."

Everyone spoke Spanish, especially near the border. I asked people where I could find work. They told me, "You're so young! Go to school." This was in Arizona. It was hard for a while. I didn't know anyone and no one gave me work. Sometimes I slept in the streets. Then I found a job cleaning houses and cutting lawns. They gave me three dollars an hour, two dollars an hour, and a bit of food.

Later, I found out that on the east coast, there was more work. So I took a bus east. I was on that bus for days. Finally, I got off the bus somewhere close to Boston. I spotted a dark-skinned guy, and I asked him if he spoke Spanish, and he said yes. I asked him if he'd help me find some work. He said in New Bedford there was fishing work that I could do. I didn't know fish, but I needed work. So I went with this guy to New Bedford.

WE ATE THE PARTS THAT THE FACTORY DIDN'T NEED

At first, no one gave me work because I didn't speak any English. I didn't understand anything. Maybe they did offer me jobs, but

I didn't understand. This was in 1990. By that time, I was eighteen years old. But since I had been so poor, with so little to eat, I looked really pale and thin and much younger. Soon, I met some other people who spoke Spanish. There weren't many Guatemalans in New Bedford at that time. There were a lot of Dominicans.

I found a cheap place to stay for the first six months with some Dominicans who were renting an apartment. I slept in the closet of that house. There wasn't room for me in any of the rooms. But it wasn't so bad because at least it wasn't cold in the closet. This was during winter.

I found work at a tire place. At the beginning, when I was still really little, I couldn't even lift the tires to load on the truck for recycling. They paid me $3.50 an hour. With the money from this job I paid for my rent and for my food. Later, I was able to save a little bit. Three dollars in Guatemala is a lot. To me, at that time, it was worth my suffering. But I was always afraid because my boss threatened me and sometimes he carried a gun. I would tremble in fear of him.

After the tire place, I began working for the first time at a fish house. They gave me work under the condition that I did everything they wanted. I stayed there for about four years. At the plant, one of my jobs was cleaning monkfish. The boats would come into the port and we would unload the fish. We'd put the fish in the cooler, and then the next day, we shared the task of processing. First we peeled them. Then we'd clean and pack them. We filleted the fish, and ate the livers ourselves. We ate the parts that the factory didn't need. The livers helped me out a lot.

The most I got paid was four an hour. And they paid me in cash.

Since before there had never been Guatemalans—I was one of the few—they told me that if I could find more Guatemalans to work there, that they would pay me a little more. They wanted me to contact my friends, to bring them there to work for cheap. First, I called my family. I told them that I was in the United States. I hadn't spoken to them since arriving here. They gave me other phone numbers of other people that might be interested in coming to work for the fish company. After a few months they came to work. The company liked the Guatemalans because we are such good, hard workers. We are also willing to work on weekends. There were some Americans working there, but we were replacing them at that company. They only worked eight hours. I got there at four in the morning and left at eleven, twelve at night. We cleaned up afterward. We did it all.

When I explained that I couldn't speak very much English, they told me I had to learn. But they wouldn't teach me. And my Spanish, too—I still couldn't speak too much Spanish then, either. I mostly just spoke K'iche' with all the other indigenous Guatemalans working there. The other Hispanics didn't like it that we spoke our own language. When we greeted each other, they thought we were making fun of them secretly. They would say, "Don't use that fucking language here." The other Hispanics working there were Puerto Ricans, Dominicans, and some Salvadorans. There were about a hundred and fifty of us, total. You don't see a single American cleaning fish in the fish plants.

There wasn't really overtime. If you worked eighteen hours in one day, they paid you four dollars for eight hours. When I complained to the manager, he started paying me $4.75. Sometimes, the manager, to get me to work more, would give me beer. He'd tell me, "Drink!" And I didn't really have experience with drinking beer. But I drank the beer as he told me to, and it heated me up while I was working. And when he saw that the beer helped me work more, he started to give me drugs, marijuana. He would say, "Smoke this, and you'll work with more energy and focus." I didn't know anything about any of this. In my place in Guatemala, none of this exists. I told him I preferred not to take any of these drugs and this made him like me less. He was selling it. He wanted the workers to buy it from him. He sold fish and he sold marijuana.

THEY DIDN'T CARE IF WE GOT HURT

On that job, I had to spend lots of time in the freezer, and they didn't give me any protective clothing or gloves. I went with my regular clothes into the freezer. I never asked for anything. That's why my employers liked me. Many things happened there. People often slipped. And it was tough because we didn't have any insurance or a doctor or anything like that. When they pay you in cash, you don't have any rights at all. If you fall and hurt yourself, they grab you and send you home. We only had a half-hour break to rest.

There were very bad accidents. I remember one of them that happened about ten years ago. I was nearby when it happened. At the plant, there was a machine for grinding the meat of the dogfish. We'd clean the fish, take off the head, the fins, the tail, the meat, and the bones. And then we'd put it all in a machine to be ground up. This machine was very dangerous, and no one ever explained to us how it functioned. The temperature inside reaches 180 degrees. Once, we were told to clean it, to clear out the bones. To do this we had to climb inside. It was like being inside an oven. I felt like I was being burned. I climbed out to save myself. And this other person, my friend, who was still in the machine—he died. He died in the machine. It was absolutely horrible. He was in the U.S. with his son. I left that place after my friend's death and I worked in other places for a while, but later I encountered the same kind of thing at other companies.[7]

At another fish plant we processed scallops, dogfish, monkfish livers, and flounder. We prepared lots of different products with the fish. The biggest danger was often the floor. Fish houses are very slippery. They didn't care if we got hurt. And they didn't want us to go to the doctor, because they said if we go, Immigration will get us.

---

[7] See Appendix C for more information.

We too were afraid that Immigration would get us. There were guys who stayed home from work six months, because they didn't want to go to the hospital, for fear of immigration officers.

At the scallops plant, my employers would hit me and the other workers, especially when they were drunk. My bosses would get drunk and fight with knives, with bats. The majority of fish processing plants are like this, with the bosses drunk and abusive. During the years that I worked in fish, I worked most of the plants. Only two or three of all of the bosses that I knew respected their workers. When I had problems at one company I passed on to another, and after that another, and another.

On one of the jobs, there was an inspector who would come to look the place over once a week. Once a week, we had to clean everything. Once a week, we had to put hats on our heads, gloves on our hands. Once a week, we had to disinfect the knives. That day, you couldn't smoke, you couldn't drink beer. And when the inspector wasn't coming, everyone would smoke in the building. People would urinate in the cooler! Then the supervisor started to date that inspector and things loosened up. Everything stayed dirty, we didn't disinfect the knives; we didn't have to wear gloves.

Most of the companies don't teach the workers how to stay clean and safe. They don't advise us about dangers, or explain how to do things in case of emergency. If you ask, "Excuse me, I need to know where the emergency exit is," they say, "Did you come to work or to investigate?"

SHINE THESE BOOTS WITH YOUR TONGUE

All those years, I hadn't seen my mother. I called her so that she could know how I was doing, because she barely knew me at all then. At that time I was about twenty-five years old. I decided to try and go home. I wanted to see my family. I went by plane. It was 1996. It was easier to travel then. When I got back, I saw that peace had been established, but still there were the same things—the corruption, the racial discrimination, the selfishness, and the torturing.

Once I had money in New Bedford, I ate pretty well. I came back to Guatemala a little fat and so the authorities said to me, "You— where did you come from? Aren't you fit to fight?" And so they grabbed me for the draft, to work for the government army. No one goes voluntarily. If they see that you are fit and able, they take you. I didn't want to serve, but an official told me that if I refused, they would kill me. They said, "You are going to serve your country."

In the training, they didn't give me enough food. I had to suffer hunger for three, four days. And they said, "You have to shine these boots with your tongue. You have to kill this dog with your teeth." They were saying to me, "If your mother is a guerrilla, kill her. If your father is a guerrilla, kill him. If your brothers are guerrillas, kill them." One has to be an assassin, completely.

So I escaped. I ran away from the camp. They taught us how to escape from the guerrillas. I used the same techniques on them. I disappeared without a trace.

I came over to the U.S. again. I went with a coyote this time. He brought me from Guatemala to Arizona. I had to pay twenty-five thousand quetzals, approximately three thousand dollars. I paid, but, unfortunately, Mexican immigration got me at the border. They eventually told me I had to pay them if I wanted to be let off. They sequestered me. They grabbed me. They punched me.

They sent me back to Guatemala—again. It would have been better if they'd stolen from me. At home, I had another run-in with the military and I said to my mother, "I am not going to live here. They're going to kill me for sure." And so when I finally came back to the U.S. after that trip, I told myself I would never go back to my country.

I made my way back to New Bedford and began working again. I got a job in a processing plant that worked with skates—a fish with a spine. There were no inspectors there. There weren't any safety standards at all. It was a small company, but they processed lots of fish. Once again, we unloaded the boat, processed the fish, washed it, packaged it. At that plant, we even put the labels on for the stores.

I DIDN'T HAVE A SINGLE RIGHT

I haven't just worked in fish. There's this temp company that finds jobs for people like me, all kinds of jobs. My last job, one of the hardest, was at a company that dyes clothing products that come from Mexico. We used machines with capacities of two hundred liters of dye. They made me sweep there at first. Then they saw that I had lots of working power.

They said they wanted me to get to know the machines. These were big machines with lots of chemicals for stonewashing pants. But they didn't explain to me how to use them. They only told me, "Just punch the start button." These were old, old machines and they would sometimes give you an electrical shock that really moved you.

One time I opened one of the machines, and it almost took my hand off. And the boss was right there. "Fucking stupid," he said to me. I said, "But you didn't explain anything to me. You have to explain to me how to operate these machines."

He was paying me in cash, and, according to him, I didn't have a single right, nothing. So when he ordered me to operate a machine, I had to do it. There were a lot of injuries there, too. A Salvadoran got hurt; I got hurt. The employers thought nothing of it. Another woman, a Mayan, miscarried at that job. Why? Because she was trying to push a box that weighed three hundred pounds. And when you're pregnant, you shouldn't push this kind of weight. She was on the shift of five in the morning to five at night, pushing these boxes.

There was also a problem with drugs at that dye house. That

manager, he took a lot of drugs and he liked to have only drugged people there with him. If you didn't consume his drugs, he became your enemy. The employees were always so drugged. Once someone defecated on the stairs. I got sent to clean that up.

Once, when OSHA[8] came, I protested to one of the inspectors. I said I couldn't work in the dark. I also said I couldn't eat with all the chemicals everywhere because my skin becomes allergic. And then, when the guy left, my manager said, "If you're going to speak to anyone about working here, you can get out of here now. You're an Indian devil."

After the OSHA guy came, my bosses had made my life impossible. They didn't give me a lunch break, they made me work, work, work: "Take this, do this other thing, go sweep in that dark place." I messed up, perhaps, when I spoke up to OSHA.

But I was tired of all this. I wanted more rights. I didn't care what they did to me. I told my manager I wanted to pay taxes to the government because that's what we should do. I'm not okay with being paid in cash. I don't like to rob the government. And so the guy told me, "Okay, I'll pay you by check, but first show me your papers." Then I said, "Now you want papers? In case I'm not the same person that I was yesterday? You already know me." He began to threaten me. Then he sent me to go alone to a sketchy place where two people later came and beat me up. It was a Thursday, at noon, lunch hour.

I spoke up about my rights. I got beat up for it. But they must have heard some of what I was saying, because after that they made us a small kitchen at the factory so we could eat away from the chemicals. They also put in some ropes so that we wouldn't fall. And so it was getting better. But this was before the raids.

---

[8] Occupational Safety and Health Administration.

LIKE POISON IN YOUR BRAIN

We Mayan people, we sometimes have feelings of premonition. Sometimes we dream that something will happen. That night in March I had a dream. When I woke up I didn't want to go to work. I was lucky. I was still at home during the raid that morning. I heard the helicopters. Then my brother called me. He thought I had gone to work and he told me I shouldn't go anywhere because Immigration is around. And he told me they brought dogs this time.

After the raid, the president of the company that owned the dye house said, "You must all leave because I don't want to have problems. You have got to go."

So they sent us all away—women, men, everyone, just like that. Only the Guatemalans had to leave. My supervisor had a big smile on his face. He raised up his hands, saying, "Get out of here—leave. You are criminals. You have a really bad rap in this country. It's good that you will all leave for Guatemala—no more Indians here. Woooooo!" All the Portuguese workers applauded. There were four Salvadorans at the plant, but they stayed, they had papers. There were some Portuguese who didn't have papers and they also had to go. But they were allowed to come back later.

We were left without jobs. I was living in a house of between six to eight people at that time. But unfortunately after the raid, we were left with only three people. We had a very hard time paying eight hundred dollars in rent. Food, too, was scarce. One week it got so bad that a woman who was pregnant gave us some of her milk for our corn flakes.

Unfortunately there are still a lot of people here who have been left traumatized because their husband or their wife has been taken away. They think that every helicopter that goes by—it's Immigration hunting for them. Some of the people who were in jail, they seem scarred. They talk about bad spirits. They hear the wind knocking on the door. They think every sound is Immigration. So their senses are not whole anymore.

It is all about fear. Fear invades us. One is always afraid—they're constantly cleaning out immigrants, because someone says something to Immigration. A day doesn't pass without thoughts of this. It's like poison in your brain.

WE DIVIDE UP OUR BREAD

I now have a young son. My son is an American. He was born here. He is indigenous. The advantage that my son will have is that he will be able to travel to see the rest of our family. And it's my dream that when he gets a little older he will go to visit my mother while she is still living.

Every week I continue to send money home to my family in Guatemala. For now it's only me working.

I now have a part-time job that is eight hours a day. I do yard work and weed flowerbeds. I mulch, cut grass. I also work weekends in the fields, cleaning and weeding the cranberry bogs. Right now it's the harvest season. I'm sorting out the berries.

On Saturdays and Sundays, I begin work at five a.m. There are about forty to fifty people in the fields. There is not one single American, just illegals. Sometimes people come with no food in their stomachs and they get dizzy. There's no food at home. So we share our bread. We have to help our brothers and sisters. Hidden under the tractors in the cranberry fields, we divide up our bread.

We are supposed to make more for working on weekends. But since the raid, we don't. The man offered us $5 an hour. The minimum wage in Massachusetts is $7.50, so to offer $5 is against the law. But what choice do we have?

I have been in this country almost fifteen years now. I've worked in all different kinds of jobs. Starting with the tires, then mostly fish.

But I've also made clothes. I've even made police uniforms, firemen's uniforms, government officials' uniforms. I put the names on the jackets. I began in the fields, in Guatemala—cutting coffee, cleaning sugar cane. We cleaned sugar cane, we processed the sugar that would come here. My whole life has been work.

They treat us like slaves. If we have cars, the police come after us. They see that we are different, that we are Mayans, and they ask us for our licenses when they know very well that we don't have one. It's tough. We have to go by foot to the bank, to buy food.

There's mafia now in New Bedford and they come after us also. They have assaulted me twice in the street. They know that on Fridays, we go to cash our checks. They wait for us behind the banks. Plus, the bank now asks for so much information before allowing you to cash checks and deposit your money, we are running out of places to put it. Sometimes we hide our money under the mattresses, under chairs, under the carpets, in the refrigerator. Not long ago, there was a *compañero*[9] who was robbed of almost nine thousand dollars. Why? Because he couldn't open an account in a bank.

The temp company that gets us all jobs is run by Chinese people who are part of a mafia, I believe. They pay us, but they don't ever really say who is paying us. It's all ambiguous. Sometimes they don't pay us what we are owed. And if we want to contest this, we don't know who to speak to. We are never told who is in charge. They use this tactic to cheat us out of our money. One day I did protest, and this Chinese guy threatened me—he said, "Don't play with me. I will cut your tongue off."

NO MORE LASHINGS

Now I understand many things. I didn't study too much, but life

---

[9] Fellow worker.

teaches me, the street has taught me. Now I demand my rights. With or without papers, I feel I have the same rights. I feel American—I have never felt like a Guatemalan, because I couldn't develop myself there. As it says in that verse in the Bible, "No more lashings for the slaves." We come from far away, and we receive lashings.

We are left wanting so much, here in this country. And we have lost so much. The drug scene is really consuming us. If we don't get involved in it we become victims of it in other ways. Our women—if an American likes one of our women, he brings her to his office, he touches her hands, he touches her rear end, as they say—the vulgar word. They do everything. And you can't say anything, or they'd do it more. There are many women who become pregnant in this way. And there is nothing controlling this. The companies don't do anything. The women feel afraid that they will be deported and shamed back home. And if you interfere to defend a woman, they say you won't have any more work here, starting tomorrow. All we do is tolerate, tolerate. In the afternoons, we cry—we share with each other our wounds of each day.

Some of us are more comfortable speaking up about our rights—we know what we are entitled to. We speak to Americans, people who do have papers, people who work at organizations, people who can do something for us. The bosses of the companies are afraid of these organizations because they support us. They allow us to have a bit of control. Without the organizations, we are abandoned.

One day, recently, when they were fumigating the cranberry bogs, hearing a plane brought me back. I remembered when they bombed us in Guatemala. The trauma that I experienced will never leave me. I have it imprinted in me. And it continues here in this country. I often think, "Aren't we in a country that calls itself democratic?" What politician will have anything to do with us? When will we see a relief from all this?

Sometimes tourists come to Guatemala. We would never say,

"You don't have papers." Because I speak a bit of English, last time I was home, I worked a few days as a guide for some tourists. I welcomed them so much, I took care of them. I treated them well.

But here they say, "Go back to Guatemala! If you don't work well, get the fuck out of here and go back to Guatemala!" In this country, for example, there are terrorists, criminals. The only crime that we immigrants have committed here is to produce and to earn money. This is our only crime. It's not so big. But it's us, workers, that the government pays attention to.

And since we are indigenous, we have no borders. Though we speak English, we are indigenous. So, for me, justice doesn't exist here. The blows we receive are more than physical, they're psychological.

POLO, 23
Gulfport, Mississippi

Polo comes from a small town in the state of Oaxaca in Mexico, and speaks both Spanish and Zapotecan. He worked for a subcontractor to a subcontractor to a subcontractor to Kellogg Brown and Root—which until recently was owned by Halliburton—cleaning up the Seabees Naval Construction Battalion Center in Gulfport, Mississippi after Hurricane Katrina.

We went down to Mississippi to the Naval base at Gulfport, and started to work. Our job was to clean all the mess—the houses, the trees, everything—all that the wind had damaged, had destroyed. We collected all the trash from the streets. We cut up the fallen trees, piling them in one spot. This is the type of work we were doing. It was a big, serious disaster, and there was so much cleaning up to do.

The *bolillos*, the white people, drove the machines. We were more like the helpers. There were other people living on the base, black people. They were people who had lost their houses. They were like refugees. I imagine that the black people went to work, but with their own people, with people of their same race. We were pretty separate in our work.

We returned to our cots at about seven at night. We slept there, in an airplane hangar on the base. We weren't allowed to leave the base at all because the *poyeros*—human smugglers—guarded us strictly. They would charge us if we wanted to go out. Once all our debts were paid, then they said we could leave.

Our boss kept a notebook with our names and all the records of our hours. We'd been promised eleven dollars per hour. We worked every day—Monday to Monday—and the first three weeks we weren't paid at all. When we complained about this, the bosses would say, "It's fine, Don't worry. I'm going to the bank right now." Then they would come back and tell us that the bank wouldn't give them the money, that we would have to wait. That's the excuse they gave us.

After two weeks, they started to take away some of the cots. We were totally taken aback. Some of us had to sleep outside. We didn't know what to do. We worked it out according to who needed the cots most. The people on the floor had some blankets, but that was it. There was intense heat during the day and intense cold at night.

Well, then the boss disappeared. We tried to find her so we could get our checks, but she was gone. After three days, the military men came. They spoke to us in English. As they were soldiers, they had their guns. They came up to our cots—the few cots that we had—and took them. Then they shut off the bathrooms. And they took us out, like they were cleaning out the base.

After that the group of us stayed next to the cemetery, under plastic tarps. I felt so sad. I hadn't been paid. I had nowhere to go. I didn't know where they wanted me to go, what they wanted me to do. That's what I was thinking: What am I supposed to do now? I thought about my family because they were thinking that I was earning money, and there I was, without work, and without any payment for the work I had done. I really wanted to go back at that point. My idea was to get to Mississippi, to start working, and to earn money to send to my family. I thought that here it would be easy to earn money. I couldn't imagine this kind of humiliation. Yes, humiliation. They humiliated us.

[*Editor's Note:* After a complaint from an activist group to the U.S. Department of Labor, the direct subcontractor to KBR paid the workers a total of $100,000. Another payment of $144,000 is forthcoming. Polo is currently working in a furniture factory in Mississippi, trying to save up money to build a house for himself in his hometown.]

DIXIE

AGE: *45*
COUNTRY OF ORIGIN: *Colombia*
OCCUPATION: *School administrator, babysitter, housekeeper*
HOME: *Bowling Green, Ohio*

IT WAS LIKE SODOM
AND GOMMORAH

Dixie is a single mother of two in her forties, originally from Cali, Colombia. Trained as an educator, Dixie made the difficult decision to come to the U.S. after economic problems in her native country put her children's future in jeopardy. After a harrowing journey, Dixie arrived in New York City and began working in the fast food industry. During a stint as a mail sorter, she met her U.S.-citizen husband, Paul. At first things went smoothly, but soon, after a move to Louisiana, the couple began having serious problems. Paul did not want Dixie to send money back to Colombia. The relationship became abusive. Dixie met us in the parking lot of a miniature golf course outside Bowling Green, Ohio, and spoke to us in Spanish. The course is located on the edge of a poor area known to house a number of undocumented people.

My real name is Dethze. But most Americans cannot pronounce it. And the truth is they don't even really try. So here I tell people, "Call me Dixie."

I am forty-five years old. I was born in Cali, Colombia on June 1, 1962. I don't have any bad memories from my childhood; I had an excellent childhood, a good adolescence—thank God—a good mother, a good father, family, a good education. There was every-thing that anyone could have wanted: love, happiness, compassion, communication, everything. My papa was always there, as well as my mother, They helped us and loved us, no matter our mistakes. They paid for private school from primary through university for myself and my brothers and sisters.

My family was well-respected in the neighborhood, notably for the responsibility that my father showed toward his family. He was a worker, at the factory of Adams Gum. He would arrive home tired after a hard shift, but he would always ask us how we were doing in school and help us with our homework. We were very united as a family, with our parents supporting us, the kids. Our teachers and directors would say our parents were great examples of parents.

I graduated from a private institute in Cali, with a preschool-education bachelor's degree in 1982. I began work as a teacher at a school where my older sister Maria was the director. The school was located in a barrio on the south side of Cali. Over the years, the school expanded and began offering elementary school and even-tually middle and high school. While my sister Maria was overall director, I became director of instruction, in charge of the curricu-lum and other teachers. It was a private school, charging for the education. Although it was located in a modest area of Cali, the parents found the means to pay because they wanted to give their children an opportunity for a better education. Many public schools in Colombia are of poor quality due to government strikes and other unrest in the country.

Over the years, operation of the school became more difficult and the wages for myself and the teachers shrank. This was due to infla-tion cutting the value of our wages. Also, since Cali is one of the centers of the drug cartels, it has suffered from the violence that the country's civil war has wrought. The situation made it more difficult for our parents to pay for their children's education. We tried to raise prices at the school, but the parents balked and we lost students. People were angry. At one point we even received telephone death threats. We assumed the threats had something to do with school business, but the police never determined who it was.

By this time, I was a single mother raising two children, so the financial squeeze continued to worsen as my pay shrank. My children grew older. They had greater needs. I was trying to give private classes on the side, but it wasn't working out. We all were living together—my parents, my kids, me, and my mentally disabled sister, Luzdali. Then disaster struck. My father came down with cancer and suddenly we had huge medical bills.

Before, I had been able to support my kids and help maintain my parents' household. But by 1999 we simply didn't have enough money to make ends meet. My two younger brothers, Carlos and Michael, had already gone to the United States. I began to think that moving to America was an answer to my problems.

It wasn't an easy decision. It was very hard to leave my family, especially my children, Cristina and Augusto. But I thought, How can I give them at least what I had? How can they become educated and go to the university? How can we pay for it, if I don't do something? It was a point of pride for me to give my children this opportunity since my father, just a worker, had sent us to college. I was afraid I wouldn't be able to do the same for Cristina and Augusto. I had lost my status as a professional.

So I left Colombia in late 1999. First, though, I went to Costa Rica and then to El Salvador. I had never left Colombia before. In crossing over, I had to deal with the sort of people I had never been involved with before, people so strange, so different. To begin with, the people who help bring people over here are very poor people. They are people who live off of smuggling human beings.

This is when my true suffering began. One night, a man who was so poor he didn't even have teeth, the poor thing, he came to my house and told me that he was going to bring me to the United States. I could only bring with me the clothes on my back. And so I went. I took nothing from my old life. Only my skin.

THANK GOD, GUATEMALA

I was the only Colombian in our group. But I couldn't say outloud that I was Colombian. Everybody thinks Colombians are rich. So they are charged more money by coyotes, by police asking for bribes. So I had to learn how to speak and sound like a Guatemalan.

Crossing the border between El Salvador and Guatemala was very difficult. They put us in a cart, and covered us with baskets. They especially had to hide me because my face doesn't seem Guatemalan. Once we crossed into Guatemala, we went by bus—with chickens, cats, lots of country folk. And each time the bus stopped, the Guatemalan police got on the bus to check everyone. I had been told to pretend that I was the wife of one of the other Guatemalan travelers. And so when the police came on board, one man would embrace me, as if I were his wife.

In Guatemala we stayed up in a camp in the mountains. It was extremely cold. I was uncomfortable. I remember that I had fungus on my fingernails. We had spent many days without washing. Up in the mountains we began to see men with guns, dressed in all black. Our guides told us to lie on the ground and cover ourselves with the grass. Some of the people in my group were taken away by these men. I think they were guerrillas. Or maybe they were part of the military. I was very confused; it was hard to know who was who. All I know is that some of the others were lost. Among us were two women and one small boy, and the rest were all men. And the men always wanted to try to abuse the women.

I was hopeless. I didn't have money or any communication with anyone I knew. We stayed twenty days in the mountains, with only water from the well and cornmeal for food. After this, we came down from the mountains. We went by bus, but soon we were stopped by immigration officers, who asked us to get off. At that point I could not escape. They grabbed me and threw me down, and took me to the police. I didn't even know if I was still in Guatemala: I didn't know where I was. I was held for two days. They interrogated me. I always told them I was Guatemalan, as I was told to say, but they didn't believe me. Eventually they wanted to get rid of me and so they brought me in a car to a town outside Guatemala City and dumped me there.

The name of this town was Gracias a Dios: Thank God, Guatemala. There wasn't much there to be thankful for. It was like those places from the Bible, Sodom and Gomorrah. It was a town like that. A nightmare place, full of poor and desperate people. A squatter camp, really. It was a town full of refugees on the move. So I was there with no money. I had to ask strangers around me if they'd give me some money. And the people treated us poorly—they just kept walking right past us.

There, I made a good friend, a girl. And she told me that the only way to make money to go north was prostitution. And I said, "Sorry, no, I can't work in that field."

Finally, a woman in Gracias a Dios gave me a job. I told her my story, and she told me I could clean her house in exchange for room and board. I worked there for three months. The woman treated me badly. She made me sleep in a room outside, with mice and rats passing right by me.

Eventually I met a coyote who agreed to smuggle me. The man said that he'd charge me four thousand dollars and that he'd take me to Manhattan. I promised him that one of my brothers would pay him as soon as we arrived. He agreed and we took a bus that brought us all the way to Mexico City. I rode with the luggage, squeezed between all the suitcases. That was a place so small, I don't know how they fit me in there. How many hours? I don't even know. If I had to, I'd say it was about eighteen hours in that bus. When we got to Mexico City the police stopped us. They took us all out. They got me and put me in handcuffs. They took me to the station for the night and put me in a cell where terrible things were going on. People were urinating and defecating everywhere. The next day they took me to a prison for women. I was detained there for two more months.

I finally had to confess that I was Colombian. I thought that they were going to deport me, but they said they weren't going to because it would have cost too much to fly me back to Colombia. Instead, they put me to work in the prison. I worked making the beds. I worked in the kitchen. At that point I became friends with a Honduran woman. She and I then made friends with one of the policemen. This policeman helped us escape from that prison. He let us out and told us to flee to a particular hotel. That night I was sick with a fever. I had lost I don't know how much weight. That night, the policeman came and brought me medicine and everything. And he also told us about a man who could take us to Texas. Two days later, we went north on a train.

We arrived at another part of Mexico, I believe it was the entrance to the United States. And when we got there, I stayed in a safehouse for a week. A house with many other people waiting to come to the United States.

Then, one night, very late—it must have been around three in the morning—they took some of us out of the house. When we got to the river—I don't know which river—they told me to take off my clothes and go across. At first, I refused. I didn't want to take off my clothes. But one of the men forced me to strip down to my underwear. He said I would need dry clothes on the other side. He put my clothes in a plastic bag. They had car tires. Inner tubes. They put me in one of those. I crossed the wide river. One person pushed. The current was very strong. One guy from Ecuador started screaming because he had fallen off his tube and was drowning. They had to fish him out.

When we reached the American side, they said it was too dangerous to come up on shore just yet. The coyotes said the immigration people would be looking for us. So we waited on the edge. I submerged myself there, in deep, black water. Only my face was above the water so I could breathe. I don't know how long we waited. Maybe about an hour. Then it was safe to move forward. But I could hardly move. I couldn't even run. I had lost all my shame, but I had to go on. The bag of my clothes was lost. All I had was my bra and my panties, nothing else. Someone told us we were in Texas.

We crawled through the brush like snakes, to a safehouse. But just when I thought it was over, the border patrol discovered us. There was all kinds of shouting. In that house, I hid behind a washing machine with another woman. We were lucky. We stayed there, totally quiet. This woman covered my mouth because I wanted to cry and scream. And there we waited until it was all over, until the next day when we saw that it was safe. We showered at this house. For the first time in so long, I slept in a real bed.

After two days, a man came and asked us where all the other people were. We didn't know! Only two people left, he couldn't believe it. He went and bought us some new clothes. Then he brought us by car to Houston.

By then I was already so tired. I only wanted to go home to my children. I had been doing this for more than six months; I was like a disappeared person. But in Houston there were even more problems. I stayed in a house with many other women waiting to be taken to other places around the country. Men were coming all the time. And every guy that came to that house, he expected some woman to sleep with him. One of the guys approached me, and he too wanted me to sleep with him. I wouldn't do it. I didn't like him. I was afraid of the diseases, and everything. He tried to force me. He said that it would serve me well to give him what he wanted. The other girls told me that it would be better to do as he asked to ensure that he would help all of us. But I really couldn't. I drank a beer. I tried to be friendly. The guy kissed me. I let him. He wanted to go with me to my room, but another girl was there with one of the other guys. All over the apartment, people were having sex. It wasn't easy, but I held that guy off.

I stayed days in that place. The head coyote told me that if my brothers didn't send them money, I would have to stay and work in the house as a babysitter and employee. Finally, I was able to contact my brothers and they were able to help me. They sent money.

I was put in a van and driven across the country. From Texas to Manhattan. It took four days. And all along the way we stopped to drop people off—North Carolina, Georgia, Virginia.

I DIDN'T KNOW ANYTHING

I arrived in New York in April 2000. I stayed with my two brothers. Soon, I was already working. I was able to get false papers that allowed me to work. In Queens, they come up to you, secretively offering these papers. So I got the papers, and started working at Wendy's. They paid me five dollars an hour. I worked at Wendy's from seven in the morning until four in the afternoon. Then, at night, I worked at a McDonald's. On my days off, I cleaned houses. It was all very grueling. And I wasn't any good at any of it. I burned the potatoes. I burned the meat.

It was traumatizing to make the transition from working as a professional in Colombia to working like this. For the first time, people made fun of me. My dress was totally different. At first, I wore stockings, high heels, and makeup to work at the Wendy's! People laughed and laughed. I didn't even know how to clean a bathroom before I came here. Honestly, I didn't know how to fry an egg. In

Colombia, I paid other people to clean my house. It was very hard for me—they all called me stupid in some of the jobs I've had here. I didn't know anything, not even how to sweep. One time my boss was explaining to me, "This is how you sweep, this is how you clean the table, this is how you clean the toilets. You have to clean the insides of them like this."

I remember one night, at the McDonald's, my hands became paralyzed. I had contracted rheumatism from all that work. It was very painful and frustrating. I had to cut back on my work for some time until my hands recovered.

After Wendy's I was able to get temporary work with a company that sorted mail. They had a facility where they sorted, organized, and mailed envelopes for other companies and organizations. They had rush times of the year and so would add workers for temporary months-long terms. It was at this company where I met my husband, Paul, an American.

Within a couple of months we had started a relationship. He would do nice things like take me to some of the homes I cleaned or pick me up from a job I had where I worked a late shift that finished at eleven p.m. At the beginning he was sweet. While we always had something of a language gap, he helped me with the English classes I was taking. In the beginning, we always found a way to communicate.

After about six months, we got married. My two brothers hosted the reception. This was in April of 2003. We had some members of Paul's family and a number of our common friends.

Our plan at that point was to leave New York and go back to Paul's hometown in Louisiana. He said the cost of living was cheaper there. He said in New York we would always be struggling to make ends meet. In Louisiana, we would eventually have our own home.

I was still sending much of my money back home. In good months, I was sending as much as a thousand dollars back home. Paul wasn't very happy with this. But when he married me he knew that

I was supporting my kids and my parents back in Colombia. I told him that this wasn't something that was going to change.

But in Louisiana, we didn't get our own home. In fact we lived with Paul's sister. In her trailer, with her kids. We slept on the sofa in the living room. Not surprisingly, we had some marital tension.

YOU DON'T RIDICULE YOUR WIFE

Our big problem, of course, was money. The small town we lived in was poor and Paul couldn't find much work. And the jobs he did find didn't pay very much. He said he was going to try to get unemployment benefits, but for reasons I don't understand he was not able to receive those benefits.

As for me, it was also very difficult. I couldn't find work either. I began to become very worried about not having any money to send back to Augusto and Cristina in Colombia. The other thing was that I no longer had any papers. One of my employers in New York had taken them and not given them back. And in New York employers never seemed to care very much about papers anyway. But in Louisiana, they did. But now I was married to an American citizen. I had heard that citizens were able to get papers for their spouses. But Paul never, to my knowledge, did anything with Immigration or other government officials to see if I could get immigration papers that permitted me to work, even though we talked about it.

I was becoming more and more anxious about this situation. One day, I told him that we were running out of money, and that he needed to find work. He became very upset and threw my things out of the bedroom and into the living room and shouted at me to get out. He did this in front of his sister's kids. In my upbringing, you don't ridicule your wife like that in front of others. I was very ashamed.

I felt out of place and had no friends to turn to. Paul was talking to various family members about our problems and they started to intervene. They didn't sympathize with me because they saw me as a foreigner clinging to Paul, kind of holding him back. Because of my limited English I couldn't really talk to them. Paul and I started arguing a lot more. Almost every day, we would fight about finances and about his lack of work. He would verbally abuse me during these arguments and continued to try to kick me out. Soon, the fighting became so bad that his sister said that it might be best if we left the trailer.

I told Paul that I intended to move to Ohio, because I had a friend named Clara, who I'd met in New York, who had moved there and who thought I could find work in her town. I was desperate to find work, so that I could help pay our bills and continue to help support my family in Colombia. I did not intend to divorce my husband. I decided to leave because I wanted to make it better financially for both of us. We were having trouble, but I didn't want to lose my husband and my marriage. I loved him; I didn't marry him for papers or some other reason. In fact, I was trying to save the marriage.

Paul realized his hometown in Louisiana was not the same place he had remembered. He didn't have the same friends anymore. Some had families and other obligations; a couple were drug addicts. He began to realize there really wasn't anything special for him there and he decided to come to Ohio with me. My friend Clara agreed to let us both come and live with her.

So after Louisiana, we moved to Ohio. I thought things were going to get better. However, one day during an argument about finances, my husband shoved me and I fell. I believe that this was the first time that he actually physically abused me. Clara heard this from another part of the house. Later that day, she talked to me about it. She didn't think my husband should treat me that way. And she said, though she was my friend, she wasn't going to allow anyone to be treated that way in her house. She asked us to move from her home.

Again I was mortified, not only because Paul had demeaned me but that he had done so in front of others. But I don't blame Clara for what she did. I took it more as a wake-up call that I needed to figure out how to change things. After that, because we still didn't have money, we went to live with one of Paul's new friends. Paul has a way of making friends wherever he goes. We moved in with a man named Steve and his son, outside Bowling Green. Then Paul and I both found work at a Days Inn.

After we moved in, another argument resulted in Paul hitting me. Steve's son heard the altercation we had behind a closed door and told his father about it, saying he had wanted to intervene. Steve told Paul about what his son had witnessed, but Paul simply said it was none of their business. He told me about this without any obvious emotion or being ashamed or embarrassed.

I was upset. I thought that when we left Louisiana and his family dynamic and the difficulty finding work, it would be like the sweet period we shared in New York. I did not call the police at this time. I did not know that I could call the police; Paul said the laws were different in Ohio, and that if I called to complain about something he did to me, the police would take us both to jail. I was also afraid that the police would find out that I was in the United States illegally, and that they would tell the immigration authorities. During our worst arguments, Paul frequently threatened to call the police and have me deported. I was afraid of the consequences of calling the police.

Because we now had regular jobs, we found our own apartment. In the week before Christmas, we had a fight because he wanted to watch TV after getting home late from his shift and I needed to sleep to get up early for my shift. He turned on the TV and the noise was very loud, so I asked him to turn it down. He went crazy. I don't really understand why. I don't know why the TV was so important that night. He threw everything he could grab of mine, including my clothes, the dishes, the photos of my kids, even the Christmas tree, out the door and into the street. He demanded that I leave that night. I said I would leave tomorrow, that I couldn't leave at three a.m. I didn't have a car or anyplace to go. He threw me out of bed and I went to the kitchen to sleep.

At this point I was beginning to see that things hadn't changed much from the difficulties we had in Louisiana.

Nevertheless, basically our life returned to a more or less normal pattern as we made do with our very different work schedules. But things still weren't really getting better. I heard that Paul's friends—some worked at the Days Inn so I heard what they were saying—were telling him he was stupid for letting me send money to Colombia.

Sometime in May, he raised the issue of me sending the money to Colombia for my family. He was so mad. He grabbed me by the neck and threw me out of the bed.

I decided that I had to call the police. The police came in about fifteen minutes. One officer talked to me and one officer talked to Paul. It seemed that the police took Paul's side. I don't know exactly what he told the police officer he spoke to and I didn't understand everything the officer was saying to me. But I understood that as it ended, one of the officers told me not to bother my husband anymore. I didn't know what to do, so I did as he said. I didn't have any cuts or bruises at that time to show to the police. They didn't really offer to help me. He said to sleep in the living room and Paul would sleep in the bedroom. I understood from Paul after the incident that if I called again, the police would call Immigration on me.

I DIDN'T WANT TO BE A FAILURE

I think it was on Mother's Day we had another fight. He threw my things all over the place. He slapped me hard. We had this white plastic basket for storing clothes. He dumped my clothes out and started hitting me with it. When he hit me with the basket, I ran out the door and to a neighbor's home; I think it was about seven in the morning. I knew this person spoke some Spanish and had been friendly in casual encounters around the apartment complex.

I went to his door and said, "My husband has gone crazy, please can I come in?" I stayed there, hidden, until Paul left. I could see out the window toward our apartment. When I saw him leave, I went back to our apartment. I called 911. I told them about the problem, but said I needed to go to work. The police officer on the phone offered to send someone to meet me at work, but I didn't want any trouble at work given my status.

In November, we had an especially bad fight that began over feeding the fish in the aquarium that Paul had. He accused me of doing something with the fish food. That degenerated into a fight over a bunch of our past problems. I went to the bedroom to get away. Paul came to the bedroom and he hit me so hard, I thought in that moment that he could kill me. He ended up hurling me over the edge of the bed and I bruised myself badly.

I left him for good the next day. I still loved him, but I knew then that I had to leave. I had hoped that one day he would change. I prayed to God he would change. But even my going to church was a point of tension between us. It was one more reason that set me apart from him and the women in his past.

I tried to be a good woman for him. I tried it all, the max and the minimum. I don't even myself understand how it is I came to leave. I had to force the leaving. I didn't want to be a failure. I didn't want to be alone. I didn't want to walk away from my marriage. But finally, I knew that I had tried everything.

I've moved to another part of town. Now I keep my distance from Paul. I try to find babysitting and housecleaning work, and contribute to the home I share with a new friend and her son. I help out at the church, especially with their nursery. Since my background and education is in the care and education of little children, I do my best to contribute. I continue to financially support my two now-adult children, my mother, and my sister, with what money I can set aside. My father died this year and I couldn't return for the funeral.

Since leaving my husband, my life has only gotten harder. But what choice do I have? It has been seven years. Seven years that I have lost the youth of my children and the love of my family. I've become a different person here. I remain, deep down, the same person—I have love and charity for others—but I've also become more of a fighter.

There's something else, too. It's a shame that I can't quite confront the fact that part of my motivation in coming to this country was selfish. True, I thought I would make money, and I did. I am proud to say that I sent both my children to university.

But the truth is, I also thought this would be a kind of adventure. After losing my status as a professional, maybe I was looking for something better for myself. And when things started to go so wrong for me here, I didn't want to admit to the others back home in Cali that I had failed at what I had set out to do. These are things I haven't been able to tell anyone. I would love to go home one day. But this time in America is something I can't really explain.

[*Editor's Note:* Dixie recently became a legal immigrant. A provision of the Violence Against Women Act (VAWA), permits victims of domestic violence to self-petition for legal immigrant status due to abuse suffered at the hands of a citizen or a lawful permanent resident. With the help of legal counsel, Dixie successfully documented the beatings and abuse of Paul. The United States Citizenship and Immigration Services, a division of the Department of Homeland Security, granted Dixie a provisional status with work authorization. Dixie still cannot visit her two children and elderly mother, whom she has not seen since she left Colombia more than eight years ago. An application for lawful permanent residence is the next step. As an LPR, she would finally be able to travel to see her family.]

EL CURITA

AGE: *28*
COUNTRY OF ORIGIN: *Guatemala*
OCCUPATION: *Housepainter*
HOME: *Bay St. Louis, Mississippi*

FIREARMS WERE NORMAL
FOR LA AMERICANA

El Curita—a nickname he uses—is a stocky twenty-eight-year-old man with a goatee. When we spoke, he was wearing a polo shirt and long denim shorts. He is from a small town in Guatemala, and came to the U.S. about three years ago. After working as a housepainter in Virginia, he received an offer to work in Mississippi repairing damage inflicted by Hurricane Katrina. He, his sister, and his brother-in-law journeyed to the Gulf Coast, where they lived in a trailer with their boss, "La Americana." They soon realized the job was not what they had imagined. They were held against their will and paid a fraction of what they were owed. Our conversation took place late at night in El Curita's new home—a storm-damaged trailer which he rents for $425 a month with his brother-in-law in Gulfport, Mississippi. He spoke in Spanish. Behind him are black velvet wall hangings of China and Tokyo, which a friend bought for him in a market.

It's done through a telephone call. That's how the contact starts. And then there's another contact, and another, and then another. Some call themselves "Lobo," others "Aguila." They don't use their real names, so it's never known who's in charge. When I made contact with one of these people I had to give them money up front. You pay the amount that reserves your ticket; the rest is paid later. That's how the journey starts. Or the adventure. I don't know which is the better word for it.

My nickname is *El Curita*. The people in my town—Santa Cruz El Chol—gave me that name because when I was very young I always helped out at the church and so became known as "The Little Priest." Santa Cruz El Chol is in the Baja Verapaz department of Guatemala, about forty kilometers from Guatemala City. I was born there, the seventh of nine children. But when I was seven years old my mother was kidnapped by guerrillas and held for two days. The town became too dangerous, so my family moved to a safer place, a town called San Jeronimo. I lived there until about three years ago.

There are decisions that destiny obliges one to make. When I was twenty-four, I made the decision to travel to the United States. I wanted to take some of the burden from my parents' shoulders and try to give them a better life. They had struggled in poverty and worked their whole lives for me and my brothers and sisters. My father worked as a laborer on a farm in San Jeronimo. My mother was a domestic worker, cleaning houses, cooking, doing laundry for other people. Though my father went to school up until his third primary year, my mother could neither read nor write. We were poor, and growing up, life was full of complications. I know there were others whose poverty was much worse and who went through many more difficulties than we did in order to survive. We didn't enjoy privileges the way other children did, but we never wanted. My parents always provided for us.

Still, I wanted my parents to have an easier life. I wanted to work in the U.S. and make money for them so they could live with greater dignity. Many people from San Jeronimo had left to go to the United States, but I was the first in my family to make the journey. Later on my sister came too.

GOD WILLED US

After all the telephone calls had been made and I had paid to secure my place among those making the journey north, we gathered. Most of the adults were between thirty and forty years old. There weren't any other older people, but there were kids. I remember there were two girls, between six and eight years old. And there was a pregnant woman. Only ten of us left Guatemala. Later, when we crossed the Mexican border, we were sixty. By the time we traveled across the desert to the U.S., there were one hundred and forty of us.

The desert was tremendous. We walked almost nonstop for four days and nights. After walking for the first two days we heard motorcycle engines. And then we saw them: the motorcycles had three wheels and were ridden by U.S. Border Patrol officers. Everyone dropped to the ground. It was an intense moment because we knew that those officers weren't kilometers away, but only a few meters from us. The men who could take away our hopes of a life in the U.S. were just a short distance away.

There were three of the three-wheeled motorcycles, so the guides told us to use our heads. "A Border Patrol officer only has two hands," they told us. "We are one hundred and forty. They can only grab three of us, but whoever gets grabbed is fucked. The other hundred and thirty-seven are on their own." That relieved us a little, even though we thought, What if I'm the one who gets grabbed? But God willed us to be where we were because they went by without spotting us.

A lot of people hurt themselves. The branches of certain plants and small trees that grow in the desert have no leaves, only thorns, and you can really feel them, especially when they hit you in the face. But there was no time to shake them off because we couldn't stop. We had to keep walking. There was no time to stop and check to see if you were injured or bleeding, to clean up a wound. When

I left Guatemala my feet were white. But after walking through the desert they became purple. Other people got blisters on their feet and couldn't walk any longer. I don't know what they did to keep going because even without blisters, sometimes it felt as though I just couldn't walk another step. We didn't walk at a regular pace, but went very fast. And we were only allowed to rest and sleep for fifteen minutes. A guide would say, "Rest," and before he could even finish saying the word we were already stopped. We had to take advantage of every second we had to be off our feet.

I'll tell you about something strange that happened on the desert journey. It was our habit to pray as we walked. Our group was made up of people who practiced different religions, but I believe we are guided by the same God. So we prayed the whole way. Once, after we had run out of water, we came across a creek. The guides gave each of us a gallon jug to fill with creek water and carry for ourselves. In the desert a gallon of water is nothing; it doesn't last very long. And some people accidentally made holes in their water jugs. That was a miserable thing to see because those people couldn't keep their water from leaking out. The next day we were on one of our very brief rest breaks when we saw another group nearing us. It surprised us because they were all kids, fifteen or twenty of them, walking like zombies. As soon as they spotted us they started yelling, "Water, water, water!" Thanks be to God we had found the creek the night before. That incident made me wonder if the creek was real or if God put it there just so we could fill up our jugs for those thirsty kids.

We passed government camps on the journey through the desert. We walked right through the middle of military training grounds in Arizona. The guides told us about the guard tower, and about when different guards would be posted in them. The guides were really smart. They had everything studied out.

Finally we passed through a tunnel under one of the main Arizona highways and arrived at a farm. We slept there. Then a van came to take us to California, to a place called San Diego.

BETWEEN SADNESS AND JOY

In San Diego, we stayed in a little house that had three rooms, a small kitchen, a living room, and a bathroom. All one hundred and forty of us stayed in that tiny house. The heat was tremendous. We only had one small electric fan to circulate air, and what little air that fan generated got sucked up instantly.

From that house the guides began sending us out to different locations in the U.S. The first group that went was Guatemalan, about six of them, and they were very happy to be going. They left for the airport at five in the morning. But later on that day, about six o'clock in the evening, we saw on the television news that they had been caught at the airport. We thought to ourselves, "How could they not have been caught?" They had all been wearing the same color clothing because those in charge had bought them all identical pants and shirts. We didn't want to travel by plane after that, but we couldn't change the guides' plans.

The day I left it was about three in the afternoon. I got on a plane that flew from California to Baltimore, Maryland, where I arrived at eight in the morning. I had a friend I was going to meet there, so after I landed I got a taxi and gave the driver directions to my friend's place. The taxi driver was Italian but spoke a little Spanish, thank God.

It was about ten o'clock at night when we got to my friend's house. I knocked on the door and my friend came out. He told me, "You can't stay here." And the taxi driver was waiting to be paid for the fare from the airport. The driver, God bless him wherever he is, was a good man. He saw my situation and handed me his cell phone and said, "Call around and try and get a phone number for someone who can help you. You're here now, you can't go back." I called Guatemala and got some telephone numbers in the U.S. and called those. I made all of these calls between ten and eleven at night, in Baltimore, without knowing a soul and without being able to speak English.

Around midnight I was finally able to get in touch with one of my uncles who lives in Virginia. He spoke with the taxi driver and asked him how much he would charge to bring me to him in Virginia. "Three hundred and fifty dollars." "Three fifty?" "Yes." "Okay. You can bring him but you have to bring him like a king. I want him to eat, I want him to drink coffee, I want him to…" And the taxi driver said, "Okay, okay, okay. Don't worry."

We got there at about four in the morning. My uncle made me a cup of coffee. There I was, forty days after I left my house in Guatemala, in another house far away, drinking coffee. I couldn't believe the journey was over. I was in the United States. I felt in between sadness and joy.

LA AMERICANA

A month went by and I couldn't find work. There was nothing. My uncle's place was far from the center of Richmond, so it was hard to get around to find jobs. I talked with a cousin of mine who lived in Richmond itself, trying to see if he could find me a job and some way I could get to and from it. That's how I got work at a grass-mowing business. I worked for that business for five months. The work was hard, partly because my coworkers and I labored in the summer sun. Later on I was able to find another job as a house painter. That was a much more relaxed job, much less difficult than the mowing business.

A Filipino guy rented me a house. He told me that if I painted the house he'd give me a discount on the rent. He saw that I could work, so after I'd painted the house I rented from him he told me about a friend of his who wanted her house painted, that she had a friend who also had a painting job, and so on, and so on. So I went to work for the Filipino. I painted houses for three months, working with his crew. We also did little side jobs we got on our own.

Once we painted a house that the Filipino had been paid ten thousand dollars to do. He only gave the crew eight hundred. And that kind of job required spray tools and rollers, equipment we didn't have. We had to paint the house by hand, with brushes. After the low pay for that big ten-thousand-dollar job the Filipino didn't pay us at all; he wanted the crew to work for him for free, telling us that if we complained we'd get into legal trouble because we didn't have insurance or a permit. One day I simply told him, "I'm leaving." That was it. The more you bow your head the more people like the Filipino want to dominate you. So that's where the story ends with that guy.

I went on to work for another painting company. My boss there saw an ad on the internet: a woman who had a cleaning company needed people to clean buildings, take out the trash, things like that. My boss didn't have much work for us at the time, so he made contact with the woman who'd placed the ad. They worked out a contract. His crew—me and the others who worked for him—would work for the woman three days a week while still working doing painting jobs for my boss's company. We were sort of "lent" to her. Little by little we got to know the woman and learned to trust her. She spoke some Spanish. I won't use her real name. I'll call her "La Americana."

One day, La Americana asked if I was interested in working down in Mississippi. She said I'd be paid good money because there was a lot of work available due to the damage done by Hurricane Katrina. By this time my sister and her husband had joined me in the U.S. from Guatemala. I lived with them in an apartment. La Americana told us that if we wanted to work for her in Mississippi she'd pay for our housing, food, everything. We hardly had any time to think it over because she wanted to leave almost immediately. That's how La Americana talked us into it. We all agreed to go with her. But it all happened so fast we didn't have time to get all our things together. When we left we only took what would fit into La Americana's truck. The rest of our belongings stayed behind. She had promised us that we would return after thirty days. We didn't have a lot of money, but we brought what we could, which was about two hundred dollars. La Americana had assured us that after the first week of work she would pay us.

THE OWNER OF OUR LIVES

We traveled to Mississippi in La Americana's truck. When we got there we lived with her in a trailer she and her boyfriend had. La Americana and my sister each had their own bedrooms and my brother-in-law and I slept in another room. We weren't allowed to talk with other people. La Americana warned us not to speak with them, saying that Mississippians were bad people and that the Hispanics in Mississippi were different from those in Virginia. And she told us that Mississippian police were really bad, that we should always avoid them. We were not to speak with anyone but her and if the police or anyone wanted to know our address we were not to tell them, or tell them that La Americana was our boss. She told us to pretend we didn't know her. All of this made us doubtful about having come. It made us suspicious.

The working hours were long. The shortest days were ten to twelve hours. Some days we worked for sixteen or seventeen hours without a break. We did three big jobs for La Americana, and lots of little ones. Our first big job was painting a bar near the beach. It took nearly a week. We would start at seven a.m. and sometimes work until four the next morning without stopping. But we kept on, believing we would be getting good money. The next big job was painting a church. It was a huge church and we worked on it for a month. But when the job was done La Americana only paid us two hundred dollars. Our last big job was painting a mansion. That took three or four months. An American family lived there. They were very kind to us. They didn't speak Spanish; we spoke a bit of English. But we couldn't talk to them about our problems.

Sometimes she told us that we could be paid two thousand for a job, depending on what it was. She paid by the job, not by the hours we worked. But instead of the full amount, she would pay us only fifty or a hundred dollars, doling it out a little at a time. She would promise us one thing and then give us something else. That's how she began to change as the days went on. Little by little she went from being our boss to being the owner of our lives. During the one year we worked for her, she paid us only twenty or twenty-five thousand dollars. That was for the three of us, working seven days a week.

OUR FEAR GAVE HER POWER

La Americana didn't want us to make any of our own decisions. During the times we weren't working we were shut in our rooms in the trailer and not allowed to leave, not even to see the sun. And when we didn't listen to what she said, she yelled—especially at me—in a way my mother or father never would have. I told her this on a few occasions, asking that she show me a bit more respect. But she showed me no respect, as though I didn't count. She might show respect to anyone else, but not to someone like me, a Hispanic like me.

We endured her abuse because we had to if we wanted to eat. Anytime we opposed her or voiced our concerns about how unfair it was to have to work such long hours, she would find a way to punish us. Once she penalized us for speaking up by giving us only rice, eggs, and tap water to eat. That's all we ate for more than a week. She would go through our belongings, too. We organized the things we owned, but our belongings were always in a different place than where we'd left them. There were times when even our underwear was mixed up and we knew La Americana had been rummaging through our stuff.

We had no car and had to rely on La Americana to drive us back and forth between work and the trailer we lived in. We wanted to buy a car of our own, and when La Americana was in a calm mood I would try talking to her about this. But she always said no, saying we didn't need a car because she could drive us anywhere we needed. She didn't want us to have any independence. Part of the reason she paid us our wages bit by bit was so we would never have enough to buy a car. I think she was afraid that we would run off. She made sure we didn't have any opportunity to leave.

We asked La Americana to let us go back to Virginia. She said, "Go on and go. Go however you can." She wasn't afraid to say such a thing because she knew we had no means of transportation. She knew we couldn't just walk away. In Mississippi it isn't a matter of just jumping on a bus. We were a forty-five-minute drive from Gulfport along an empty road. If we did decide to leave we were afraid that La Americana would come after us in her truck. She kept guns in her bedroom closet. If we left on foot she could drive after us and kill us on that road and no one would hear our cries; no one would say anything if we just disappeared.

Firearms were normal for La Americana. Sometimes at night she would sit in a chair with a gun. If she heard a noise or if she saw someone outside on the road—especially if it was a person of color—she went and got a gun. On a day La Americana and her boyfriend left for a place in Mississippi called Diamondhead, her guns almost got me deported. Their truck had broken down along the way so they called me to come get them. I drove their other car, a Nissan. I didn't even think of escaping in that car because it wasn't my property. If I took something of hers, I could have even more problems.

As I drove on Interstate 10, I neared a state policeman parked on the side of the road. I got nervous and made sure I had my seatbelt on and that I was going the speed limit. But when I passed the patrol car, it began to follow me. The siren switched on. I got scared and pulled over and called La Americana. But when the policeman got to my window I couldn't talk any longer because he told me to shut off my phone. He asked for papers—registration and things. I told him the truth, that I didn't have a license or anything. I don't speak much English, but what little I said the patrolman understood. He let me go, telling me to be very careful.

When I finally got to where La Americana and her boyfriend were, they both laughed at my being pulled over, like it was some kind of joke. La Americana said, "Did the cop give you a ticket?" I told them he hadn't and La Americana asked why, almost as though she would have preferred it if the policeman had given me a ticket or taken me to jail. She went to the trunk of the car and opened it. Inside were two firearms. I didn't know those guns were in the car and at that moment I became very angry because I knew if the cop had found them that would have been a ticket directly back to Guatemala. I would have been arrested before the police had asked any questions.

La Americana was a violent person. One time I called 911 because she got into a fight with her boyfriend. She was holding him by the neck, yelling for us to help her, yelling that he was killing her. But she was the one hurting her boyfriend, not the other way around. The thing is, if she could lie about him, she could lie about us. She could harm us and then say she was defending herself. She manipulated things to suit her own truth. That's where a lot of our fear came from. Besides La Americana's yelling and leaving us without food, we were afraid of her because she owned guns, because of her violent ways. Our fear gave her power over us.

THANK GOD THE BABY WAS BORN IN GUATEMALA

La Americana's boyfriend was bad, too. He would call my brother-in-law like a dog. When he wanted to be brought a tool or something, he wouldn't ask or even speak; he would just whistle or snap his fingers, as though he were calling the German shepherd he and La Americana owned. When my sister became pregnant, La Americana remarked that their dog liked kids and so my sister needed to stay in the U.S. to have her baby. To La Americana, my sister's baby would be nothing more than a toy for her dog.

My brother-in-law and I wanted my sister to have the baby in Guatemala. But La Americana said my sister couldn't leave, that the child was conceived in the U.S. and so must be born in the U.S. She told us she would talk with a lawyer. We were frightened La Americana might try to steal the child, that because we were undocumented she could have found a way to do something to us and keep the baby for herself.

In order for my sister to leave the U.S. for Guatemala she needed a passport. She had no citizenship papers, not even a Guatemalan passport. The only way to get one was to travel to the Guatemalan consulate in Houston, Texas. We saw this as an opportunity to escape from La Americana because we knew she wouldn't go to Houston. But she was smart. She told us, "Two of you go, but one needs to stay behind with me." I traveled to Houston with my sister. But we weren't going to leave my brother-in-law behind; we had to come back for him.

It cost seventy dollars for bus tickets to Houston. La Americana said hotels would charge us fifty a night and that it would cost us about thirty dollars for food. So she gave us only three hundred for the trip, the exact amount she thought we needed. The thing is, the money she gave us was our money, not hers. It was the money we had earned working for her but which she had not paid us.

My sister did get back to Guatemala and had her baby there. It's about to turn one year old. Thank God the baby was born in Guatemala. When La Americana made the remark about her dog liking kids, that my sister should have her baby here so that her dog could play with it—I never felt good about that.

SCARS IN OUR SOULS

As my brother-in-law and I got to know more and more people, we tried to figure out a way to escape from our situation, to ask for help. But it wasn't as easy as approaching someone and explaining the kinds of things that were going on in our lives. No one could really understand unless they had experienced what we had. Truly, you would have had to have lived it firsthand to know how we suffered with La Americana for such a long time. We didn't have physical marks we could point to, nothing outward to show how we were being abused. But we had scars in our souls. Those wounds only God can heal.

We asked people who worked with La Americana, people besides us, for help. No one helped us except one guy. His advice was to run off with the truck, the tools, everything. We didn't want to turn into criminals. So we went on putting up with our situation, our imprisonment. But La Americana made us criminals anyway. She started making us steal for her. If she saw something she wanted, like a ladder, she would tell us to take it. I told her, "You know what our legal status is, we can't steal." If we were to be caught we would be the ones accused of thievery. La Americana could just leave and let us pay the consequences. But if we didn't steal for her it meant another week without eating.

When we did eat our meals, it was away from La Americana and her boyfriend, in our rooms. But there were times when she would cook and tell us that what she had made was for everyone. Once, after my sister had gone to Guatemala to have her baby, La Americana prepared dinner and invited us to eat with her. It was scary. La Americana didn't eat what she'd made. Neither did her boyfriend. My brother-in-law and I ate and then got very sleepy. Drowsiness overcame us. It wasn't a natural sleepiness, but something powerful. Our eyelids got so heavy we couldn't keep them open. It wasn't normal. We thought for sure she had put something in our food. But we never said anything to her; we knew she was capable of doing such a thing. She did those kinds of things casually and then washed her hands of her deeds without a second thought.

We decided we had to escape. I say "escape" because that's exactly what it was, an escape. We were prisoners.

A DOOR OPENED UP

One day La Americana had to go back to Virginia. I think she had had some trouble with the law there. It was while she was gone that my brother-in-law and I began going to church. It was a Catholic church—Our Lady of Fatima—and it opened up a very different road for us to follow.

When La Americana returned to Mississippi, my brother-in-law told her that he was studying for baptism in the Catholic Church. She told him he could continue going to Our Lady of Fatima for catechism. That's how we were able to go to Mass on Mondays. But La Americana knew when we attended Mass. Five minutes after Mass ended, our telephone would ring: it was La Americana checking to see if we had already left the church and how long it would take us to get back to the trailer. We couldn't be even five minutes late or she would scream at us.

In Biloxi, I began working with someone who also worked for La Americana. He was a kind man. My brother-in-law and I were able to get close enough to him to make comments about the horrible situation we were in. We told him we wanted to buy a car to escape. He gave us a telephone number and said, "Call this person and they will help you." I called the number. The guy I spoke with asked me how I was going to make payments to him if he sold me a car: every week? Every two weeks? I couldn't make any arrangements with him because my brother-in-law and I never knew when La Americana would pay us or how much we would get when we were paid. Once the guy understood our predicament he told me about someone who could help. Her name was Vicky Cintra; she was the coordinator of an office that helped immigrants. And that's when a door opened up for us.

We agreed to meet up on a certain Monday because Monday evenings were when we went to Mass and La Americana wouldn't suspect we were anywhere but at the church. On the Monday we were to meet, my brother-in-law and I didn't go to Our Lady of Fatima but instead went the opposite direction, looking for the office we'd been told about. We still didn't know for sure if all of this was connected with La Americana somehow, if it was part of one of her underhanded plans.

We found the office. From that time on, we were able to associate with people whose words gave us some relief. The people at the office made us feel that we were human beings, that we mattered. I may forget things that have happened in my life, but I will never forget the moment we made contact with the people at that office. We were shaking and crying, we were so scared. With their help, my brother-in-law and I were able to come up with a plan.

The people at the office told us to buy a telephone card so we could make calls without worrying about La Americana's tight control over our phone use. That's how we were able to stay in contact with the office. Finally, one day, we contacted the office and told them that we were ready to escape. We were scared, afraid that our plan might be doomed, afraid of the uncertainty of what was going to happen.

COLOR MATTERS MORE

La Americana would take walks in the afternoons, so she was always gone for a certain amount of time. The day we were to execute our plan she came out as usual for her afternoon walk. I don't know whether or not she suspected we were up to something, because a second after we had called the office to tell them we were ready, she came back to the trailer. The office people had told us they would arrive to get us in thirty or forty minutes, good timing because of La Americana's regular afternoon walk. We would be alone. But for some reason that day La Americana returned after only ten minutes. This made our escape plans more difficult because she would be there when the office people came. But there was no turning back. The plan was in motion and we had to move forward. It was the moment of truth: whether to continue to stay chained up or try to gain our freedom.

The people from the office couldn't find our location. My brother-in-law had to sneak away, running out toward the road to help guide them to where we were without being seen by La Americana. I stayed, trying to create distractions so she would not suspect that my brother-in-law had gone off to assist the office people. When they finally arrived I was so nervous I could hear my heartbeats in my ears.

Things got tough. La Americana saw the two office people drive up and told them they were trespassing on private property. It was Vicky Cintra and her husband Elvis. La Americana told them that if they didn't leave she would call the sheriff. Then Vicky confronted her about the situation she had put us in. La Americana claimed she didn't know what Vicky was talking about. She denied everything. I remember she told Vicky that she wanted to hear these accusations straight from the horse's mouth. She wanted me to speak for myself. So I did, face-to-face with her. But she pretended that she couldn't understand what I was saying, as though she didn't understand Spanish. "Let him speak English so I can understand," she said.

That's when tempers began to run high. I had been too afraid before, but now I was angry and had the bravery to tell La Americana to her face that I was tired of all her screaming and the pressure she had put on me and my brother-in-law, her treatment of us, how we were her captives. I told her that those days were over. La Americana got angry and things got very tense.

La Americana called the sheriff. My brother-in-law and I were afraid to leave with the office people before the sheriff arrived because

La Americana could tell him that we had stolen something and then we'd be fugitives from the law. So we waited for the sheriff to come and resolve the standoff, thinking that he would bring peace and justice to the situation—do his job. But it didn't happen that way.

A deputy sheriff arrived. He pointed the finger at me and my brother-in-law. He made us responsible for the confrontation. Instead of asking questions to try and find out the facts, he just stomped on us, taking La Americana's side. I think he preferred the color of her skin to ours. I remember he asked my brother-in-law something, and when my brother-in-law began to respond the sheriff laughed at him and said, "Huh, he doesn't even speak English." Just like that. A little while later he asked me in Spanish how old I was. He'd asked the question in clear Spanish, perfectly. Then I knew what was really going on. I thought I had seen racist people before, but that day I believe I saw in the sheriff a true racist.

When the sheriff asked if we were legal, La Americana yelled out that we were illegals. Vicky told the sheriff he was there to investigate a crime and not the legal status of a person. The sheriff started calling the Department of Immigration to report us, but Vicky told the sheriff he couldn't do that, that it wasn't right.

Then another deputy sheriff and a security guard from the complex came. Together they teamed up against us. I remember one of the deputies lingering around Elvis, Vicky's husband, hovering over him. The sheriff said he thought Elvis was armed. It wasn't true, but the sheriff frisked him for firearms. He was looking for something to use against us, inventing things so that he could say we had some kind of criminal motive. Thank God he didn't find anything because he was searching for any excuse to arrest us.

The sheriff took La Americana's and Vicky's driver's licenses and called in on his radio to check them. The report came back that one license had been suspended. The sheriff had no doubt in his mind that the one whose license was suspended was Vicky's. But it was La

Americana who had the suspended license. Vicky asked the sheriff, "Why don't you arrest her?" But the sheriff answered that La Americana wasn't driving and so had not broken any law.

The sheriff asked me for my keys to the trailer. He told me he would go with me to get my documents, my ID, my passport, everything. He said he'd go with me. But it was a lie. He simply took my keys and gave them to La Americana. Then he laughed at us once more because he had taken the keys with a lie. He told us that we couldn't get our things unless we had a judge's order.

I suppose color matters more than real justice. If you're not white with blue eyes you don't count in the U.S. We saw that firsthand. But if you strip us of our skin we look the very same.

Vicky told the sheriffs we were being held against our will. La Americana denied everything again. But since she was denying that she was holding us, she could not stop us from leaving. The office coordinator just dominated the situation. She was very strong with the law at her side. She didn't allow anything else to happen to us. She didn't ask La Americana for permission to take us. She just did it.

When my brother-in-law and I got in Vicky and Elvis's car, we finally felt free. On the drive, memories of our horrible year with La Americana swam in our heads. We knew we had to take those memories and throw them away, one by one, because a new life was starting.

From La Americana's trailer, Vicky and Elvis drove us straight to the office, where they looked for a place for us. Then they took us to America's Thrift Store, so we could buy some clothes. They found us a place to live, sharing a trailer with other people they had helped. Afterward they helped us find our own trailer. Soon after, Vicky and Elvis learned there was an arrest warrant out for them. The sheriff had filed criminal charges for trespassing and disturbing the peace at a business. But La Americana didn't show up in court, so a few months later, the charges were dropped.

LIKE STRAY CATS

All our material possessions had been taken from us. My brother and I had nothing. We had not been allowed to go inside the trailer to get any of our things before we left. The only things we had with us were our work clothes, nothing else, not even simple everyday things people need, like toothbrushes and toiletries.

My brother-in-law and I had to wait months before we could collect what remained of our things because the law prohibited it. We even tried legally soliciting a court notice, but the courts told us they could not contact La Americana. It's an awful feeling to know that your belongings are yours but you aren't able to have them. They became La Americana's things, things she kept or threw away.

Later on, a lawyer tried to help me and my brother-in-law recover our belongings, driving us to the property where we had lived. La Americana was no longer there but we were still so afraid of her that we insisted the lawyer park her car far up the road so we wouldn't be spotted driving in. Our lawyer had spoken with the manager of the property where we had lived and the manager told her that there was nothing inside the trailer, just garbage. It was true. La Americana had taken absolutely everything: clothing, television sets, photos, our passports and personal documents. Everything. She even took the telephone numbers I had for my family in Guatemala. I found out that she had called some of them including my sister and my brother. My brother called me, scared after he had spoken with her. La Americana was very smart. She knew how to manipulate us, to strike fear in our hearts by telephoning our family members as though to say, "I know where you and yours live."

Inside the trailer we found what remained of our things in a jumble on the floor where a trash bin had been purposely upturned. I found a wet photograph of my mother there. The things that belonged to us that La Americana and her boyfriend didn't take they had scattered over the floor so we would have to search for what few little things we could find, so we would be like stray cats rummaging in the garbage.

A GRAND NATION

That year with La Americana was an eternity for us. I consider it the darkest year of my life. We didn't know if we would ever be able to return to Guatemala. I don't know how to put it, but in a way she is still governing a part of us. Even though we're no longer under her control, we're still afraid of her and of what our future now holds. What will happen? What will become of us? We're relearning what it is to determine for ourselves what direction our lives will take.

I'm now working at a place owned by someone who felt bad for my brother-in-law and offered us a job at a store. Our current bosses are very different people from La Americana. They're our bosses, not our owners. When they chastise, you know it's because you made a mistake. If we're reprimanded, there's a reason for it. It's really something to be able to work for a boss instead of an oppressor.

But there are nights when I wake up remembering the terrible moments we went through. Sometimes I wake up at two or three in the morning. No one can know what it was really like unless they were to walk in our shoes. The law didn't help us because the law requires proof. What proof was there that we were being abused? There weren't any physical marks on us. As violent a woman as she was, maybe it would have been better if La Americana had done physical harm to us so we would have something to offer as proof.

The truth has weight. The truth holds power. We don't know when or how, but we're sure the truth will bring forth justice. We are waiting now. One FBI agent and two immigration officers came to interview us. They are looking into a case against La Americana. The officers didn't say they would deport us, but even if they do I'm not scared. For us that wouldn't be as harmful as what La Americana did. As for the future, it's clear. After seeking justice, I want to return to my family in Guatemala. My brother-in-law does, too.

That's my story. I'm able to tell it now because I've been able to slowly return to being the person I am, something of the person I used to be: the kid who used to laugh, the mischievous kid, the kid who thought the United States was a place where justice existed, where there was respect for human rights. There was a year in my life when that kid didn't live. But here I am, El Curita, the little priest, trying to move forward even with the fear that lingers inside me. I grew up believing that the U.S. was God's nation, a grand nation. For me, the U.S. was like a toy that you aspire to have, the most precious toy. Now I don't know if justice really exists here in the U.S. or if what I believed to be true was only a delusion in the mind of a little Guatemalan kid.

[*Editor's Note:* The Criminal Section of the U.S. Department of Justice's Civil Rights Division, which prosecutes acts of human trafficking and forced labor, began investigating El Curita's case in the spring of 2007. In October 2007, the Justice Department informed him by telephone that it would not pursue his case further. It issued no written findings or decision. Vicky Cintra of Hispanic Interest and Services told us that a Department of Justice employee said of El Curita's situation, "He must have seen all that in the movies."]

JULIO, 46
Kern County, California

Julio has been deported seven times in twenty-eight years, every time returning almost immediately to the same small Central Valley farming town. A year ago, he was badly injured in a job-related truck accident. After two weeks in the hospital, his arm still badly dislocated, he was determined to get back to the fields. But on that first morning back, his longtime employer fired him, purportedly for missing those two weeks of work. This was the first time since he was six years old that Julio had ever been unemployed. He has begun to study English in an ESL class.

I've crossed the border eight times. The first time, I just jumped on a train to Mexicali. There I paid three hundred dollars to a coyote. We passed through the border, jumped the fence. That's the easy part. There were twenty of us. Once we passed, the coyote told us we had to stay in the desert because there were lots of border patrols out there. He kept saying, "Maybe tomorrow, maybe tomorrow." But tomorrow never came. We were hiding, sleeping on the ground. It was hot in the day, just a little shade, only a few trees. There was no eating for maybe two days, no food, then one sandwich, then nothing for many more days. Finally somebody would bring us something to eat, but then I'd see an old man—there were two old men with us—and I'd give him half my food. I needed water, but I didn't care about eating. We walked for miles, then stayed, then walked more, then stayed. There were no cars, no roads, just desert.

For three weeks it was like that; we all waited together. But I couldn't wait anymore. That's when I went off by myself and got lost in the desert. I was alone for four days—no water, no food. I walked for two whole days, no stopping. I drank from my urine, I think that helped me. And I chewed on my backpack, I think that helped too, the saliva from the chewing helped. But for two days I didn't drink any real water. Finally I got to a concrete canal. There's a little water, you know, but it's shit water. It looks like chocolate. I drank it and thought, Oh my goodness this is no good. Later I saw some cows, so I followed them for a long time and they led me to a tank of water. I drank from that trough like a cow, down on my hands and knees.

On the third day the sun was very strong, but I was very, very cold. When it got dark I finally laid down to go to sleep. I dug a hole to sleep in, for protection. I couldn't see anything. I was shivering, shaking. When I woke up, it was still really dark. Dark. I touched something cold next to me; I reached my hand out, patted it. It's a body. I touched the chest, felt the ribs. I thought, Am I dreaming or what? I kept feeling around, I still thought I was dreaming, then I touched the eyes. Oh, I can tell it's not a dream. Somebody's dead, they died there. When I'd dug the hole to sleep in, I guess I uncovered somebody who had died out there in the desert. I jumped up and went running away.

On the fourth day I finally saw some other Mexican guys. They told me where to go, told me to walk over and jump on the train. The first time I got confused and I caught the train going the reverse way, it was going south to Mexico, the wrong way. I thought, What happened? Why is the sun over there, not here? Uh oh. I jumped back out and headed north again.

Now, after being lost in that desert, nothing scares me anymore. I was alone. I was crying, nobody saw me. I talked, nobody heard me. I lost my fear. No more being scared, ever. Sometimes though, I think about that body out there in the desert. A body nobody finds.

LORENA

AGE: *22*
COUNTRY OF ORIGIN: *Mexico*
OCCUPATION: *Student, office worker*
HOME: *Fresno, California*

SABRINA NEEDS HER
IDENTITY BACK

Lorena is a twenty-two-year-old college student who hopes to study medicine. She left her home in Puebla, Mexico at the age of six, walking across the desert with her mother, stepfather, and two brothers. The family now lives in Fresno, California. In addition to being a student, she works full-time in a real estate office. The interview for this story took place on a weekday afternoon, while Lorena was working. The first part was conducted in her car, as she drove from her office to a warehouse. At the warehouse, Lorena continued to tell her story in English as she sifted through boxes, trying to locate an old file her boss had requested.

I have a very young mom. I'm twenty-two and she's thirty-eight. She had just turned sixteen when she had me. She had my brother that very next year, a few days before I turned one. Then two years later, she had my youngest brother. She's really like my sister. I've never missed having a sister. I always hear everybody else saying that they wish they had a sister that they could talk to, and I never really had that need.

My biological dad was, or is, an alcoholic. He used to beat my mom and us, so my mom took us to stay with my grandparents, in Puebla, Mexico. They had a very poor house, very basic, just cement walls. It was a two-story house, but it was open. You went into the house, and the first floor was the patio area. You walked directly to the stairs, which went up to the kitchen, and then a bedroom. But downstairs to your right was another bedroom. That's where my great-grandpa and my mom and the kids, us, slept.

One time, my father kidnapped me to get back at my mom. My mom had gone to a party or a dance, and she left our door open slightly, because we didn't like it completely closed. If she had left it closed, we would have woken up and flipped out. I remember my little brothers were asleep. The youngest was two, and my other brother was four. So we were very little. And my father came in in the middle of the night. I remember I was in shorts and a little tank top or something. No shoes, no sweater. I don't remember where he took me that night, but I do remember the next day he took me to a bar. Before that, we went to somebody's house, and he asked for a pair of shoes for me. The shoes were gargantuan, like clown shoes. That next day, we went to his sister's house, and we just happened to get there when my grandma was there, too. So that was the end of that. But I remember when we got home, everyone kept making fun of me because I had big, huge clown shoes.

I remember my little brother, the one that's just one year younger, telling me, "You know the reason why he took you? It's because you don't sleep with your head covered." That's a four-year-old's explanation. My brother always slept with his whole body covered.

To get away from my father, and to try to do something for us, my mom decided that she needed to come to this country. She came here by herself the first time, when she was twenty-one. She crossed the border, just went through the desert, like so many do.

I remember that period when she was gone. And I specifically remember one time that my grandmother was walking me to school.

I heard an airplane go by, and she told me, "Oh look, there goes your mom." And I said, "I know, she's been gone a long time. Two years is a really long time." She was only gone for two months, but I was just thinking it was two years because I was so young. I was six years old at that time.

There was a lot of blackmailing from my dad while she was gone, with him trying to take us all from my grandmother. So when my mom met my stepdad while she was here in the U.S., she married him right away. Not married legally, but married like the Mexican way—just move in together. My stepdad fell in love with my mom very quickly, and when he found out that she might lose her kids, he said, "Well, we can go to Mexico and pick them up. Then we can just come back and live here."

I remember when my mom came to get us. It was in the middle of the night. That was the first car I had ever seen. I don't even remember what kind of car it was, but I remember the color exactly. It was brown, like a chocolate brown, and it was really shiny. I was just enamored with the car. I was like, "Wow, that's a real car, and it's here. We're really cool." Of course, I wasn't thinking "cool." I don't know what I was thinking, but it was the equivalent of "cool."

My stepdad very rapidly took me in, more than my little brothers. He had me on his lap in no time, and we were just talking and talking. I don't remember if my grandma or grandpa had told us anything about us leaving. I remember that by leaving, that meant that we got our mom back, but we would be losing our second mom. We called our grandma Mom for a long time, too.

I vividly remember how heartbroken my grandma was, knowing that we were leaving. We were like her children. And it was just like in the movies, when the little kids are waving bye from the back of the seat. I think about it still, and it just breaks my heart. I knew I wasn't going to see them for a long time, but I didn't think it would be sixteen years.

THE BOTTOM OF THE FOOD CHAIN

I remember walking through the desert. It was my mom, my step-dad, my two younger brothers, and me. I was six, so my brothers were five and three. I was so hungry. That is something I don't ever wish on anybody, that kind of hunger. And the only thing I could think of was, if I'm hungry, then my brothers must be hungry. I started get-ting worried. We were literally in the middle of the desert.

That night, we fell asleep in between bushes. It was early in the morning, like six or seven o'clock, when I woke up. We were in the middle of bushes on top of other bushes, so we were completely cov-ered. It was all dry, so it was really noisy. And so nobody could move. I remember waking up, and I kind of jerked my foot to the side a little bit, so the bushes made a loud rustling noise. And there were actually INS agents on the other side of the bush. When they heard that rustle, they looked in the bush, and we got caught. There were other people with us. I think it was seven, eight of us. But they weren't family, so I don't remember who they were.

I felt horrible. This was totally my fault, and I knew it, and I just could not live with myself. I remember my mother and stepfather getting their hands tied with those plastic handcuffs. I wanted to kick the INS agents, because I was thinking, We are good people. People that get tied up are bad people.

They walked us to the van and they took us to a cement holding cell. It was a big room, and they were holding a lot of other people. There was this lady with a baby, a brand-new baby, like less than three months old, on her back. And my mom was begging her for a little bit of Gerber that she had for her baby, because we hadn't eaten or drank anything in I don't know how many days. At first, the lady didn't want to give us any because that's all she had. She didn't have very much more for her baby. But then she did give us some. And I remember my mom feeding us that Gerber with her finger.

That night they let us go, dropped us back across the border. Not even a day went by and we tried it again. Fortunately, the second time we were successful. I remember walking through a canal, but there was no water. One of the coyotes was holding my hand, and he asked me if I was tired, if I wanted him to carry me. And I said, "Oh no, I can do this. This is easy." I said, "This is as easy as the three-times tables. Three times one, three times two, three times three." I remember they were making fun of me because I said that.

We got to somebody's house, and they let us take a shower. My mom bathed us all. From there, we got to a little tiny trailer. A one-bedroom trailer. It was for the three kids and my stepdad and my mom. It was in Lamont, which is about twenty minutes from Bakersfield.

My youngest brother was crying. He didn't like my mom. When we got to Lamont, I forget what my little brother called my mom, but she said, "No, I'm your mom." And my brother said, "No, you're not my mom, my mom is Juana." That's my grandma's name. That broke my mom's heart, of course.

The first weeks, all we could afford to eat was soup and beans. I understood that we were poor, and I understood that we were kind of at the bottom of the food chain, so I never demanded stuff from my parents. My little brother, though, the one that was five, like the third time that we ate beans back to back, he was frustrated. He said, "Beans again?" But he said it in Spanish, and he said it like a little kid. We still make fun of him for that. He was just frustrated with beans.

I started school that very next day after we arrived at Lamont. And I remember being very scared, because as soon as I walked into the little school office, everyone was speaking English. Even though Lamont is more of a Hispanic-populated town now, back then it wasn't as much. Everyone was speaking English, and we didn't know English. So I really felt lost. But I got a wonderful teacher, who was the perfect American girl-next-door. Blond, blue-eyed, everything.

She tried so hard to speak Spanish and to try to make me understand. She really comforted me.

A lot of the kids were mean. Especially the girls were really mean, about me not knowing English and not being able to understand what the teacher was saying. We used to sit in groups. I think we were taking a spelling test, or a cursive test. I was writing something down, and I happened to look up to think, and one of the girls, I still remember her name—Laurie Greiger—she grabbed her paper, and she said, "Don't copy off of my paper." She said it really loud so everybody could hear. Little things like that. And little things like, "Oh, you're not good enough to talk to me because you don't know English."

The very first years my mom and stepdad worked in the fields, picking everything that was in season. Everything from lettuce to grapes to cotton to carrots, everything. Soon after that, they got a job at the local packing house. That's a step up from farm labor, so that was a really good thing. They were there for a long time.

Then my stepdad got a job doing construction stuff. And my mom started working at a clothing factory. She was working in that factory with a fake Social Security number. Her supervisor knew about it, but she was a really good worker, so the supervisor just said, "I'm not INS. It's not my job to be verifying those, so as long as you don't give me any problems."

She was there for about five years, until one of the workers that was in the same situation got herself documentation and decided to make problems for everybody else. She kept telling the boss that if she didn't do something about all the people that were working there without documentation, she would go to the police. So they had to let all of those people go, and my mom lost her job.

That's when she started sewing for a lady who sells clothes at the local swap meet. She would start work at five o'clock in the morning, and sometimes she wouldn't finish until eight, nine o'clock at night.

They made sweatpants and sweaters from really cheap cotton. Some of the clothes they made were knockoffs. Not really name-brand, like Louis Vuitton or anything, but Levi's, Ecko, Tommy Hilfiger. My mom got paid about ten cents per pair of pants, or ten cents per sweater, so she had to make hundreds and hundreds of pieces of clothing for it to even be worth it for the day. After that stopped working out, she got a job at a bakery, where she rings people up and cleans the bakery and stuff like that. That's where she's been ever since.

MY JOB AS A HUMAN BEING

My first job was working at that same bakery. I started when I was about sixteen. I did the exact same thing, just cleaned, swept and mopped, rang up people. That was really hard for me, because I had never done any type of physical labor, but I got over it, and it just became a routine. I was only there for a few months. They really liked me, but the owner of a Mexican meat market would go there to buy bread to sell at her store. She watched me ringing up people, and could see I was quick. She asked me if I would like to work for her on the weekends, and I said, "Sure." And for a while when I was in high school I was working the two jobs.

I was using my cousin Sabrina's name and Social.[1] Sabrina has good papers. She's my stepdad's niece, so she's really not related to me, just by marriage. She was in Mexico, so she didn't mind, since she wasn't using it. And she could use the tax return, because she has like three kids or something. She was helping me get work, and I was helping her out. I worked, she filed the taxes, and she got the tax return.

---

[1] The Internal Revenue Service requires employers to report wages using a Social Security number. Therefore, in order to be legitimately employed in the U.S., you must have or be in the process of applying for a Social Security number. While being a U.S. citizen is not necessary to obtain a number, foreign workers must have appropriate immigration documentation from the Department of Homeland Security.

I was still working at the meat market when I started college at Fresno State, in 2002, as a biology/premed major. I was lucky that I started college before Governor Gray Davis got booted out. He was the one who signed the law allowing undocumented immigrants to pay in-state tuition. So, actually, it's doable to go to school if you work. Otherwise it would have been extremely difficult. But if I wasn't undocumented, I would be getting financial aid. I probably wouldn't have had the need to work so much, and I would have finished school by now.

I had to sign an affidavit stating that I graduated from a California high school, that I'd been here a certain number of years, and that I would get legal residency as soon as I was able to. I think that last one is for those conservatives who think we're just educating terrorists. It's pretty ludicrous. I mean, who wouldn't want to get legal residency?

During my freshman year, my advisor, who is really the reason why I'm still in school, told me about this awesome internship in North Carolina, helping farmworkers. And I said, "I have to do this."

I've always reminded myself that the only reason why I'm in school and I have a good job is because my parents did backbreaking labor so that I could go to school. I've always felt like I need to give back to those people, because those laborers out there in the fields are like my parents.

I didn't get accepted the first year, but the second year I did. I almost backed out, though, because I was afraid I'd get detained at LAX, and possibly even sent back to Mexico. I kept telling my advisor, "Okay, what if they ask me for this? They'll ask me for an ID." He said, "No, you'll be fine. You deserve this. You need to go."

My parents didn't want me to go. My bosses at the time, the owners of the meat store, didn't want me to go, either. They told me that I was putting myself at risk for something that wasn't necessarily valuable. They told me they couldn't promise me my job when I came back, even though I'd been there for three years, and I'd been a really good employee. I probably would still be there if it wasn't for the internship. I was trying to make something better, trying to broaden my horizons, and I had people telling me not to do it. So, I think that's why I did it, because people kept telling me not to do it.

I told my mom, "You know what, Mom? God's going to take care of me. I'll be fine." And LAX had absolutely no problems with me. I was picked up at the airport with another intern. We went to somebody's house and ate there. That was the first time I ever tasted tofu, and vegetarian something. It was horrible. I couldn't eat it. That first day was really difficult for me. It was all too hippie-ish.

But later, we went to the headquarters, and I met the other interns. We left for our training, which was up in the mountains, and it was beautiful. I loved it. They started training us on the causes we were going to fight for, like the Taco Bell boycott. We were fighting for a penny raise per pound for the tomato pickers in Immokalee, Florida. They told us we would be marching, and we would be picketing in front of Taco Bells,[2] and in front of stores to protest Mount Olive Pickles, too.[3] And right away, I thought, I don't know if I want to do this. It was a little too much exposure for me, and I didn't know if I'd get into any trouble. I was nervous.

After that, we all left to our respective places. I was placed with another intern, and we stayed with a wonderful family. The wife's name was Rosa, and the husband's name was Francisco. They had a little girl and a little boy. The boy was about two or three. He was adorable. And the little girl was so smart. She reminded me of me

---

[2] The Coalition of Immokalee Workers backed a four-year boycott of Yum! Brands—the parent company of Taco Bell, KFC, Pizza Hut, and other chains—that resulted in Taco Bell agreeing to pay an extra $100,000 per year to its tomato growers in Florida.

[3] The Farm Labor Organizing Committee, a union representing 8,500 Mexican guest workers, sponsored a five-year boycott of the Mount Olive Pickle Company—the nation's second largest pickle company—which resulted in an agreement to raise workers' wages.

when I was little. I loved listening to everything she said. While we were there, she started school, and it was wonderful for me to be able to see that. That's like planting a seed to me.

So the organization I worked with helps farmworkers. They knew where to send you if you had legal trouble, if your boss was being bad to you, or if you needed food. We did food drives, too, distributing food baskets to farmworking families.

I was also placed with a medical school. They were just starting a research project about pesticides and the effect they have on children, even though the children are not the ones that are in the fields. The researchers wanted to see how much of the pesticides that the parents ingest and breathe in and get on their clothing and on their skin actually ends up on the kids. They also wanted to know how educated the families were with respect to pesticides. It was really eye-opening, because a lot of these families, they didn't even know what pesticides were. And they didn't even know that they were bad. One lady actually said, "Are they bad?" You just think that's common sense. But they don't know. They don't have access to the internet. They don't even have TVs to watch the news.

Part of my job was to educate people. I'd tell the women things like, "Make sure that when your husband comes home, he changes outside, that he doesn't come in and sit down on the couch with the kids or play with the kids in his work clothes." Or, "Make sure that you wash your husband's clothes separate from the baby clothes and your clothes. Make sure that the kids don't play with those clothes."

A lot of these people lived either in the middle of fields or in very close proximity to fields, so that when the airplanes sprayed, the people would get all the drift, even if they were inside. So I'd also say, "Make sure, if you hear the airplane, close your doors. Don't let your kids go outside. Wait a few hours before you let them go outside. Don't open your windows." A lot of common sense stuff.

And we were able to help in other ways. We were helping the

people from the medical school get their data by collecting urine samples from the kids. It was really surprising how many of the families were willing to help us out. They had to get the first urine of the day from the kid, then put it in a little bag that we gave them. And if we didn't come to pick it up, it had to be kept refrigerated. At first I thought, Oh, these people won't want to do all this, but they did. They were as interested as we were to find out how bad these pesticides really are, and how much they're affecting their families, even though the kids aren't directly exposed to it.

My experience at the internship opened my eyes to a lot of injustice that I didn't want to know about before. The way that farm labor is in North Carolina is very different from how it is here in California. In North Carolina, the men in the camps still live in barracks-style homes. When we visited families, those were people who lived there year-round, that rented either a trailer or a house in the middle of the field and made a life there. But the people in the camps are all men that have been brought over to North Carolina to work.

There's H-2A camps,[4] where the workers who are here legally live, and there's undocumented camps. The undocumented part of it is so dark and kept in the back. It's like a "don't ask, don't tell" type of thing. And undocumented people are very scared in North Carolina to let anybody in. There were undocumented camps that were literally in the middle of tons of trees. Unless you knew that there was a little path through there, you wouldn't even know the camp was there.

We went to several of these camps, and it broke my heart the way that they lived. At the undocumented camps, we weren't able to go inside any of the dwellings. We were only able to go inside the H-2A camp dwellings. And they were horrible enough. Prisoners probably

---

[4] The H-2A program allows farmers to hire non-immigrant foreign workers for seasonal work. The employer is required by law to provide appropriate housing, reimbursement for transportation, tools, and other necessities. See Appendix D for more information.

live in better conditions and more comfortably than these people do. If you put any kind of animal in that type of dwelling, there would be riots. And just to see what legally is required for the grower to have for them... They're only required to have one toilet per fifteen people, and one showerhead per ten people. There are all these men, living in barracks-style homes with no privacy, just a bed. The mattresses are years and years old. They have bloodstains from other farmworkers that have been injured or even died. I heard horror stories of farmworkers that had died from heat exhaustion and tobacco illness.

When I saw all this, I told my supervisor that my mission is to change one person's life. Educate one person, so if their boss tries to be bad to them, they'll say, "No, I know you can't do that, that's against the law." If I can do that, then I've done my job as a human being. I at least wanted to give them knowledge to defend themselves with.

These people don't have transportation. The nearest store is literally miles away. The grower picks them up in a bus at whatever o'clock in the morning, before the sun is up, and takes them directly to where they're working. Then he drops them off when they're done. Once a week, on Sundays, they'd get picked up at a specific time to go into town and wash their clothes, buy groceries, buy whatever they need. So my supervisor and I would go to the camps to see if people needed anything. There were a lot of times we took people to the doctor because they didn't feel good. And there were a lot of times we took people to the store, so they could buy a calling card to call their family, who they hadn't seen in a year.

I still keep in contact with the family that hosted us. The husband, Francisco, was a farm laborer for a long time, so he knows all the farmworkers. All those farmworkers are pretty regular. They get called back every year, if they don't get blacklisted for causing problems. Francisco knows most of them, and they still ask about me by name. That's flattering.

GOD LETS US DRIVE

When I came back to California, I had to start looking for another job. I'd heard about a job as a runner at Benson-Thomas Real Estate, so I walked in and asked for an application. I'd never had an office job, and I was petrified. I didn't even know what a runner was.

They called me in for an interview that very next day. Both of the bosses were there, Grant Thomas and his partner Fred Benson, the quintessential Republican white male. And the office manager Geri was there too. It was a really intense interview. I expected them to call me the next day, whether yes or no, and they didn't. After a few days I didn't hear from them, and I thought, Oh great, I didn't get it. And it made me feel like people who are like me, in my situation, Hispanic people, we don't get office jobs. I was sure I needed to go get a job at another meat market, or maybe helping somebody clean houses, or babysitting.

Then Geri called me on the last Friday of August 2004, and offered me the job. I came in that Sunday, and Geri started training me and told me what I needed to wear.

Image was everything for Benson-Thomas. I had to wear heels. I had to wear slacks. And I just threw myself into the job. I would deliver flyers to all the listings, all the houses that we had for sale. Pick up closing packages. Pick up gifts. Pick up documents. Take documents to escrow. Take deposits to the bank. Anything that needs to leave the office or come to the office, the runner would do it.

I really didn't think I could be office material. I thought, I'm not refined enough, and I'm not the quality of person that they're looking for. The company was predominantly targeted toward white, upper-class real estate, so I kept thinking they'd eventually realize that I'm just this Mexican girl that doesn't know how to speak to people and conduct herself appropriately. I didn't think I would last. But I did. I ended up staying.

When I started working there, I was still pretending to be legal by using Sabrina's identity. At first, if they'd say "Sabrina," I would just keep working. I wouldn't pay attention until I realized, "Oh shit, that's me." I was working there for about four or five months, but then Sabrina decided to come back to the United States. My aunt, who was the middle person between the real Sabrina and me, called and said, "You need to quit. Sabrina needs her identity back." I was crushed. I loved my job. Sabrina's from New York. If she lived in California, we could both use her Social and pretend she was working two jobs or something. But she couldn't be working in New York and California at the same time.

So finally, one day, I came in with tears in my eyes. I couldn't even talk. I told Geri, "I need to talk to you." I felt guilty that I'd lied to them, and I was really scared of how they would take it. Everyone had been so helpful in training me. I didn't even know how to use a fax machine before I started there. They literally shaped me to be someone productive at an office. They treated me like family.

Geri and I went next door to a Mexican restaurant, where we used to hold meetings and interviews. I showed her my Fresno State ID and told her, "This is truly who I am. I'm really sorry that I lied to you. But I just want you to know that I didn't do it out of malice, or to hurt people. I did it because I had to, because I need to pay for school."

She asked me, "Did this girl know you were using her identity?" I said, "Yes," and I explained it to her.

I was amazed when she said, "Well, we'll see what we can do, but you're not going to have to quit." She said, "Grant won't have a problem. The only one we have to talk to is Fred." Because, like I said, he's the conservative one.

It was two days before Fred came into the office again. I was so petrified. I couldn't eat, I couldn't sleep. He came in for literally ten minutes, just to pick up some stuff. Geri said to him, "We need to talk to you."

We went over to the Mexican restaurant again. I just knew he was going to say, "Well, I'm sorry for your situation, but we can't keep you." Geri told him. She was like my lawyer. It's like she was making the case for a saint, or an angel, or a virgin or something.

And Fred said to me, "Why don't we just pay you cash?" Like he was saying, "Why don't we go down the street and get a smoothie since it's hot?"

My tears were just flowing down. I looked at him and said, "Fred, that's a big deal. You can get in a lot of trouble for that, and I don't want to put you in that position."

He said, "You've been too good to us. We can't let you go." I think it was that day or the next day that Grant came in. I was up at the front doing something with flyers. He said, "Sabrina, come here." I grabbed my notepad and my pen, and I went up to his desk. I was about ten feet away from his desk. I didn't want to get any closer. He said, "Come closer." I came right up front to his desk, and he said, "Come over here, come around."

I thought, Is he going to hit me? He was sitting down, and I was standing right next to him. He reached over and hugged me. He said, "Don't worry, we're going to take care of you. You're going to be okay."

I couldn't even explain how grateful I was. Pretty much everybody has left the company now that there have been money problems, including Geri. But I won't leave him, because he literally risked his life for me. He still could go to jail for a long time. Because of me.

Not a lot of people there know that I'm undocumented. Fred and Grant know. Geri knew. As far as the other employees know, I'm on payroll. They pay me eleven dollars an hour. And I work about twelve hours a day, every day, seven days a week. There's no overtime pay, though, no time and a half or anything like that. I can't be on the company health plan, because I'm not a legal employee there. So I use the clinic at the university for my doctor's visits. I usually only go see them for a yearly check up. The only thing that I do have to visit every six months is an eye doctor, because I use contacts. I pay for it out of pocket, which is pricey, so I ended up shopping around for the cheapest place. Now I go to Sam's Club, which I know I shouldn't go to because they're a monopoly, but that's all I can afford without any health insurance.

I've never been sick enough not to go to work. In my family, you go to work, no matter what, unless you have to be hospitalized. I haven't even taken a vacation since I started working there. I do get holidays off, though, like Christmas or July Fourth.

My boss, Grant, is the most unselfish person I know. The car that I drive is actually a gift from him. It's a Volkswagen Beetle. He leased that car for me for two years, so that I wouldn't have to worry about a car payment or an insurance payment. And I use it to drive all over town for my job. I learned how to drive in North Carolina. One of my supervisors there taught me. I don't have a license, of course, so I'm always looking out my mirrors to make sure there's not a cop behind me. The way that my mom says it is that we have Jesus's license. God lets us drive.

I've been at this job for three years. Now, I do everything from being a runner to being office manager to being chief operations manager. I don't have a job title. If you ask anybody at that office what my job title is, I swear they will say, "Everything."

A lot of people at the office, like Geri and Fred, would always tell me, "You have to assimilate, you have to become American." And I'm all for that. I'm all for speaking English. I'm all for respecting this country, because I love it. It has given me opportunities that I couldn't have. In Mexico, I would have been a mom of three or four by now. I wouldn't have an education. I know that.

But it's really hard for me to keep my identity of being Mexican. I'm very proud of being Mexican, but being Mexican now is almost taboo. I don't describe myself as Hispanic. I don't like calling myself

Latina, either. Because Latina is like, Latina with an attitude. The fighter Latina, but not the good fighter. The troublemaker. Chicana, the same way. Chicana is, "Oh, you're always protesting for something, you're always angry at something or somebody."

I really don't know what to call myself now. I'm Mexican. That's what I fill out on applications. That's where I was born, and that's legally my citizenship. Or, I guess I'm Mexican-American. I love both countries. I love my heritage. It's beautiful, and it's old. Its traditions have lasted for centuries. A lot of Americans wish that they had that. I get that a lot from my office, that they wish they had that much tradition, that much heritage and history. But I also love this country and the opportunities that I've been able to have from here.

WALKING TO THEIR DEATHS

A few weeks after I got the job at the real estate company, in September of 2004, I started an organization on campus to help local farmworkers. I glow a little when I talk about it because it's something that I created.

I had come back from North Carolina full of fire and a revolutionary spirit. We'd had students selected for this internship every year before that, but no one had come back and done anything. I couldn't understand, after seeing all that—what was going on in the fields—for ten weeks, that no one would want to come back and continue the fight. I said to myself, I have to do it. We have to keep educating people about the issues.

So I got some students together at school and talked to them about what I wanted to do. The Taco Bell boycott was still going on at that time, so we did a lot of demonstrations on campus. We visited classrooms and spoke at different events. And then, finally, Yum! Brands, which owns Taco Bell, agreed not to buy tomatoes from that particular grower any more.

We also helped with passing the Emergency Heat bill[5] into law in California, to reduce the number of deaths from heat stress in farmworkers. So many farmworkers were dying from heat exhaustion. We helped organize a press conference with one of our state senators, and we were the only student organization there. It was in the middle of a field, at twelve o'clock noon, right when the sun is strongest. All these reporters had to walk through the dirt and sit on buckets and listen to a state senator talk about why it was so important to get this law passed.

Another student and I dressed up in all black. We were supposed to be grim reapers. We had crosses and flowers and candles for three men who had just passed away of heat exhaustion, one right after the other. We were basically representing that if the law didn't pass, then when the workers walked toward the field, they were walking to their deaths. We almost passed out from heat exhaustion ourselves, but it all went great.

As a result of the law, farmers had to provide a shaded area. And a shaded area is not a tree. They had to provide a canopy or something like that. And they had to provide drinking water for farmworkers. The law also said that farmworkers could not be penalized for taking breaks if they felt sick. Before that, farmworkers wouldn't take breaks for water or to rest for fear of being sent home or not being called to work the next day.

After that, we started getting up to thirty people or more at our meetings. But now the membership has dwindled. I was president for two years, but this past year somebody else has been president. I guess nobody runs something as well as the person who created it. A lot of the passion dies.

---

[5] The Heat Illness Prevention section of the General Industry Safety Orders adopted in California on June 15, 2006.

IT'S ABOUT HELPING PEOPLE

I'm hoping and praying to be done with school next year, 2008. That would be my seventh year. It's just getting more and more difficult to keep going through this. I still love being in the classroom. I still love learning about biology. But I'm only taking one class right now. First, because that's all I could afford at the time when tuition was due. Second, with my job, there's no way I could take more than one class. That's an ongoing struggle, between work and school. I have to work a lot of hours so I can pay for school. But working so many hours takes tons of time away from schoolwork.

I used to be a straight-A student. But now, the time I have allotted after working twelve hours a day, seven days a week, is very minimal. No matter how much I want to read that chapter or how much I want to do extra research for that paper, my body just won't let me.

Last quarter, I did horribly. My job was being so demanding, and so was school, that I got really sick. I started developing ulcer symptoms. I became anemic. I was having anxiety attacks. I started thinking that I need to choose, either work or school, but my fiancé insisted that I can't quit school. And I know I can't. I have to do it for myself. Because I know I can.

After college, I'll hopefully go to medical school. I know I have what it takes to be a doctor. I have two legs and two hands. I have eyes, and I can read. So, what's stopping me? My mom raised me to never think money is going to stop us.

A lot of people ask me how I'll pay for medical school. I can't apply for loans or scholarships. I'll just deal with that when it comes. I have never once thought about what kind of house I'll buy when I'm a doctor, or what kind of car I'm going to drive. It's not about money for me. It's about helping people, especially the farmworkers, who are the ones that need it so much.

After medical school, I'll probably do either neurology or ER surgery—because I love fast-paced stuff—until I can open my own clinic. When I went to North Carolina, I decided that I want to have a mobile clinic, so I can go to those camps, and just help them. It was so painful being there. Everyone misses their kids and their wives. And then to be sick, too. Some of these people are diabetic, and so they need insulin. They need all kinds of stuff.

We risked our lives to come to this country, and I had the opportunity to go to school. Why not go all the way? I always thought I was pretty smart. Because I don't have very many tools to defend myself with, I know that knowledge is the only thing I can arm myself with. When you have an MD after your name, very few people are going to tell you no, for anything.

EL MOJADO

AGE: *29*
COUNTRY OF ORIGIN: *Mexico*
OCCUPATION: *Meatpacker, dairy worker, carpet installer*
HOME: *Dodge City, Kansas*

I KNOW I'M NOBODY IMPORTANT

Born in Guerrero, Mexico, the man who calls himself El Mojado[1] lives with his wife and four children in Dodge City, one of three cities in southwest Kansas known collectively as the "golden triangle" of the state's meatpacking industry. He has also worked in roofing, irrigation, carpeting, at two body shops and a dairy farm, and has sold chickens at a city park. He agreed to be interviewed at the behest of a Catholic nun. They showed up together at the offices of a nonprofit one evening. El Mojado, although twenty-nine, appears much older. Our translator casually mentions that the building had been a nursing home and that the basement is haunted. Luckily, it was in a room upstairs that El Mojado spoke in Spanish of his struggles and of the emotional and physical toll they have taken. As his story unfolded, his reality became painfully clear: in spite of almost nonstop work, he is no closer to the American dream than he was when he came to the U.S. eight years ago.

I was born in the Sierra de Porvenir, Guerrero, Mexico. It's on the coast. You can camp, fish, hunt. It's a small city, mostly fields. It's like Dodge City if there was no Home Depot, Dillon's, Burger King,

---

[1] Wetback. A derogatory term for Latino immigrants, referring to workers who cross the Rio Grande into the U.S.

Wal-Mart, or Sears. The only thing is, there's no beach here in Kansas. And there's no feedlots in Porvenir. Here in Kansas, at seven in the evening, every day, you're smelling the pestilence of the feedlot.

I wasn't like a normal boy who finished primary school. I felt really separate from the other kids. When I was six in primary school, we sometimes went the day without lunch. We had to sell things like tender corn on the cob, turkeys, chickens, eggs, and bread rolls. We had to sell things to make one peso, two pesos. We also had to walk almost for an hour to wash in the river.

I have a brother and a sister only. My sister is twenty-six. My brother is twenty-four. I am the oldest. My parents separated a long time ago. My brother and I both didn't finish secondary school. It was better for us to start working. My sister stayed in school and studied English and French. My mother's working to try and support herself and my sister because right now I can't even afford to send her money. My mother cleans. She cleans office buildings. A gas place. She makes enough for one person, but still she has to pay for light and bills, and for a woman it's harder as well to try and make it on her own. My sister still lives with her. My brother's already married.

My wife and I have four children. My wife is twenty-eight years old. She is very nice, a hard worker and a good cook—she makes really good tamales, which we sometimes sell. I like the way she takes care of the house. She's also taking classes to learn English. And I tell her not to leave school. For her it will be a big help. It will help me, too. She'll be able to translate. At least she gets ahead, since I can't study. We get by with what I earn. It's the only thing we count on. Three of my children were born here—the girl is five, the older boy will be two, and the younger boy will be one. My oldest son is eight. He's a wetback, too.

EVERYTHING MOVES WITH MONEY

You come here with a dream. I came here for one reason: I was told I'd earn double what I was making in Mexico. But the bad thing is that your dream never comes true. You just want to see the greens. A lot of people have died wanting to see those greens. Here everything moves with money. My wife also wanted to come here. She thought it would be a better place for children, that there are more opportunities here for kids.

We spent about eight months living on the border in Juarez before crossing over. To support my family I worked in a kitchen as a cook. I crossed first, alone, with a coyote and some other guys. I left my family in Juarez. You hear stories about the border, of women who are raped. People who are assaulted. Money stolen. So in different places, depending on where you pass there are different problems you encounter. The big problem we had was climbing a fence, which was about twelve feet high. It had this sharp wire at the top of it. I had to help a guy, a friend, who got caught on that wire. He was bleeding. He'd cut his foot. The coyote left us. He was running ahead with the others. But the truth is I couldn't leave a friend like that, hooked on this piece of wire. If Immigration had taken him down who knows what would have happened to him. I helped him off the fence and cleaned his foot with a shirt. We had to throw that shirt away.

Later, we ran across a four-lane highway. Honestly, I felt like a thief. Then we ran toward the town of El Paso to look for a hotel to spend the night. When we got to the hotel, the coyote said, "Don't come out. Don't open the door to anyone." There are people who report people who are staying in hotels in El Paso, call Immigration. Then half a day later, they put me on a bus that came straight to Garden City in November of 1999. I came to Kansas because my wife had family here. I was twenty-two years old.

My family crossed over in March 2000. My wife came over as an

American citizen. She walked across the bridge with a fake ID she bought at the border. Sometimes U.S. citizens will sell their papers. For example, if I'm a citizen I make copies and sell my papers. My papers end up in the border area. A coyote then buys them for about five hundred dollars. Then he turns around and sells them again for about a thousand or fifteen hundred. So my wife had good papers, another person's papers. When I first saw her, I hardly recognized her, she looked so ugly, dressed up like this other person on the papers.

My oldest son was three years old at the time. He also had the papers of a citizen. He passed alone, without my wife, with the son of a coyote, a twelve-year-old kid. My wife was already waiting on the other side. You see the coyotes have to separate the children from the parents because the children will sometimes say, "My mom doesn't have papers." You have to be careful with those things. And say the mother gets caught, taken down, at least the child has gotten through. When she got to Garden City my wife was crying. She had never been separated from her son like that and she was afraid that something could've happened to him. That's why it feels bad when they separate you. And you have to trust people you do not know. Thank God that we are all here and we're okay, but I wouldn't want any of us to go through that again.

VERY HOT AND VERY COLD

At first we stayed with my wife's family. Nine of us lived in one small trailer. The first job I had here in Garden City was at the Monfort beefpacking plant. My brother-in-law worked there and helped me get the job. I used my fake papers. When I first saw the cow at the slaughterhouse I was surprised. I had never seen animals like that, all cut up, with blood everywhere. There is always work with the slaughterhouse. They don't stop work because of snow or rain. So on the one hand, it's good to have work, but on the other hand, it's not good because they discriminate. They make certain people work more than other people. They do give you training, but too little training. Someone just tells you, "Move your wrist, warm up the fingers." But you never warm up your back and you're standing up the whole time. It depends on the job they give you, but I was standing the whole time for the job they gave me. My fingers would lock up. They're still locked up. But God willing, my fingers will get better because it's bad to have the fingers kind of messed up.

At the plant, I would work sometimes ten, twelve hours a day. It depended on the hours that they gave me. The salary was very little—I made about $8.00, $8.50 an hour. They told us how to use the equipment, but charged us for it. They charged for the boots, the gloves, helmet, goggles—all the equipment. The most expensive piece of equipment was the steel glove. That glove cost about $30, I think. I don't know for sure. They don't give a list of how much things are. The checks I received were supposedly for about $300. I ended up with something around $150 after they charged me for the equipment.

I was on the line. There were three of us on the line. One did the flat cut, and I would take the bone. Then when I worked on the flat, another one did the bone. While I worked on the bone, another one did the flat. And we would take turns like that. And we had to do it quickly—in less than two minutes—or else it would all end up together, the work would stack up on you. Pieces of meat would come across the table. The first chunk, about twenty, thirty pounds, had a bone in the middle. I had to separate the meat, then throw the bone on the belt. If the bone wasn't clean, the ones that were farther down the line—if they saw that it wasn't cleaned right—they would throw it back at me to clean it right. The other piece was called a flat cut, which weighed about five, maybe ten pounds. For that I had to trim the meat, the pure meat, and I had to cut the fat out from the ball of the meat.

There's two kinds of climates in the slaughterhouse: very hot and very cold. I was in processing, so the place where I ended up was very cold. It keeps the bacteria out of the meat. I wore a vest, sleeves, an apron, and four gloves. I was wet all the time. Inside I trembled. When I took off my clothes I would catch a fever. Sometimes the body acclimates to the environment. Other times, as time passes, you end up with respiratory problems. Or you get heart problems. I got a lot of colds, too many. I also got sinusitis.

They only gave us two breaks—one fifteen-minute and another one for half an hour. Forty-five minutes all together. They don't let people rest. Instead they make them work more. Sometimes I had to do work for somebody else if they were absent. And since I was new, I sometimes had to do the jobs nobody wanted to do. But I had to do them. I needed a stable job. I was afraid that they would fire me. And where am I going to go without papers?

And that's how it is. In the United States, working as a wetback is very difficult. I'm working illegally and things are getting more difficult for me. And I can't fight for my rights. I have no rights here in the United States. I don't have a right to anything, I can't fight anything. I know I'm nobody important.

One Christmas there was a fire at the plant, and it burned down. So they sent us to Greeley, Colorado to work in another plant. Monfort paid for fifteen days in a hotel, that's it. But after that Monfort wouldn't pay anymore, and the little hotels are expensive if you're paying out of your own salary. So they kicked us out of the hotel and we had to find another place to live.

For me, there are good and bad Mexican bosses. The boss at Monfort was a good guy. Because he was Mexican, he knew more or less how to treat Mexicans. He taught me various jobs. But he told me that if I wanted to earn more money I would have to put out even more of an effort. On the line, you earn more, but you have to work more. Sometimes it's better to have a Mexican boss. But some Mexicans discriminate against other Hispanics because they have papers or another doesn't. The boss at Greeley wasn't Mexican. He was like an Arab. He didn't speak English very well. He was more strict, more racist. He didn't want Mexicans. The Arab made us do the job of three people.

I had an accident. It was in Greeley, outside the apartment where I lived with my brother-in-law and an acquaintance from Monfort. A guy who would give us rides to work locked his keys in his car. The window was open about five inches. The guy tried to squeeze in through the five inches, but he broke the window. There were shards of glass all over. I pulled him out of there and I cut my hand. I had to go the hospital. I didn't have insurance. I paid all $495 in cash. They sewed me up, but left glass inside. I could hardly work, even though I wanted to. The plant wanted a doctor's note giving me permission to keep on working. I told the doctor that I couldn't work. My hand was looking really bad—green. I thought I would end up without a hand. It was all swollen. I couldn't put gloves on or anything. Now, when it's cold, my hand still hurts a lot. It still gets a little green.

I couldn't work, and if I didn't work, I didn't eat. Couldn't pay rent. I had to go back to Kansas and support my family in whatever way I could. I sold chickens. I'd go to the city park and look for people and tell them, "Look, I'm selling chicken." They would tell me to bring them a chicken, two chickens, one and a half chickens. Then I prepared the chicken with a salad, onion, rice, and sauce with a special spice mix. Or I would I sell the whole chicken. If I sold fourteen chickens in day I could pay my bills.

KEEP GOING, MOVE FORWARD

I found other jobs. I got into touching up car dents, preparing them for paint jobs at a body shop. I was mostly a sander there. We did it by hand. My boss there treated me very badly. He stole Saturdays from me. For some reason, he wouldn't pay people when they worked on Saturdays.

One day I found a hair dryer outside the shop. I asked my co-workers about it, and one of them said it was broken. And I said, "Well, someone can still use it, get parts out of it." As I picked it up my boss saw me. He asked me what I was doing. I told him it was in the trash, that my coworkers told me it didn't work anymore. He said, "What do you mean it doesn't work?" He said, "It works fine." He didn't believe me. He accused me of stealing. He fired me right then, after eight months.

I had another job working with large farming sprinklers, the kind that irrigate corn. We put in new ones, or fixed old ones. They paid me about $6.50 an hour; we worked over twelve hours a day. They never gave us a raise. They wanted us to work more so that they could make more money. We worked in snow, heat, whatever.

In 2003, I worked in roofing and made three hundred dollars a week. That manager didn't like wetbacks either.

With my fake papers I was able to work at lots of jobs. I never did my taxes, so I never got money back from the government. I was paying in, but not getting money back.

In June 2006, I applied for a job on the cleanup crew at the IBP meatpacking plant. Even though you work more, IBP pays more than at other jobs. An American girl at the office there took applications. She took my picture and checked the picture and my papers on the computer. She saw the photos weren't the same. She said, "If you don't leave, I'm either going to call the police or call Immigration." She got a person—some big American guy from the office, and he was in agreement that they should take the papers from me, and they took them. From then on I haven't had any papers.

After they took my papers, I went to work at the dairy farm. The hours were long, twelve hours. It's a job you have to be careful with, because a cow could hurt you or a fence could hurt you. I cleaned the pens, took the poop off the cows. I was in charge of the corrals, maybe fifteen corrals, more, with half an hour to clean each corral. I rushed to finish it all in one day. I had to keep going, move forward. Someone would check if the corrals looked good. I had to take care of everything—the cows, the machinery. They would tell me, "You have to do the work perfectly. And if you can't, leave. Find other work," they said. The truth is that, no, I wasn't perfect.

It was a lot of pressure. The pay was little. It turned out to be about $6.50 or $7.50 an hour for twelve hours a day. There was no insurance. When we started there, we had to sign a sheet that said that we could be let go at anytime, At any instant. But if we chose to quit, we had to give them two weeks' notice.

I had headaches, I felt very tense, I had nosebleeds. My ears hurt. I had to go to the doctor. They drew blood. They gave me pills. They gave me a letter for the boss. The foreman told me he didn't care. "You still have to work. Many people come in sick." He said, "I knew a person who drove a tractor. He was sick. He kept driving that tractor, and he just died in that tractor. You don't have to worry about it. God is good." My foreman said I could come back. I told him I wasn't going to come back. I had to keep my health.

Right now, I work in carpeting. Again, I work about twelve hours a day. It's very hard on the knees, on the back. The knees get swollen. You can dislocate your back because of the carpets; they're very heavy rolls that you have to carry. Sometimes you don't have equipment to carry them upstairs or anything, two people have to carry them, or one person. But I have less stress with my boss on this job because he's Mexican. He understands immigrants, because he knows a little bit about God. If one knows about God, a man can understand other people better.

A JOB TO LIVE ON

If I'm discriminated against by my bosses, I can't do anything. Supposedly there are lawyers and all that. But if I were to seek help, they would get rid of me fast. Because at those jobs, if I get a lawyer involved for whatever reason, that would mark against me for other jobs. And here in the United States, word spreads really quickly wherever you are. I would never be able to work. The best thing to do is put up with the discrimination and keep looking for a job to live on. My family needs to eat from my daily earnings.

Truly I don't see a difference since when I got here. I don't have more money. I don't have any land. I was supposed to earn double what I was making in my country. For the eight years that I've been here—nothing.

The trailer we live in is okay enough, but it's missing lots of details. There are three holes in the roof that leak. The insulation underneath is all broken. If I had seen how the trailer was, I wouldn't have paid $2,000. I pay $180 for the lot rent and cable; $82 for water and trash; $140 for electricity and gas. I pay more money to the dentist to get my children's teeth cleaned.

I'm also not done paying my coyote. He lives in the area. I paid about $12,000 for the whole family to come over. Right now I still owe $2,500. My coyote will come to our house to collect, or we'll go to his house to pay. Cash. Depending on how I get paid, he expects to be paid. If I am paid bimonthly, he needs to be paid bimonthly. The coyotes have friends that inform them how much we make and when we get paid. And I can't tell on him for anything. He would call the police on me or Immigration on me. My coyote's legal here. If I say he's a coyote and I don't have papers and he has papers, it's logical they're going to believe him and not me.

That's the world. That's the life of the immigrant. That's a Mexican. People from El Salvador, Honduras, Guatemala—they pay even more. A Guatemalan is twice a wetback. Guatemalans pay five thousand dollars to come here. The Salvadoran is three times a wetback. The Salvadoran has to go through Guatemala, and then to Mexico and then…

THINGS AN AMERICAN WOULDN'T DO

Immigrants need documents. They need at least an ID or license. But there's no way to get a license. Here in Kansas, you must drive to get to the store, to the hospital, everywhere. And everything we do is a crime. You don't have papers, it's a crime. You buy fake papers, it's a crime. You live a crime.

The Americans want us to do the job harder, faster, but for less money. If we at least had insurance or a raise… We come here to find a different life. We work hard here; if we worked this hard in our land, things would be better for us in our land. At least in our land, we're not discriminated against like we are here. My dream is to own a home, land, for my children. But the truth is, it can't be done.

The U.S. is nice to get to know. It's beautiful sometimes when it's green. I've gotten to know the culture. But these days it's hard to work here. In 1986, there was an amnesty.[2] Now they don't want to do any more amnesties and the government's getting harder. Now immigration officers go to jobs to look for you. They didn't used to. Yes, you broke the law. Americans with papers can go to Mexico and drive. They are able to work there, too. Why can't we work here? A lot of Americans in Mexico have hotels, restaurants. They live well there. Nobody bothers them. And here, nobody wants us here; but over there, they really are living off of us. We do things an American

---

[2] The Immigration Reform and Control Act of 1986 made it unlawful to knowingly hire an undocumented worker, while also granting amnesty to illegal immigrants who had entered the U.S. prior to 1982 and resided here continuously since then.

wouldn't do. The wetbacks. Instead of helping us, they seem to kick us to the curb, want to throw us away like trash.

Who works the oranges? Who works the construction? Dairies? Fields? Hog farms? Cleaning homes? Who does that? Immigrants. I don't think anyone who has papers is going to be doing that. An American, when is he gonna be picking oranges? Who is going to milk cows for ten hours straight, then get a five-minute lunch?

YOGESH, 24
St. Louis, Missouri

Yogesh came to the United States from India when he was eleven. He was here legally until the age of twenty-one, when he became, in effect, a legal orphan. No longer a dependent, he was stripped from his parents' green card application, which has been pending for seventeen years. His parents are here legally, and hold work permits. But the only way in which Yogesh can become a legal U.S. resident is through a change in the law. He hopes that proposed legislation called the DREAM Act passes (see Glossary for more on the DREAM Act). Yogesh graduated from college last year.

First my parents came to the U.S., to St. Louis, without my brother and me. We stayed on at my uncle's. My parents thought it would only be a matter of months and then they'd send for us and we'd join them. So a month went by, another and another. Eventually it became two years. It was hard living without our parents. Every time they'd call, my brother would cry after we hung up. It wasn't that my uncle and aunt didn't love us—I mean they treated us just like their own kids—it was just that it wasn't the same.

I've been told the reason it took so long is that my parents were promised things by a lawyer. Actually he was only pretending to be a lawyer; he was a notary. And he gave them the wrong information about immigration. He kept telling them they would be able to get green cards soon. And once they had green cards, it would be a lot easier to get us over. But the green cards weren't going through. In seventeen years, my parents' green cards still haven't come through.

Both my parents were putting in a lot of hours every day at jobs. My father was working as a cashier. My mother found a job as a secretary. It hasn't worked out too badly for them. They recently bought a house. But I think they have their regrets. Especially given my brother's and my situation. They have work permits and now that we are no longer dependents, we've lost our legal status.

I started college in autumn of 2001, hopeful that it was only a matter of time before my family's immigration trouble would be resolved. There was talk then on Capitol Hill of some way of resolving the status of undocumented immigrants in the United States. But then September 11th happened. I remember the day very clearly. We were glued to the TV. The following weeks would only worsen the situation as we heard and read about stories in local papers about people being deported due to immigration violations. We had heard that people in a situation similar to my father's, who had to get their work permits renewed every year, were denied their renewal permit. We didn't know what to expect. Every other week we would hear about an immigration raid that had taken place somewhere in the Midwest. So now we were waiting again, but not sure for what.

My own situation is still waiting. Now, it's five years after 9/11. But I've become optimistic lately because I would be covered by the DREAM Act, if it passes. I actually met with Senator Dick Durbin from Illinois about it. The weird thing was that when we met, the senator himself told me he didn't even know how his mother came to this country. He only knew she came from Lithuania. And there was Senator Durbin's senior counsel, or his policy director—I forget his exact position—he said that his grandfather had actually come to this country in an illegal way, I think, from Lebanon. He said someone had told his grandfather, "When you see the Statue of Liberty, jump in the water and swim for shore." And that's how his grandfather entered into this country.

So I was taken aback by all that, but also it gave me some reason to hope. Paperwise, I don't have a status. But this doesn't mean I'm not American. Because I mean, I'll say it: there's no way I could go back to India. I don't know what I would do.

JOSE GARCIA

AGE: *37*
COUNTRY OF ORIGIN: *El Salvador*
OCCUPATION: *Cook, substance-abuse counselor*
HOME: *Mount Vernon, Washington*

IN THAT NEIGHBORHOOD, IF
YOU'RE NOT PART OF A GANG
YOU'RE GOING TO SUFFER

At four-thirty in the afternoon, in the public library in Mount Vernon, Washington, one hears both fluent English and Spanish. Jose Garcia stands next to the information desk in the lobby. He's thirty-seven years old, a native of El Salvador who has been in the United States for twenty-four years and currently works in a restaurant and as a substance-abuse counselor. Wearing baggy pants and a black hooded sweatshirt, he stands with his hands in his pockets. He carries a file folder with photographs, which he later explains are of graffiti and gang tags. He speaks English with a slight accent, and pauses occasionally while he searches for a word. As part of his work in the community, he often speaks about his past to recovering addicts and to children in the public school system. He seems gratified by the opportunity to discuss his childhood in El Salvador and his reasons for first coming to the United States.

I grew up in Jucuapa, in the Usulután province of El Salvador. My mother got very sick when I was born. She died soon after. I never knew my father. I grew up with my grandmother and my two aunts,

Marta and Luisa, and they gave me a lot, but I always knew that I didn't have a real mom, so it was kind of hard for me to know that I was living in a house that I didn't belong in. They gave me a lot of love, though, and they always showed me how to do the right thing. I called my Aunt Marta "Mom."

In those days, my aunt was making probably less than a dollar a day. She grew tomatoes and onions and she tried to sell them and make a profit, and I don't know how she did it, but we always had— well not always, but most of the time—food on the table.

It wasn't an easy life. When the civil war came in the early '80s,[1] it became even harder because not that many people had money, and sometimes you couldn't go into town on the bus because of the fighting between the army and the guerrillas. Sometimes the gun battles would go on for weeks.

But we had a nice house. We had water, electricity, and it was a luxury to have that because, like I said, my aunt didn't make that much money.

My grandmother passed away when I was five. My aunt Luisa, by this time, she was living in San Salvador, and every time I went back to school, she used to buy me clothes. I never had new clothes, but they were all right. They were used clothes Luisa would buy at the swap meet or the secondhand store, clothes that people sent from the United States to El Salvador because that's a way people make money over there.

Our neighborhood was quiet. It was quiet because for some reason, in those days, people listened to their moms. We grew up with the mentality that if you don't listen to your mom, then something wrong is going to happen to you. God's going to get mad at you.

It was nice. I've got nothing but good memories from that time.

---

[1] From 1980-1992, the Salvadoran government was embroiled in civil war with leftist guerrilla organizations.

After school, we'd play football, soccer, from three o'clock probably until it got too dark to see the ball.

JUST THE BODY, NO HEAD

I remember the first time I heard about the guerrillas. We were out there playing. They dropped something out of a plane. It was like a bomb, but it wasn't a bomb. When we ran over there to see, we found a lot of papers, propaganda, flyers about the FMLN.[2] They were fighting the government; they were saying the people should have more rights, that imperialism was killing us, taking our land.

This made a pretty big impact on most of the people my age because we heard about rebels in other countries, like Cuba or Nicaragua or Russia, but we never thought we were going to see anything like that in El Salvador. Especially in our town, because everybody knew everybody, and it was such a quiet town. But it didn't take a long time before they started putting up a lot of graffiti. It was from different groups like the FMLN and the LP-28. Even the BPR, the *Bloque Popular Revolucionario.*[3] I still remember that.

I think I was around ten years old when they dropped that paper bomb. Everything happened so fast after that. Next thing, probably a month later, they started finding bodies in the town where I lived. Sometimes just the body, no head. Other times you'd see a man's body with a woman's head. And it started happening almost every day. What the soldiers used to do was, they'd pick somebody from one town and drop the body in a different town. It was rough because

---

[2] Farabundo Martí National Liberation Front. A coalition of leftist parties and guerrilla groups formed to oppose the government during the Salvadoran civil war.

[3] LP-28 (*Ligas Populares 28 febrero,* or, Popular Leagues of February 28) takes its name from the day government forces killed over one hundred people protesting the fraudulent 1977 elections. LP-28 and BPR (Popular Revolution Bloc) were part of the guerrilla resistance in 1970s and 1980s El Salvador.

you could see the dogs and the pigs eating the bodies. Other times they threw the bodies in the river. I don't know if this is true or not, but there was a story that a few people found rings inside the fish. The fish were eating the bodies. Nobody wanted to eat fish after that.

Most of us were afraid because we never knew if it was going to happen to us. Almost every day we'd wake up with the news that soldiers had taken three or four people from our town. Then they came and took my cousin; he lived next to me. He wasn't my real cousin, but we grew up together like brothers. We were all part of one big family. I heard them come. It was maybe around one in the morning. They were kicking in the door. Next thing we know, my cousin's mom, she started crying through the wall, letting us know that they took him.

He was about twenty. I think he was part of one of the rebel groups. So the government came and killed him.

Most of the people who got killed in my town were killed by the government. They believed that the whole town was supporting the guerrillas. We couldn't go much outside of town because there were a lot of checkpoints that the government had, and if they asked for ID and then you showed your ID and they saw that you were from Jucuapa, there was a good chance they'd take you.

I remember one time, I went to San Salvador with my aunt Luisa, and the army came to town, and they took everybody. Aunt Luisa told me it was probably six hundred soldiers that came into town. And they took everybody from their houses, and took them into the city, to a big park. Then they put the fathers and the daughters and men, women, and children in one line, and they started putting paper bags on people's heads. When they put the bag on your head, you knew you were gone. They were going to kill you. That day, I believe they took probably two-hundred-something people. I believe only a few of the bodies were found. The rest, nobody knows what happened to them.

My older brother was a soldier for the army. He used to tell me things. Once he was sent by his commander to kidnap two girls and kill their family. His commander wanted to have sex with the girls. My brother refused to do it, so the commander found someone else. They kept the girls somewhere close to the river, and the commander used to go there and rape the girls twice a day. That would happen for two or three weeks, until finally they killed the girls. My brother reported the whole thing to his other commander. And you know what happened? They punished my brother. He wasn't supposed to say anything. He left for the U.S. soon after that. He passed away in the '90s. He'd never been well psychologically after that.

Before the civil war started, I don't think anybody in El Salvador had any desire to go anywhere else. El Salvador's a beautiful place. Even making just a little bit of money, you make enough to live well over there. In my days, you didn't need that much money. Like I said, when that stuff started to happen, it was something new to us. Nobody wanted to leave their town and the people they grew up with. I don't think anybody would have left if there hadn't been fighting.

IF YOU LOVE ME, YOU'LL GO

I was around thirteen when we finally came to the United States. It was 1983. My four sisters, they came first. I didn't want to come here. I didn't know my sisters that well. I didn't feel comfortable with them. But then one of my sisters came back to El Salvador to get me. I refused at first. But finally my aunt convinced me. She said that what was happening in El Salvador wasn't going to stop. She was worried that if I stayed, I'd get killed. She basically said, "If you love me, you'll go. And over there, you'll go to school, you'll get a job. Then you can send me money, and I can go over there, too."

We took the bus. The bus from El Salvador to Guatemala, and then from Guatemala to Mexico. Every time you get stopped by the

Mexican Immigration, you were supposed to give them some money. If you didn't have enough money, they'd send you back. That's why it took us a long time. From Mexico City, we took a bus to Tijuana, where we paid our coyote. It cost five hundred dollars each. My group had about twenty-five people in it. They made us stay at a ranch in Tijuana while we waited for the best time to cross. At the ranch, for three days they didn't give us much of anything. No food, no water. At night, we used to go around and ask the people for water.

We almost got killed twice. The guy that was supposed to take us, he got sick, so they sent us with another guy, and he didn't know the area very well, so he took the wrong way. I remember we started walking around ten p.m., and the car that came and picked us up on the other side of the border didn't pick us up until probably six or seven a.m. We walked about nine hours. And in the process, the guy got lost. It was so dark. There were these things in front of us we thought were big rocks. Next thing we know, one of the rocks starts moving. We were walking right through a herd of bulls; I think they were rodeo bulls. They started chasing us. I don't know how we didn't get killed. I know one guy got hit by a bull. He didn't die, but he was hurt.

After we crossed the border, they packed us all in a motor home. The tire blew while we were driving on the highway. The thing started shaking real bad. The windows broke. Next thing we know, we went and hit these two big trees. My sister, she was bleeding from her nose, and she had a cut on her forehead. From there, we started running.

I think this was in San Isidro. Not so far from the border. We ended up on somebody's property where they had a bunch of dogs. We could see the people walking around, and the dogs started barking at us. We hid in a tunnel. I don't know if the people saw us, but after a while, the police came. It was dark by then. They were right at the entrance to the tunnel and we could see them shining their flashlights.

It was the kind of tunnel the bilge water goes through, the water from the city. It was a big tunnel, made out of cement. It was dark in there, and the water was nasty. We didn't go in very far, because we were afraid. We didn't know what kind of animals were in there. Probably rats, big ones.

We stayed there I don't know how long, but I remember it was cold. Because we didn't have any jackets, we all just got real close together. I think we stayed all night and left early the next morning. The coyote came back for us. Then we got put in another motor home, and they took us to L.A.

A GREAT WAY TO INCREASE PROFITS

At first, I didn't like L.A. because I didn't speak English. I didn't know my sisters that well, and they didn't do much to help me get used to the new culture. I was thirteen, the city seemed so big to me, especially where we lived. My older sister, she was married, and when I first came here, I was staying with my other three sisters in an apartment in West L.A., next to LAX, the airport.

For me, leaving my family, my town and everything, living with my sisters, it was awful. I remember the worst part was the nightmares. I used to wake up four or five times a night, screaming, seeing my aunt Marta killed, without her head.

My sisters had a drinking problem. They used to drink a lot, so they didn't care if I went to school. They were more interested in me going to work. They didn't care if there was food in the house or anything. A few months after I got here, one of my sisters, she got me a Social Security number so I could start working. At that time it wasn't that hard to get a job, even if you didn't have any papers. But you had to know somebody. If you're Hispanic, from Mexico or El Salvador or Guatemala or wherever, the only way you could get a job was if you had a friend or family working somewhere already. My two brothers-in-law, they've been working for the same two restaurants for more than thirty years. They weren't legal then, but they are now.

One of my brothers-in-law, he got me my first job at a place called Coco's. My brothers-in-law, my brother who passed away, my sisters, we all worked there at different times. I remember the first time I worked there, I was so little, so skinny, that I only lasted for a week. The guy who hired me knew I was only thirteen. I didn't have any problems washing the dishes, but I had a problem cleaning the tables because you were supposed to clear the table all at once, all the dishes, and I couldn't lift the bin. It was just too heavy for me with all those dishes and glasses.

After Coco's, I worked for a lot of different fast food places, probably seven different restaurants over the next few years. I worked for McDonald's, Burger King. I worked for Denny's. I worked for Red Robin. I tried to find a job I could work at night because I had started going to school during the day. So I'd go to school all day and then work from three or four in the afternoon until sometimes midnight. I usually ended up quitting after a few months because it got to be so hard.

It was frustrating sometimes. This happened to a lot of people that I knew. Even if you worked seventy hours, they'd only pay you for forty hours. If you don't like it, too bad. You don't have papers, you don't get overtime. And they make you work more than if you had the papers. And another thing was that in most of the restaurants in my area, probably only the manager had papers. Hiring people without papers is a great way to increase your profits. The managers make money, the company makes money, and they don't care if you're happy or not. If you need a job, well, take what we got to offer you. I knew people that had papers back then, and they were making six, seven dollars. Everybody else was making four eighty-five. Eventually, a couple of years later, I ended up back at Coco's. I kept losing jobs. I was trying to stay in school. Coco's was the only place that would take me and I needed the money.

I was probably about fifteen when one of the manager's friends, he made me have sex with him. He did it to four people that I know of, me and three of my friends. He used to buy us beer, and he had hard liquor for us back at his house. When we came back to his house with him, he would start to touch us. Then, after it happened once, he would tell us, if you don't come back and do it again, if you don't show up on this day, I'm going to tell your family what we were doing. The manager was white, but the guy who did this was from El Salvador. My sisters, they knew the guy. He was a friend of theirs, too. Back then, because there weren't that many people from El Salvador in the area, we all knew each other. He did this to me five or six times before I finally quit. Afterward I never told anybody. I was too ashamed. Also, I was afraid. In all the places I used to work, they used to talk a lot about Immigration. If we ever made any trouble or complained about anything, they'd threaten to call Immigration.

A few years ago, I heard the guy got stabbed by another employee at Coco's. When I heard that I figured he must have kept doing the same thing to other people who worked there.

EVERY OTHER HOUSE WAS A DOPE HOUSE

Not long after I came to the United States, when I was fourteen, I was introduced to marijuana. I didn't care for it at first. I told myself, stay clean, keep going to school, get a good job. I wanted to send money home to my aunt in El Salvador. Then came cocaine, and heroin a year or two later. I remember the first time I went to juvenile jail, they didn't try to deport me. Maybe because I was so young, only thirteen or fourteen. It happened not long after I first came here. It was a dine-and-dash. I was hungry—we never had anything to eat at the house—and I asked for food at a restaurant and didn't pay.

I remember the judge, he said, "Next time don't make me go through this." He told the district attorney, he said, "Next time, if you need somebody to pay for a kid's meal that badly, call me at home, and I'll pay for it." They were supposed to release me, but the paperwork got messed up, and I ended up staying in juvenile jail for four, almost five months. When I came back in the courtroom, I remember the judge, it was the same judge, and he said, "You have to release him right now." He said, "I want to see you take those handcuffs off, and I want to see him walk out of here with my own eyes."

A year or two later, I was using crack cocaine. One night I was messed up and I guess a little out of control. One of my sisters called 911. When the police came, I panicked and I went and hid in the closet. That time, the second time I went to juvenile jail, I was held for ten days before I was released.

By the time I turned sixteen, my drug addiction was too much for me. I stopped working. I was using heroin. I was using crack cocaine more than ever. I was using marijuana. I was drinking every day, and I kept going to jail.

In the neighborhood where we lived, maybe every other house was a dope house. And then you start hanging around with people that have been in the United States for seven, eight years, and they start telling you, "Man, don't be stupid. Why should you be working for $4.50, $4.85. Look what a nice car I got, look at all the money I got, and you could be doing the same thing."

Not long after I started getting involved with drugs, when I was still a teenager, I got involved with a big gang in California. I was introduced to the gang members by my cousins, and they told me I could make a lot of money with them, selling drugs. In Los Angeles, in that neighborhood, if you're not part of a gang, you're going to suffer. Being part of a gang was a way to protect myself from all the other gangs in the neighborhood. But more than that, I didn't want to be abused anymore. I felt like I'd come here, and I was doing my best and working hard, and there's nobody who can help me. My sisters, they didn't take the time to send me to school and take care of me. All the places I ever worked, my employers just took advantage of me. And then somebody comes along who can help you, who can offer you the good life, and you feel like it's payback time. You know you're doing something bad, but you start to feel like if somebody has to die, you'd rather it was somebody else.

At eighteen, I got married to my first wife, an American citizen. She was born in California, but her family was from Puerto Rico. A few years later, after I got out of prison for the first time, I applied for a green card. We paid the fee, but I never finished the paperwork. My wife tried to finish it for me, but I needed to go to the appointments with Immigration, and I never did. I was an addict. I couldn't focus on anything, paperwork or whatever.

For years, being in that position, I kept trying so hard to stop using drugs. I even tried to kill myself. During my twenties, I went to the hospital three times, and they saved my life all three times. They thought I'd overdosed by mistake. But I'd tried to overdose so I could die. I thought that going that way, with an overdose, that it wouldn't hurt, because I'd heard about people overdosing on heroin, and I thought that's what it would be like. I thought it would be peaceful. I thought I'd just fall asleep, and it would be over.

It was crazy, but I remember I used to think that if they deported me, maybe it would save my life. I used to think that maybe if they sent me back to El Salvador, maybe I'd be able to stop using drugs over there.

IN PRISON

Right now, I'm thirty-seven years old. I was thirty when I stopped using drugs. I did drugs for fourteen years. Most of the time I was in jail.

I don't like to talk about this stuff because I'm not proud of what I did. But I believe God works in mysterious ways, and maybe if somebody reads something in a book, if they hear a story about somebody like me, maybe it can help them.

I spent twelve years in prison. I went to jail three times—for three years, for six years, and then for three more years after that. I went to jail twice for receiving stolen property and once because of drugs, for possessing drugs. I never went for big stuff. I always went for small stuff. One time, the second time I went to prison, I was walking with a friend, and we found a VCR in a trash can. We cleaned it up. We were trying to sell it to buy drugs. I was holding it when the police came, and when they saw I had a prior record, that was it. My second son, he was born on the second of January, 1992, and I went back to prison on the third, the next day.

All the time I went to prison, they never tried to deport me. They never sent me back to El Salvador. They always told me there was a good chance they would deport me, but they always just sent me to rehab instead.

Finally, my wife, she got tired of me going to prison. She waited for me for a long time, eleven years. She was everything for me, my ex-wife. It hit me hard when she told me one day, "You know what? I don't want nothing to do with you." She said, "I don't care if you write the babies letters. When you get out of prison you can come and see them, but I got a new boyfriend, and we're going to get married." I was shocked.

And finally I decided, I said, "You know what, I don't have nobody else." Because people from my gang, they're there when I'm in prison, but they don't really care for me.

Leaving the gang, I was more scared for my family than me. I was more afraid they were going to hurt them. Or that they were going to kill me, and my kids were going to grow up without a dad. But most of the people I knew when I was in the gang, they knew that you don't have to worry about me telling everybody or somebody or the police or anybody what we did. They knew me. If they sent me to do a job, and I did the job, and I got caught, and police wanted information about why you did it, don't worry about it, I did it because I wanted to do it. So they couldn't get no information from me.

AS GOOD AS ANYBODY

After I got out in 2000, I told my homeboys, if you guys want to kill me, that's fine, but I'm tired of this shit. I don't want anything to do with drugs anymore. I don't want to sell drugs and kill my own people anymore. I don't want to kill nobody anymore.

The guys in the gang, they knew the way I was. And I told them, "You know what? All I need is one chance. Just give me an opportunity to help the community, to help our people."

I was thirty years old. They have an electronics class in prison, so I got a diploma for electronics. They had culinary arts classes, so I took those, too. I got my GED in prison. And I took classes in drug and alcohol counseling. When I got out, I passed the test. So I'm a drug and alcohol counselor, too.

I did good for a year. I started getting involved in the community, working as a leader, as a community leader in L.A. I opened a halfway house, a rehab program for people who didn't have no money or no papers. They want to get clean, they can go in there, they didn't have to pay nothing. I went and got two jobs, so I could pay for the food and everything.

A lot of people started getting clean. I said, You know what? This is working. And a lot of people I used to hang around with, they saw what I was doing, and they said, you know what, that's good.

It's funny because finally I decided to let my spirit in El Salvador go. I'd love to go back home someday. Even just talking about the place, I get sentimental. But so many people are dead now. I used to be mad at the president, at the government. The government here, too, because the U.S. was the one sending guns, so they could stop the communists from coming into El Salvador. And finally, I said, You know what, I know what happened was wrong, and a lot of our people got killed, and we didn't have nothing to do with communists or the government, and we paid the price for it, but it's time for me to let it go. This is my problem, right here, in my heart. I got an addiction problem, I got an alcohol problem, but my main problem is right here, in me.

I've been in Washington for three years. My sister lives here. She moved here eight years ago. One time I was talking to her, telling her about the rehab programs I was doing. And she said, "There's no program like that here for the Hispanics." So I told her, "I'm going to go move there, and if I like it, I'll stay there and see if I can start a new program."

So here I am. I started working for a restaurant. I'm a cook. Then I worked for a rehab program. I worked there for seven months, and then I started my own organization. I still cook. I keep pretty busy.

Probably about four months after I got here, I met my wife, my new wife. My daughter, she's going to be two years old next month, and my son's going to be four months.

My new wife, she's from El Salvador, too. She's been here for five years. She has TPS status, temporary protected status, for people from El Salvador.[4] She's worked for some of the various restaurants around here, different chicken places. We're not legally married yet, but we've been together for two years, and we're going to get married soon.

My oldest son, he's seventeen, and my other son is fifteen. They're both in California with my ex-wife.

I've spoken to an attorney, he tells me that in California, it's one

---

[4] See Glossary for more information.

of the few states where they can seal your record, so if I can get some money together to do it, I want to send some paperwork back there to see if they can seal my record, so my felonies won't be used against me if I apply for a green card. But because I have more than one conviction, I understand that I probably won't be able to get my record sealed, so we're probably going to have to try to get asylum.

A friend of mine just got asylum because a lot of people are getting killed in El Salvador, people who used to be part of a gang here. When they get deported, they get killed back there because they were a gang member here. They believe the government is doing that there, so sometimes that helps you get asylum here.

This attorney, he told me that those were the only two options he could think of for me, for me to try and get my record sealed and apply for a green card, or for me to try and apply for asylum. But he said he's looking into other options, and if I hire him, we might be able to do something else. I might be able to tell my story to Immigration and apply for asylum retroactively—but the lawyer says this is a long shot.

I've only started to do this stuff now because I knew it would be hard for me. Back in California, when I got out of prison, I knew that it would take a lot of work for me to show the government or Immigration that I could be a positive part of the community and not a harm to the community. I knew it would take a lot of work for them to see that I'm for real with what I'm doing, that I'm not just playing games.

I remember when I was a teenager, and I went to juvenile jail, they would ask me where I was from, and I would tell them Puerto Rico. Then, the first time I applied for a green card, they couldn't find any record of me in the system. There was no record of me going to juvenile jail or to regular jail. I think about that, and I hope it's still the same today.

I think it's probably true that if I got stopped tomorrow or picked up by Immigration, and they asked me for my papers, I'd get sent back to El Salvador. I try not to think about it too much, but I know there's a good chance. A few times, they've done those immigration checkpoints in Washington, and I believe fifty or sixty people got caught and deported last time.

My faith is what's keeping me strong, what's helping me not to worry. I believe that if something happens, I can help a lot of people if I go back to El Salvador. I would have to get used to life over there. It would be lonely. Most of my family, they're gone. Most of them have moved here. But I also believe that I can help a lot of people if I stay here. Every week, I get twenty-five to forty people in my drug and alcohol class, and probably 60 percent of the people that go to my class, they stay clean. I believe that has a positive influence on the community.

I go to schools, and I talk to them about drugs and alcohol and gangs. Right now, I'm also raising money for scholarships for kids of different races. In a way, the reason I'm doing this is because I want to show the government or those people that think that all Hispanics are bad, that if we get the same opportunities, we can be as good as anybody.

This other program that we want to start would go to schools and focus more on culture, and show the difference between being a *cholo,* or a gangster, and representing your culture. A lot of people, from California, Mexican-Americans, they think being a *cholo* is part of being Hispanic, Latino, or Chicano, and that's something that I'm working on here. I say no. If I'm dressed like a *cholo,* and I'm a gangster, I don't represent you. But maybe, if you see a person that owns a restaurant, or he owns a store, and he's doing good, that's somebody who's representing you.

The people in the government, they're talking so much about immigration, and that's good. I respect the law. Now I do. And I believe that we should come to the United States the legal way. Even though most of the people that come here, they don't do it for bad reasons. Most of the people that come here, I don't care if they're Chinese or El Salvadorans or Guatemalans, they do it because there's not enough food over there. But I would like the government to understand that if they don't give these people a chance, if they don't give them the opportunity, these people can choose to go the wrong way. Because I know a lot of people, I know a lot of good people, they're doing bad things now because they don't have another option.

And if something happens with this immigration thing that's going on now, we're just going to do more to help the United States. Like, my friend used to tell me, you give a Mexican a bicycle, that's half of a restaurant. You give him a trailer, that's a whole restaurant.

ELIZABETH

AGE: *36*
COUNTRY OF ORIGIN: *Bolivia*
OCCUPATION: *Teacher*
HOME: *Fairfax, Virginia*

YOU'RE THE WORST THING HERE

Elizabeth grew up comfortably in La Paz, Bolivia, and became an English teacher. Her daughter, then eight, was diagnosed with a severe form of arthritis in late 2002. After trying a range of treatments and doctors, Elizabeth decided her best hope lay in the United States. In 2004, Elizabeth came here by herself with her daughter's medical records and the hope that American medicine might hold some answers. Her quest quickly turned into a nightmare of sexual abuse, exploitation, and incarceration. She agreed to be interviewed while in immigration custody at a county jail in Virginia. After months in jail, Elizabeth appears pale and thin as she speaks in a mix of Spanish and English.

My mom is a nurse and my father is an accountant. We never had money problems. Like any family, we did have some problems sometimes. The main thing was that I got married very young. I was seventeen years old. And I had two babies. Actually, I had three, but one passed away—the second one.

When I gave birth to my second baby, the doctor told me that I would not be able to get pregnant again. But we had always wanted three. It was important to us to have three. So we tried and tried, and I got pregnant with my third baby—a girl. I had many problems during the pregnancy, but I gave birth to my daughter and now she is sixteen years old.

Because I got married, I didn't finish high school. Then I had problems with my husband. He left me with the kids, so I had to go to work. I trained at the American Bolivian Center to teach English and I started working as an English teacher at a public school. First, I worked with the beginning levels, and then on to intermediate, and then advanced English. I went back to the city to take more classes, to improve my speaking skills and grammar. I was there for about four years, taking courses and practicing teaching. I finished my certificate in 1999. Then they gave me a job there at the Center as an official teacher.

At the Center, we taught American culture, language, everything. Working with the American Embassy, we helped Bolivian students apply for scholarships and take the required tests to study in the U.S. Each of the universities from the U.S. sent their information to us. The American Embassy helped us with the visa and the papers. We gave cultural and practical advice about how to get to the U.S. We were a resource for study abroad and cultural exchange opportunities.

I SOLD ALL MY BELONGINGS, EVERYTHING

A few years ago, we discovered that my daughter has a serious form of arthritis, which is rare for someone so young. She started showing some symptoms when she was eight years old, beginning with two fingers. The middle finger of her right hand, and the middle finger of the left hand, I remember. At first, I thought that it was just something small. I didn't pay much attention to it. Two or three months later, it was the whole hand, all the fingers except the thumb. Her fingers were very red and swollen at the joints. Then, they started to deform. She couldn't write. She couldn't even move sometimes. Her legs, her arms were completely damaged with this illness. Her limbs stayed bent, curling.

It's as if you want to hold a glass, and your hands stay in that position—she couldn't straighten her fingers. She would say, "Mom, I'd just rather be in bed." She didn't want to walk.

We went to the doctor three months after the first symptom appeared. The doctor was very surprised. She didn't want my daughter staying in her office. She wanted to talk to me privately. She said she was very sorry, but my daughter has arthritis, and it's chronic and very aggressive, and that she didn't know how exactly to treat her.

After the diagnosis, I took her to many doctors, and tried many different medicines—pharmaceutical drugs, special diets, natural herbs—but there are no pediatric rheumatologists in Bolivia. Also our technology is behind the times. To treat my daughter, for instance, it's necessary to test a sample of her synovial fluid. This was impossible in Bolivia.

At work one day, I was crying about my daughter. The doctors had just told me that her illness didn't have a cure. It was 2002, November or December. My boss asked, "Why are you crying?" When I told her what was going on with my daughter—that in Bolivia there is not sufficient treatment for my daughter's condition—my boss said, "Elizabeth, we will try to help you to find a hospital out of the country where your daughter can get the treatment she needs." At that time, my daughter was very, very weak—she was losing her ability to walk. She had been in and out of the hospital, seeing many different doctors, and I was running out of money. I sold all my belongings, everything.

My boss gave me her business card, and I remember exactly what she said: "You know I work for the American Embassy. I'm an American citizen and I have connections. Go to the wife of the president of Bolivia. She knows me. And let her know what's going on with your daughter—she'll help you." And with that business card, and with the reference from my boss, I went, crying, to ask for help from the president's wife. She paid for six months for my daughter in the best hospital—a Belgian hospital in Cochabamba. The doctors worked very hard. They found that there was also a problem with my daughter's heart. She saw a cardiologist who explained to me that her mitral valve was dysfunctional. As I understand it, the fevers my daughter suffered are caused by the inflammation in her joints, and these fevers had damaged her heart. They told me they would do their best to keep the heart working, and to keep the arthritis under control.

I didn't have any money and I thought, the six months will end, and she's going to need more and more. I left my apartment; I asked my mother to take care of my children; and I decided to come here to the United States. I told my boss, "Please help me with the visa, with the embassy. I don't have money except for four thousand dollars that I will use for the ticket and to give my mom enough for two or three months with my kids. I will go to the U.S. and I will work and I will get help for my daughter." I was determined to come here, for my daughter.

I applied for the visa and since I was working for the American Bolivian Center, it was not difficult to get. I couldn't bring my daughter with me because she was in the hospital.

I FELT LIKE A KID

I arrived here on October 23, 2003, in Miami. I was all alone and I felt lost, so I called my boss. She is Mormon and she called someone from her church. Lawrence was his name, and he picked me up from the airport and took me to a church where I could stay. The person taking care of me was Lawrence's father. He was very old. He couldn't even see. I had no idea how to get to hospitals or anything when I first got there because I was figuring out the new place. I was new. I remember once I got lost in Miami. I was really scared. It was ten or eleven at night and I couldn't get to the place I was living. It was so frustrating for me because I am an adult but I felt like a kid.

The first thing I did was find a library to get to the internet. That way I'd be in touch with my family in Bolivia. Also, I could get information about hospitals through the internet. Close to where I was living was a library, and I got a library card right away. I had half an hour each day to use the internet.

I communicated with my daughter by phone. I called from the church right away, with a calling card. My daughter always blamed herself. She said, "Mom, you went away because of me." And I said, "No, I'm okay, I will be back with many things, with money and information."

Whoever I talked to, I talked about my daughter. In Miami, I was referred to a hospital in Maryland. I got information about that hospital and I found out that there was a special research program there on illnesses that don't have cures. I wanted to know if they had any research about childhood arthritis. But the problem was how to get around. Here in the USA, the distances are so great. In my country it's not like that. There are many buses in my country.

I left Miami three weeks after I arrived. I went by Greyhound to try to get to the hospital in Maryland. During the trip—it was like twenty-four hours on that bus—I got sick. I was feeling so bad that I couldn't continue the journey. I got out of the bus in Richmond, Virginia. I stayed in the hotel that was closest to the Greyhound bus stop. I was there for two weeks with a stomachache, a fever; I couldn't eat anything. I think I was sick from some shellfish I ate at Red Lobster. The hotel manager said, "I am sorry, but you have to do something. I can't have you here like this, or I'll call the police." Two, three days in the room, the manager said that was fine. But I was there two weeks.

So a lady who worked at the counter of the hotel, a black lady, she told me that her mom could rent me a room. She said, "It will be cheaper for you to go live with my mom. She'll charge you fifty dollars per week."

I accepted the invitation, but when I got there, I couldn't get used to living with them. They had different habits and I was sick. I needed medicine and rest. I was sick in my bed, and they were making noise, dancing all night. Many, many guys came through the house, smoking and doing things like that. It was so foreign to me. I had enough money in that moment, but I knew that money wouldn't last long. I stayed there just four days. I didn't complete the week, but I paid her for the whole week. I remember that.

I turned to my own mother for help. I called her, and told her what was going on with me, so she and my sister found some help. My sister said that she had a friend and this friend had a brother over in New Jersey. And she said, "He is going to help you. Go to New Jersey." And she gave me a number. I called him and I said, "I am Paula's sister and I am here in Virginia, I am sick and I don't know what to do." He told me to take a Greyhound and get to Newark and that he would pick me up there. I don't know how, really, but I did it.

I WANTED TO SHOUT AND I COULDN'T

The guy told me how he was going to be dressed, so we met when I got to Newark. I'm not going to use this guy's name because he's still out there. He brought me to his house. He told me that my mom already talked to his uncle in Bolivia. He said that he would rent me a room. But since I was sick, he said to take it easy, to take the first month to get better, and the next month we would talk about the rent—something like that. He seemed very nice, at the beginning.

He told me, "You get my room because we don't have rooms available right now." I protested, and he insisted, "But you are sick, Elizabeth, so take my room now, and I'll sleep in the basement." I said, "Okay, thank you very much." If I needed medicine, he went to the CVS and got me pain relief for the fever, and Pepto for my stomach, things like that. He was always taking care of me.

I was in bed for two more weeks. I couldn't even stand up, let alone go to hospitals to talk to doctors about my daughter. I didn't leave the room, except to go to the bathroom, but I soon understood that the house was very, very big. Downstairs, a Colombian guy lived; upstairs, three guys from Turkey—altogether, seven men living in the house and just me, the only woman. And I thought, Okay, they know my mom, they talked to my mom in Bolivia. I felt safe for the moment.

I had been there, still recovering, for about a month, when I asked the Bolivian guy if I could use the internet to write to my sister. "Yes," he said, "The computer is in my uncle's bedroom." And I went in, and I was using the computer, and he brought me a glass of Coke and he said, "I put in a little wine, is that okay?" "But I am taking medicine," I said, "so I can't drink alcohol." "No, it's just a little," he said. And when I tried it it was very light. I said, "Okay."

But in that drink he put something else. When I tried to stand up from the computer, when I had finished my emails, I fell down. I remember he brought me into the bed, and I couldn't feel my body. I wanted to shout and I couldn't. My voice wasn't there. He put something in my drink and I felt very bad. I don't remember. I don't remember really. When I woke up the next day, I was in his uncle's bed. I was naked.

I didn't know what to do. I was thirty-four years old, and he was twenty-five. I'm older—would anybody believe me? I felt very embarrassed. I didn't know what to do. I wanted to leave the house that night. I was packing to go and he told me, "No, you're not going to go anywhere. If you go somewhere else, I will call your mother and I will say that you are a whore, that you were not only with me, but also with other guys in this house." That didn't stop me, but then he said, "Okay, you're going to go? Where to? You might notice there are no beggars here like in Bolivia. The police will stop you and if you don't have an address here, they will arrest you for vagrancy. They will tell you, 'Miss, if you don't have an address, you're going back to your country.'" And that stopped me, because I didn't want to go back.

He wouldn't let me leave and things got worse.

I made a call one day because we were arguing and he hit me, he hurt me. I had seen on the TV a number to call about domestic violence and I called that number. I told them that somebody was hurting me and that I'm not from this country and everything. I was crying, and I told her that I had been raped and she said I had to get a test for HIV—she gave me the number of a social worker.

The tests were all fine, and the social worker told me to go to a shelter. She gave me her business card and everything. But I went back to the house with him, I don't know why. The thing was that I didn't want my mom to know about this. If I reported it to the police, he would talk to his mother over there in Bolivia, and my mom would know everything that was going on. And the thought of my daughter, sick in bed, to hear about her mom like that... And my mom was taking care of my two kids. It would be too much for everyone. So, I was thinking about that, and I said, "No, nobody will know about this. Okay, you win," I said. And he said, "Okay."

I remember it was December 28, my birthday, and I was expecting a call from my mom and I told him, "I'm not going anywhere. I'm going to stay here and wait for this call from my mom." My mom was trying to find someone else to help me. I didn't tell her what was going on, I just told her that I couldn't get good work, so I needed to go somewhere else. My mom was trying to reach somebody else she knew in this country. I was awaiting that call. And the Bolivian guy said, "Elizabeth, it's your birthday. I want to take you out somewhere."

I said, "No, I can't go. I have to wait for my mom's call." He was very angry. He went out and got drunk, and didn't come back until twelve, midnight. He kicked my door down. He started hitting me because he wanted to have sex with me again. He said, "Wake up, I want to talk to you." He started throwing all my things everywhere. He pushed me out of the bed and onto the floor. He left the room and he came back with a belt. And he started whipping me with the belt. I was trying to run away from him, and when I reached the stairs, he pushed me and I fell down. I fell down all the stairs. He pushed me down twenty, twenty-five steps. He came down, and started kicking my legs. He said, "Open your legs." He kicked me in my head. I wanted to get to the front door, to try to run away again. He put the belt around my neck—and he said, "Where are you going? If you go now, I'm just going to pull this, and you won't go anywhere." He was pulling the belt—I couldn't breathe. I asked him, "Please, let me leave." At the time, I thought he was going to kill me. He was very drunk. Very, very drunk. He finally stopped and had another bottle of wine or something. Eventually, he fell asleep in the living room.

I DID THINK ABOUT GOING BACK

I was working at McDonald's at that time. Another guy in that house had gotten me a Social Security number. I didn't have the card, but I had a number. I went to work a few days after my birthday. When I got there, my manager saw my bruises, and she said, "No way. This is not going to happen to you anymore." She called the police immediately, and the police helped me get out of that house and into a shelter. It was January 2.

At the shelter, I told the social worker everything. And I focused on my visa, because it was January. I entered on October 23 and I just had three months to stay here. So, on January 23 my permit to stay in the U.S. would finish. I asked the social worker about a lawyer to talk to about my legal status. And she suggested that I go back to my country, because of my emotional situation and everything.

I did think about going back. I didn't have any money at the time, so the social worker said, "I will get you a ticket. I don't know how, but if you want to go back, I'll get you a ticket. That way you won't lose the opportunity to get a ten-year visa."

I couldn't reach my goals to find help and information for my daughter, I couldn't do anything. I felt so frustrated. What was I going to say to my daughter? I was so sad. So I decided that I wouldn't go back, that I would extend my visa.

When I was living in the shelter, all the expenses were paid by the U.S. government. And my lawyer said, "Immigration will check this—they'll say, 'She's living in a shelter, she's not producing anything for us.' They'll say no to the visa extension, that's for sure." I said, "I will try myself."

I went to the library, I got the forms to extend my visa, I filled them out myself—I didn't know if I did right or not, but I did it. I bought the money order. It was the first time I used a money order. I put the whole application inside and I sent it. I didn't know that I had to get the receipt. But I sent the whole thing. I needed an address, but I couldn't give the address of the shelter. That was their policy that I never give the address. So, I put the address of an Indian lady I had met in the shelter.

In the shelter, sometimes ladies who are living there suddenly disappear—they decide not to live there anymore. And my Indian friend did that. She disappeared. One day she just didn't come back to the shelter. So, I couldn't get the answer from Immigration if they accepted my extension or not.

I ALWAYS SAID YES

I was still living in the shelter when the person from the Mormon church came again to help me. He came and picked me up from the shelter. He gave me food and a place to stay for a while. When I had my strength back, the man said, "Do you want to be here in New Jersey, or over there in Virginia? It seems better for you over there—your embassy is closer to that place and that guy is still here in this state. And I don't think you'll be safe with that guy near you." I said, "Okay, I'll go to Virginia."

I got here to Virginia in March 2004. I rented a room on a road where other Bolivian people lived, and I started working. The lady who rented me the room cleaned houses. And so I went with her, to help her. I felt comfortable being with her because she was a woman.

She paid me cash. But later I realized that she wasn't paying me very much. She was paying me twenty-five dollars for two houses. Twenty-five dollars in one day. For me, at the beginning that was great. I didn't complain. But later, I met people who told me that they sometimes pay fifty dollars a house. "Okay," I said, "I'll get another job."

I went to work painting. I remember I painted a dentist's office. They said it would be easy for me because everything was white. It was my first painting job—it was very easy. My boss was very nice to me. I didn't have any tools—she bought all the tools I needed to do the painting. I also did cleaning—working for this company that cleans all the Home Depots.

At the beginning, I usually just worked eight hours a day because I couldn't drive. It took me time to get to work. If you count that travel time, I was out of the house the whole day, from seven in the morning to seven at night, but my job was just seven or eight hours.

That was in 2004. Though I didn't have much time to research my daughter's illness at hospitals, at least I was making enough money to pay rent. Everybody wanted to give me a job. And so I never said no. I always said yes. And I always sent money home. I was sending two hundred dollars every week, for the special treatments my daughter needed. With that money, I paid for the hydrotherapy that helped lessen the pain in her joints and strengthened her muscles. And I was also able to send enough home to pay for her school.

In 2005, I got a job at an Italian café, a restaurant. Since I knew English, the guy said, "Okay, you're going to work here. You'll be one of my servers." It was my best job. I practiced my English. I met lots of nice people there. My boss taught me everything about a restaurant, everything about Italian food. It was easy for me because I just worked nine hours. I started at eleven in the morning and finished at three o'clock, and then, I was back there in the evening from five to ten. I made good money. I made $120, sometimes $160 on a good day. It wasn't a job like painting or cleaning. I really enjoyed that job, but I left because I finally found a hospital that I thought could help me. They had the equipment for doing the test my daughter needed—the synovial fluid sample test. They can analyze the sample and figure out what kind of arthritis she has. They had that test because they worked with cancer patients. I called them and they gave me an appointment. In July of 2005, I asked for a week's vacation from my boss to go to Miami and he said yes.

FEELING SAFE

When I was traveling by Greyhound, I had to transfer in Jacksonville for the bus to Tampa. Immigration got me for the first time. It was July 2005. The Immigration officer was standing outside of the bus checking—not checking everyone—but asking, "You, you, and you—let me see your passports." And I gave him my passport. He said, "Wait, hold on." And he called someone from the office, and then he said, "Oh, sorry. I know you asked for a visa extension, but it has been denied."

I said, "I didn't know." I had no way of knowing. I told him what happened in New Jersey, and he said, "Well, what are you going to do?" And I told him I was going to the hospital—I showed him all the papers of my daughter's situation, and he said, "All right, Elizabeth." He didn't arrest me. He said, "You have to take care of yourself. You are traveling alone. You are a woman. Something could happen to you." He didn't ask me for anything else. And I got back on the bus.

At the hospital, I learned that my daughter's fevers might be due to an infection she had when she was a baby. The doctors can't say for sure what the causes are, but the fever is inside. The doctor said that the inflammation of each joint was causing the fevers. It's not a fever that you can recognize from the outside. It's an internal fever. They told me about a special thermometer to use to check her temperature.

I talked to my mother about how my daughter was doing in the hospital in Cochabamba. She said that after doing blood tests and x-rays, the doctor prescribed some medicine for the arthritis, but it was very strong medicine, meant for adults. Later, we found out that this medicine would interfere with my daughter's bone development, and so I had to look for alternatives.

In 2006 I hired a lawyer. At first I didn't want to go to court, I was really scared. So I asked my lawyer, "Is there a way to avoid going to court?" And my lawyer said he could change the address to put off the court date, and I said for him to please change the address. I gave him my papers and he didn't do anything. It was two days before the original court date and I asked him if he had changed the address and he said no. He said, "Elizabeth, I'm sorry, I couldn't do anything. I was very busy. So we have to go to court."

I was so confused, so depressed, I didn't know what to do. I went to court and I was thinking that my lawyer would explain my daughter's situation and why I needed to stay in the country. First, he arrived one hour late. When he got to the court, he only signed some papers. I was trying to give him my daughter's medical records, and he said, "No, no. I didn't prepare anything. We are going to tell him that you have an American boyfriend. And you're going to get married in the near future. And your boyfriend is in Miami, we're going to change the address again. He will deport you, order your removal, if we don't say something."

And so he told the judge, "This woman wants to change her address because she's moving to Miami to be with her boyfriend—he's an American citizen." And the judge accepted that. He said I could stay, and he gave me a court date for the next year, January 2, 2007. He said, "We accept it. Do you have an address?" "Yes, we have an address." "Okay, we'll send her the letter, letting her know when the next hearing will be." I gave an address of a friend in Fort Myers.

Since I was free, I was feeling safe, and I forgave the lawyer. He said, "I'm sorry if I didn't do my work, but I was very busy. But now you have a chance to get someone to marry you." I said, "But you know I don't have time to get someone to marry me. That is not why I am here."

I started a new job as a sales representative for a wholesale, prepaid phone card distributor—those cards that we use to call our country. My boss hired me because I know about computers. I called all the customers and asked them if everything was all right with the cards, took their orders, everything. I worked very hard. I worked with him from nine in the morning to eleven, twelve at night. For that guy I worked not only as a secretary, but I was also a babysitter and cleaning lady for him and his wife. I was doing everything. I was with him from Monday to Sunday, working. And I made good money because he was paying me well. My boss was very pleased with me. He said, "Elizabeth, you are doing a good job. All you need is a driver's license. Get your license and you will do deliveries for me also." And so I did. I got a license to drive. And with the pay from the job, I was able to buy an old car and then I could do deliveries.

But sometimes this guy focused too much on money. He just wanted money, money, money. Sometimes he didn't care about people. Even customers or people he worked with—he treated people like machines. At the beginning, I didn't mind. I came here to work and make money, I wasn't here to get friends or things like that. So if he doesn't treat me well, who cares? If he pays me well— for me, that's enough. But unfortunately in September 2006, I had an accident.

I crashed into a tree with my car. Maybe it was my fault, I don't know. I was doing deliveries for my boss and I went far. I went to Richmond, Arlington, everywhere, doing deliveries. One of the tires of my car was very old and when I went over a bump, the tire exploded and I crashed into a tree. The airbag didn't work, so I got hurt, and my car was pretty wrecked. I had full coverage, so the insurance paid for everything, but I had to pay a six-hundred-dollar deductible. I paid the six hundred dollars, and they gave me a rental car, and my boss said, "Elizabeth, you have to keep doing deliveries in the rental car." I said, "I can't do that. If something happens with the rental car, it's going to be my fault and I'll have to pay. If you want me to do deliveries, give me your car, and I will do the deliveries." And so I was arguing with him about this and I left the job.

After a short time, he wanted me back. I had gone to work in a gas station as a cashier, but he called me and he said, "Elizabeth, I need you. You are the only person who knows everything here. I will raise your salary, and I will give you my car. Please come back."

So I went back, and I was working with him again. But my car was still in the body shop. I was trying to reach the guy in Florida to get the letter about my next court date. When I finally reached him, I authorized him to open my mail. I said, "Just let me know the court date. I need to know." He told me it was January 20. I asked, "You sure it's January 20?" He said yes, and I believed him. But I told him to please send me the letter.

So, I fixed all my things to go to Miami on January 18. The letter got to me on January 16, and when I read it, it said the court date was January 2—I had already missed it. I didn't know what to do. I called my lawyer and he said that the judge already ordered deportation.

I called another lawyer and I asked him to reopen my case. And he said it would be very, very, very hard—maybe impossible to reopen my case.

Then, on April 9, Fairfax police stopped me and said that my license plate was suspended. When I gave him my driver's license, he also told me that I had a deportation order. So they arrested me that day and they kept me at the Fairfax county jail. I was there two days. On April 11, Immigration picked me up and brought me to the nearby immigration office. They asked me if I was aware that I had broken the law, that I had missed my hearings. I said yes, but when I tried to explain to them what had happened with my lawyer not telling me the date, they wouldn't listen to me.

NOBODY WANTS TO LISTEN

They treated me like I was a criminal. They didn't give us anything to eat. I was there with other women, and they were asking for something to eat, and the officers threw two boxes of uncooked lasagna at us. "Eat, if you want," they said. "You're not in a hotel." We were all crying. They treated me very badly. People who hurt me—they never went to jail. I didn't hurt anybody, so I don't think I deserve that kind of treatment.

On April 12, they transferred me here to Hampton Roads, to this federal detention center where I am now. I wrote a letter to the person in charge of my case in Immigration, letting him know about my situation. Now I want to reopen my case. I want to fight. I wrote a letter to the judge also explaining everything. I wrote him three pages letting him know why I am here, and asking him for mercy. My daughter doesn't have time. Her condition is getting worse. And I'm trying to make money for my daughter's treatment. Here they have all the technology—they can do the special tests. I don't know if he will answer my letter. But I tried.

Now I'm trying to hire a new lawyer. Maybe that way I can re-open my case. And I can ask for a voluntary departure or something that allows me to come back some day. Or maybe something will happen, God might touch the judge's heart and he might allow me to stay a little bit longer. I don't know.

It often feels like nobody wants to listen to me. Nobody wants to just stop sometime and ask, "What's going on with this lady?" Every person is a different case. I know that some people who come to America do bad things, but not all of us are like that. And they treat us like, "You're Latina, you're the worst thing here."

I want to tell everybody that Latinos are here. We are not all criminals. We are helping this country. And we are really grateful to this country. My daughter is walking now. Through my hard work here in this country, I made enough money to get her the physical therapy in Bolivia. Many people here may have the same situation as me. Many women left their children in their countries.

I haven't talked to my daughter since I've been in jail. I haven't written her—I don't want to because I'd have to put the jail in the return address. I don't want to. I used to call my daughter three times a week, sometimes more. Now I'm not calling her anymore. My family doesn't know I'm in jail in Virginia. The most important thing for me is the life of my daughter, and I don't want to give her bad news—the news that I failed. Doctors are trying to help her in Bolivia. I don't want to disturb her treatment.

I've never been in jail before. I never get to go outside. I haven't been outside once since I got here.

Some officers discriminate against Hispanic people. They treat us like, "Go home. Why are you here?" There was an incident with one of the other Hispanic inmates here just two days ago. Flora was my roommate, but right now she is in trouble and in isolation. She was walking in the big dining room and the night guard pushed her—didn't say excuse me or anything. And so my roommate spoke up, stood her ground. The officer then ordered Flora back to her cell and ordered lockdown on Flora for one week. They put her in the red uniform, which indicates "dangerous inmate," and the officer says she's going to press charges against her, extend her sentence. That's no way to treat us. I'm afraid of the officers. If you fight or argue with them, they just get you. I don't know if I will leave or what will happen to me.

[*Editor's Note:* Elizabeth was deported to Bolivia in July, 2007. She recently got her job back at the Bolivian American Center and once again works closely with Americans in Bolivia. Over the phone she told us, "I try not to have feelings about the situation, or the connection with this to my job. I do still work alongside the U.S. Embassy here. We promote American culture. My family knows nothing about what happened to me over there either. I don't want to worry my daughter's heart. She has suffered enough."]

NSOMBO, 39
New York City

Nsombo fled to the U.S. from Cameroon after being imprisoned in a political roundup at home. He trained here as an AIDS nurse and worked in that field for a while, but now drives a shuttle bus to help support his U.S.-born teenage daughter. He was recently picked up, however, and sent to an immigration detention center.

In Cameroon long ago, I was taken to jail for nothing, rounded up by the army in Operation Harmattan when the government was trying to stop citizens from protesting. I was lucky not to disappear or die. Now, I have learned that if you do not belong to any strong group in the U.S., you can find yourself in a similar situation.

They call it detention in the U.S., but it is a jail. When you arrive, they put you in a cell by yourself. They give you a physical examination, take your clothes off, and give you jail clothes. In this section, you don't see other people. After many hours, they move you to a big room called "the pot." Here, people play checkers or cards or talk to each other. You feel relieved to be with other people.

At five in the morning, they wake you up with a loud noise. At five-thirty, you have about fifteen minutes to eat. Then: "Everybody back in the cell!" The temperature is never adjusted. You wear a jumpsuit and this is all you have. Some nights they give you a cover but other nights you just sleep in your jumpsuit.

You can write letters if you have an address to send the letter to, or make a collect call if you have a number. But if you don't have any contacts, no one to call, you just wait. Even if you have a lawyer, your contact is very limited. But still, people go to court almost every Friday. Sometimes they come back without being seen by the judge. Your picture goes to the judge before the person is called. Color plays a big part. If your skin is whiter, you're treated differently.

If you do see the judge, he will talk, the immigration lawyer will talk, the prosecutor will talk on behalf of Immigration, the judge will decide. You will not talk. You want to explain everything but everything you say is a lie. You can be deported without ever being heard. But they only deport you when they arrest someone else to put in jail—your replacement—so that Immigration employees can work.

That jail is supposed to be divided: one side is for American people, the other side for immigrants. You wear different jumpsuits. But they mix people up. Some on the detention side are actually citizens who committed a crime. Some lost their citizenship because of the retroactive law—if you committed any offense in the past ten, twenty, thirty years, they can take your citizenship away, even though you were punished long ago and now you have papers.

One time, this boy, maybe twenty years old, changed the TV channel and another guy hit him on the head. The boy fell, bleeding from the mouth, and they took him away. The one who did the beating—a criminal arrested for cocaine distribution—was released later and he got his green card back. It doesn't make sense.

Jail was like a nightmare to me. I prayed more than I've ever prayed before. I used the small amount of money I had to pay a lawyer. The lawyer ate that money and sent me a letter in jail: "Sorry, there is nothing I can do." All the years I have worked in the U.S., most of my money went to lawyers.

There are about thirteen million Americans overseas, foreigners like all the foreigners who come here. The human being is a nomad, a traveler—he goes where he feels free. The American was not an American before. The system makes Americans believe that their job has been taken. But foreigners like me pay taxes that don't even benefit us. The people who are benefiting from our taxes are complaining that I am taking a job that they're not even interested in. The job belongs to the person who is willing to work.

DESIREE

AGE: *32*
COUNTRY OF ORIGIN: *Mexico*
OCCUPATION: *Waitress*
HOME: *Berkeley, California*

THAT'S MY MOM'S GIRLFRIEND

Desiree has a broad, sweet smile and a quick laugh. She moved to California from Baja, Mexico when she was eighteen, and her friends now call her a co-conut: brown on the outside, white on the inside. We sit in the sunny kitchen of the apartment in Berkeley that she shares with her nine-year-old daughter and her domestic partner—a Mexican-American woman—both of whom were born in California. During our most recent interview, Desiree's daughter stays with us for a while, but she's sent upstairs when the subject veers toward Desiree's immigration troubles and the looming threat of deportation. We speak in English as Desiree laments that because she and her U.S.-citizen partner cannot be legally married, they are preparing for the worst.

I came to the United States in 1992. I crossed the border legally, with a passport and a six-month visitor's visa. I took the bus from La Paz to Tijuana, about a sixteen-hour drive. I passed the border by car—that's always safer—then I flew from San Diego to San Jose. There's always a lot more problems when you fly in, even if you're coming legally. They check every single thing you have—not only the luggage, but your paperwork, your ID. It's always been an issue. But at the border, by car, they don't even track it or anything. Of course, that was back then. That's all changed now.

I thought I'd stay in the States for six months, maybe a year at the most. I was young, sixteen years old, and I came to join my older sister. She'd moved to Berkeley in 1991, and she was very strict, so my parents thought maybe she could help me get my life back on track.

HALFWAY CRAZY

I'd say I grew up too fast. My mother went away when I was four, supposedly to go to the university in Mexico City. For many years she was gone, for much longer than college should have taken. She left me with my father and my three siblings in our town of La Paz, in Baja, Mexico. My dad was hardly around at all; he worked for the county during the day and was a street musician at night. I was the youngest kid and I wasn't brought up with any kind of guide. I had to figure everything out for myself. I'm angry now.

I don't think I really had a childhood at all. I don't remember playing with kids. I mean, not like my daughter does, not at all. No best friends or anything. I was very, very tomboyish. The boys were mean to me. That's how I learned to be very tough. I was so tough that I ended up saving my brother in fights. People thought he was the youngest because he was so shy. I was the talkative one, and I'd say, "Come close to me and I'll beat you up." I got to be strong on the outside, but I was already strong on the inside. There's a word they called me, it's very mean to say, about a girl who plays like the boys, it's called *marimacho*. It's like saying "dyke," but you feel it on your skin like a deep cut. It's like calling a boy a *coto*, like queer. The thing is, I never wore skirts and my hair was always short—I didn't even think about things like that. I didn't know how to dress like the other girls, and I had no mother to help me.

I had quite a few experiences with boys when I was young. There was a hide-and-seek game, like truth or dare, but it was a kind of abuse, looking back. The older boys would say, "I'll give you a bag of chips if you let me touch your leg." That kind of stuff. It didn't go much further, but it still stuck. They'd try to do more, but I'd walk away and wonder, What was that all about? What were the good feelings they were getting out of it? For me there was no pleasure, just hurt.

By the time I started junior high, I wasn't behaving like a tomboy. I started puberty in the sixth grade, so things were different. I couldn't be a rough girl anymore. I became very shy after that. In junior high and high school, I kept to myself. I had a lot of stuff that I was holding back inside of me.

When my mom finally came back to live with us, she was always drunk. Every day. I would come back from school and she'd be drinking already, half a bottle of Presidente. She'd have that with Coke. She'd be crying and playing the music loud, and she'd say to us, "You guys don't talk to me, you don't love me." She'd start going off like that. My brother and I would just look at her. You see, my mom was trying to be a mom, but it was too late, period. She wasn't really our mother anymore. She was crazy all the time. Drunk and wild.

My dad would just get up, go to work all day, come back, eat, and go right back out again at night to sing in his quartet. My mom would say something to him and he would just walk out on her. When she was really pissed off she'd throw plates and break bottles. She never did work after college—her degree was in political science. That's one of the things I can never forgive her for. I mean, if I decided to better my life, to sacrifice, I'd do it for my daughter. I would have gotten my degree and used what I'd learned, what I'd gone to school for. But my mother never took advantage of her education, after all those years away from her family. Supposedly she had worked on a campaign while she was in Mexico City. When President de la Madrid ran for office,[1] my mom says she worked for him. She said

---

[1] Miguel de La Madrid was president of Mexico from 1982 to 1988.

that's when she got the habit of drinking; there was always a cocktail party here, a cocktail party there.

I graduated from junior high. How I did it, I don't know. In my first year of junior high I flunked math. By the time I was sixteen, I was becoming more rebellious. That's when my mom sent me and my brother to a Christian camp that some friends told her about. They were praying all the time. Anything I said, they'd say, "Oh no, that's wrong, you need help." They put me in the middle, put their hands on me and prayed. I said I had a boyfriend, and they were like, "Oh we have to pray." They were telling me that boyfriends were bad, that you should wait until you got married. I thought that was so crazy. I wasn't having sex, and you can't even date until you get married? They'd say, "Oh God, take these crazy ideas out of this poor girl."

When I got back home, I thought I was *posedia,* possessed. They'd sold me these tapes and books. I was reading them like crazy, and playing the music over and over. If somebody said something to me, I'd go off. I wasn't eating, I wasn't sleeping, I was just crying all the time. My mom got worried and went to our church, to the Catholics. The Catholics thought I was possessed, too. They didn't know why I had gone to a Christian camp, but I shouldn't have gotten that crazy. All these Catholic people came to our house and started praying for me. It was a battle between the Catholics and the Christians, for me.

The priest prayed with me and gave me holy water, and I started feeling more comfortable. I was traumatized by the Christians, but the Catholics were just saying, "This is a stage of your life, you'll go back to the real you, don't worry." Then the priest offered to send me to his camp. My mom said, "Let's give it a try, she's already halfway crazy. She'll either go back to normal or finish what she started."

The Catholic camp was a completely different environment. The leaders were telling you about life and how to behave, they told you not to use bad words, to be nice to everyone, to be caring and sharing.

They asked us challenging stuff. What's the most pain you've had in your heart? I let myself loose. It was more like therapy. I loved it.

That's where I met my best friend, Christina. She was twenty-four, and had just graduated from college in Guadalajara. She treated me well, like a person. At least a couple nights a week, I ate at her house. Her parents were from Spain. It was a lot different than our house. At Christina's they had salad, then the soup—always four or five dishes. I never had all that before. I'd try to look okay, but I didn't even know how to use a napkin. Whenever I went to her house I felt like I was walking on clouds.

Christina and I became very close. She'd tell me that I was smart, that I had a voice, that I could make decisions. We'd read books together. I wanted to be with her all the time. I don't think it was any kind of sexual thing, but she opened my eyes.

My mom and dad thought Christina was a bad influence. They called the priest and asked, What's going on with her? She spends too much time with that older girl. My mother said, "Oh Father, I have to tell you, this girl is driving me nuts. She doesn't listen to me, she's angry and she's talking back." The priest said, "She's become the seed you planted." My mom went crazy.

I spent my last year of high school fighting with my parents and hanging out with Christina and the Catholics. I hated school. My parents didn't know what to do with me. That's why they decided to send me up here to the U.S., to learn to behave.

A LESSON ABOUT ALL GOD'S CHILDREN

At first I lived with my sister. I just went to school. For five months I went to adult ESL classes at the back of the Methodist church. And at the high school I took another class every night from five-thirty to nine-thirty. The teachers were all very nice. I think you'd call them hippies. They wore funny clothes and smelled kind of funny, like old grannies, but they were very sweet to us, very patient. The classes were interesting. I was like, "Man, this is cool."

When I was in adult school, I met this Mexican-American woman whose family had been here for a long time. She had quite a few brothers and one of them was very interested in me. He was a legal resident. He was always telling me, "You should marry me and I can fix you up and stuff." I thought that sounded good. But when I moved up here I was still a virgin, and this guy wanted me to lose it with him. He was a nice guy, but I didn't like him in that way, and I told him so. He said, "Well, they're going to ask about us. They'll check to see if we live together and stuff, to see that we're really married." I didn't marry him, but he helped me a lot. He took me to the Social Security office. He said, "My name is Blah Blah and I'm a resident. This is my girlfriend, she's visiting me from Mexico. Here's her passport, everything is legal." So because I had a real passport, I was able to get a real Social Security number. Back then you were able to do that. The thing is, on the top of the Social Security card it said: *Not valid for employment.* But it was good enough, it worked to help me get a driver's license. I went to the DMV, they looked up my numbers and my passport, and it was all okay. That guy really helped me through that situation. Because of him I have an ID, a Social Security number, and a driver's license. I renew it all by mail.

My first job was at a restaurant downtown. One of my friends from the adult school told me about the position of prep cook. I thought, I'll take anything. I used my real Social Security number, but I had the "not valid for work" part taken off the card, and I had a fake green card all ready to go, too. When you first come here you get involved with people that tell you how to do certain things, like get fake papers of all kinds. When you apply for a job you make copies of the cards, your Social Security number and an ID. You don't have to bring the originals; employers just want to keep copies for proof if something comes up. They can say, "There it is, she brought it in." Then they can wash their hands of it. Obviously, they know it's not real. When they take out taxes, they know who's legal and who's not. They have a number they can call to see if it's a real Social Security number. That lie about, "Oh, we didn't know"—no, believe me, they know.

The prep cook is the person in the kitchen who prepares the vegetables for the cook to put in a recipe or onto a plate. That was the first job of my life and whenever they asked me to do something, I caught on very fast. It's my pride not to make mistakes. But after a few months the owner wanted to open a window to sell take-out. He wanted me to take the orders and I was like, Are you crazy? I mean they had clam chowder, white and red; calamari; fish and chips; they had hamburgers, hot dogs, cheese sticks—so many things I'd never heard of in my whole life. My boss had a lot of confidence in me—too much. But I didn't have my English yet, so it was impossible. I had to quit.

I started working with my sister at McDonald's. Every chick who went to look for a job there ended up sleeping with this guy, the head manager, in order to get the job. He tried it with my sister, but because she was already in a relationship, she just said, "Hell no, either you give me the job or you don't, period." She said, "Just wait, there's going to be some changes here." They finally fired the guy for that reason.

I started at McDonald's as a cashier. Usually you start in the back, where you don't have to understand what the customer is saying to you, but I had influence through my sister since she was an assistant manager. My sister would write down things, like "ketchup," "mustard." Those are funny and hard things to learn at first. Onions and tomatoes. There's a high school right down the street from that McDonald's. When the students came in they gave me hell. They'd come up and say, "Give me a cheeseburger." Then they'd come back in a few minutes with just a piece left: "I told you, fucking Mexican, that

I didn't want any onions in this." The way we were raised, we have no shame in the way we react, and my sister would scream, in front of the other employees, "Are you fucking stupid? Don't you understand what the guy said to you when he ordered it with no onion?!" She gave me hell. She'd make me feel even more terrible. The kids would start out with me and my sister would finish it. It was such pressure to go to work every morning, just to think about the kids coming up to the counter, saying stupid things, calling us Mexicans this and Mexicans that. When it came time to take an order I'd try to really be there and understand them, and then they'd still say, "You fucking Mexican..." Then my sister would say, "I told you..."

The thing is, I had a lot of reasons to learn English; that's why I put so much into learning the language. There was no way around it. Sometimes you have to feel the pressure, something has to push you. To me it was pain, anger, and humiliation. I didn't want to be always in the back, in the kitchen. I looked forward to the time when I could talk to a white person in America in the same way they talked to me.

I worked a lot of jobs in the beginning. I worked as a prep cook at a health food store on six mornings, and at McDonald's from three to eleven. On my two days off from McDonald's, I worked at another restaurant, in the back. I only had Sunday mornings off. When I first started I only had a bicycle for transportation. I had to go through heavy traffic and it rained a lot that first year. I weighed about a hundred pounds, wearing size zero. I kept working that hard for a long time. I liked making money, the sensation of buying anything I wanted, the freedom of not expecting anything from anybody. Just me.

HOW AM I GOING TO SURVIVE WITH A BABY?

My daughter's father was my first true love. I met him at a taqueria where he was part-owner. His restaurant was the only place nearby that was open late. I'd go there to eat and chill, to rest from my night shifts. There'd hardly be anybody there at eleven o'clock, so sometimes we'd talk. One time, I'd run out of money and I asked him if he could "loan me" a taco. I was so embarrassed, but he thought that was funny. I swore to him I'd pay it back in two days, and I did. After that, we became friends. He was like a *rancho* guy, from a very small town. He only went to school until sixth grade. He didn't have his papers either; we had that in common. He was a nice, cool, down-to-earth guy. That was the first time someone really cared for me that much. There was a lot of love there. We were both virgins at the time we met.

That was a three-year relationship, but we never lived together. I had my own room in my sister's house and he would show up after work. Within four months he asked me to marry him. He was very serious about it. He was living with his sister and two brothers, and they saw that he was getting home late every night and his sister said, "You have to pull on your pants and be a man." He got "the talk." But I'd seen so much trouble with my parents, the last thing I wanted to do was get married at eighteen years old. I said, "Why don't we just keep going and within a year or two we can work something out?"

After a while he started drinking and partying with his friends a lot. I thought maybe he just wanted to have his times, but apparently he had met this girl at the taqueria, another customer who came once a week. She was a citizen and she went to college. He told me he wanted us to take a break. He said he'd call to tell me what he was thinking. But he never called. After about a month and a half, I called him. He said he wanted to explain things, so we went out and something ended up happening, sex-wise. Next time I saw him he said, "I have to tell you the truth about this new girl." He told me he wanted to be with her. But it was too late, I was already pregnant.

He didn't want anything to do with a baby. He told me I shouldn't keep it. He offered me money to take care of it, to have an abortion, but I decided not to. I don't know how to explain, I just couldn't do it. It was a very hard decision, because you're at the point of finding out you're pregnant and you're all by yourself trying to figure out what to do. Knowing that I was making seven dollars an hour at that time, that made it even crazier. I thought, How am I going to survive with a baby?

It was hard to tell my family. I didn't want them to think I was a crazy girl, a wild girl. My family thought that if I was a single parent no guy would ever take me seriously again. That's how it is in Mexico, people put a tag on you like a car, you have too many miles on you. If you already have a kid it shows everybody you've already had sex. You can play around and date people, but you just can't have a kid. But my mom told me that my older brother's girlfriend had an abortion when he was younger and they didn't want to carry another one in their thoughts. They said they'd support me in any way they could. But that didn't mean they were happy about it, that's for sure. I decided to keep the baby, crazy as it seemed.

THEY WERE ALL WHITE LADIES

Later in my pregnancy I found another job—the restaurant work was too physical. I worked at a place that sold women's sportswear by catalog. They didn't have anybody to help with the people who made the clothes. They had all these Mexican girls to work the sewing machines, but they didn't know how to communicate with them. I was translating and I became a shipper, too. It was okay, but it was still only paying seven dollars an hour. I didn't have insurance there, so I got on Medi-Cal, just through the pregnancy.

When you get Medi-Cal, they give you options for which clinic you should go to. I wanted to have a midwife, so I decided on this one office, and that's where I met Gabriela. She was the social worker there. She comes and asks you, "Are you feeling okay?" and you chat before the midwife sees you. She would weigh me, ask how my pregnancy was going, how I was doing emotionally. She says now that she can tell what kind of people need the most help. Every time I went there I was about to cry—every single time. I was so depressed, but Gabriela would always be so supportive. She told me about free yoga and aerobic classes for prenatal women. I asked her, "Well, do I have to show my immigration stuff, because I don't have any."

She said, "Oh no, you don't have to show any of that." I always ask that, just for reference, to get it out of the way. Medi-Cal has people like me in a different category; after my name there was a letter to define that I wasn't legal. They knew all along, and Gabriela knew, too.

Gabriela and I became friends in the doctor's office; I looked forward to going to talk to her. She always had a piece of chocolate and she'd say, "This is for you." I thought that was very nice. But there was no sexual feeling of any kind, from her side or from my side either. I thought of her as one of my saviors. I was always very grateful whenever someone did something for me at the time, because I was nobody.

I did do the yoga and aerobic classes, but in my situation it was hard to be around all these women who had their husbands. We had to sit around next to each other and everybody would have to say something about their pregnancy and their life. Sharing something like, "Okay, my name is Desiree and I am seven and a half months pregnant and I've been feeling this and that." Most of the other ladies said, "Well, my husband and I, this is our first baby." I was like, Oh man. Every time they came to me it was difficult. That didn't stop me from going, but it was very hard for me to be there sometimes. I had to be brave enough to say I was a single parent. Especially being Latina. They were all white ladies. I felt out of place.

I had my baby on the seventeenth of August. There's a sentence we say in Spanish: The baby comes with a sandwich under their arm. It's a way of saying that babies always bring something good for the family, either luck or prosperity. But to me, it didn't feel like that.

The day my baby was born she drank water from the bag—the IV. When she came out she was almost dead, her lungs were clogged with a liquid that was toxic for her body. They revived her, and spent all day at the hospital clearing the stuff out of her lungs. When we went back home the next day, one of my roommates told me he was going to move out. That was the first thing that happened when I was walking up the stairs with my new baby. There was nothing I could say. I was the one in charge of the lease, and there was no way that I could find somebody to move in that fast, to get the money back in time. Through my pregnancy, after all my bills, I only had $500 saved and I had to pay $450 for rent. I ran out of resources. Out of money. Faith. Everything.

So there I am the first night home. I started worrying about the rent that night, and then my baby—she wasn't breathing again. I had to call 911. The ambulance took us in the middle of the night, just me with my new daughter. They gave me a thing to put inside her nostrils, and every time I saw that she wasn't breathing well, I had to squeeze it out. She got better a little bit at a time, but I couldn't see the sandwich under my baby's arm—not at first. But now I am so thankful for the kind of kid I have. Because after all that, there's been nothing else. She's nine years old now, and she's such a great kid.

IT'S FREE, THIS TIME ONLY

The sporting-goods factory where I was working went out of business right after my daughter was born. That's when I started working at a bike helmet factory. They were paying pretty good, $7.75 an hour. And they gave me insurance. So I went to the dentist, I went to see my midwife again, my daughter and I got our checkups. I made enough money to make the rent, just enough to get by and provide for my daughter. Then the helmet factory closed down, too. They moved the factory to Chicago where the labor cost less. Here they were paying everybody over $7 an hour, but there I heard they were paying something like $4.50 for the same job. So I started working full-time in restaurants again.

That's when I started working at Emilio's. I've been there six years now. It's a nice restaurant; it was a move up. A friend asked the owner if they needed any help, and they said that one of the girls was leaving for college, so I should come by and see if it could work out. I told them when I got there, "You know, I've only been busing tables at other restaurants, I haven't ever been a server." They gave me one shift, but only two hours of training.

I got there at three on my first day, and the girl who was training me was off at five. So from five on I was by myself. It's complicated to learn to be a good waitress, and they have a big menu, but fortunately it was in Spanish—all the names of the dishes. Most customers can't say the names, so they just point at the menu. So, okay, I'd write it down. People would ask, "What's in it?" I'd think, Oh shit. They'd ask, "Does it come with everything?" I'd always say yes. I'd have to go back and ask the kitchen, "Does it come with this?" They'd say no. I'd say, "Can you put it on there for me, just this one time?" That's how I learned. People were getting guacamole and all kinds of extra stuff. Anything that sounded right to me, I'd say okay. But when I came back with their plate I'd say, "You know, this only comes with this and that, but there it is for you." It's free, this time only.

I still always had three or four jobs, but I started cutting down on the other restaurants, and getting more hours at Emilio's. I started feeling more secure. Doing that job proved to me that I had learned enough English. That was my biggest fear before, that I wouldn't be okay in front of customers.

MY DAUGHTER COMPLETELY LOVES HER

I worked with some gay people, and had some gay friends, and I thought it was fun to hang out with them. They were outspoken and very liberal in their thoughts, and open about their feelings. I could see that good side, but the bad side seemed more like 60 percent. They seemed lonely to me, and these friends were heavy smokers and drinkers, and I thought maybe it was because they were gay. I was curious about lesbians. To me it seemed sad to be a lesbian. That's how I saw it then, from my point of view, being a Latina. I especially knew it would be crazy with my parents and family members. And then, with my kid, I thought I would never be able to do it, that I'd ruin my life and hers.

Then I ran into Gabriela again in May of 2005. I went to a club, a gay bar, with a busboy from work. He and I were dancing. I kept thinking I saw Gabriela. I keep looking at this woman and saying, "Man, I know that girl." I was so happy when I realized it was her. My heart was pounding. I went over to say hi to her and I gave her a hug. I said, "Oh my God, I haven't seen you for years."

She said, "Oh, Desiree, what are you doing here?"

I said, "Well I'm dancing."

She said, "Do you want to dance?" and I said sure.

After that, we started spending a lot of time together. It was something about the way she treated me. Every time I was with her she would bring me peace. Pretty soon, I don't know how it happened exactly, but the way she treated me, that's what made me more and more attracted to her. The way she was with me and my daughter was so nice and so caring. My daughter completely loves her and she always makes sure we're both taken care of in every way. I started realizing how much I cared for her.

I told my sister first, because she was the closest thing I had to a family member who could listen to me without judging me. She said, "Careful with the family, and watch out for your daughter." Later I called all my family and told them what my situation was. My dad was quiet, my mom was crying, but I told them, "Come on, you knew all along." They knew all along, of course they did. My younger brother said, "You're a great sister. Anything you like, that's part of you and you're my blood." But my older brother came at me with this big Latino attitude. He said, "No, you're confused. You just want to try something different." I said, "Well, if that's what it is, I'm following it. I'm not saying I'll be with a girl my whole life, because I don't know. Who ever knows?"

He said, "We're worried for your daughter, we don't want her to be traumatized by you being like that." He talked like it was a disease type of thing. My whole family was kind of confused about it, and I was confused too, but I felt freed by telling them what I felt, right there.

I got a lot of negative stuff from my mom, with all her Catholic talk. I still get that from her. Now she tells my daughter that Gabriela and I are sinners, that we're going to go to hell. It doesn't really surprise me; her only brother died of AIDS when I was still living in Mexico. He was number seven, the youngest, with six sisters. He'd watch my aunts dressing up and putting on makeup, and he got into it; he was wearing their shoes and their clothes. He was born that way—very, very sensitive, very gay always. His sisters said terrible things to his face about it. Later, when people in the streets called him names he just shrugged it off. My uncle had heard it so much already, he didn't care anymore.

I CAN'T WAIT AROUND HOPING

My daughter knows that a lesbian family is a little hard to live in. Inside our family it's great, we have so much fun, but in the outside world it's hard for her. Gabriela and I try, but we know that we can't protect her always. We're trying to let her know that we're just regular women who love each other and that there's nothing wrong with who we are. She pretty much gets it, but when we're at her school or with her friends, we try not to rub it in. We let her decide if she wants to talk about it. People don't ask her too many questions. She'll talk about "my mom and Gabriela." People will ask her, "Who's Gabriela?" and she says, "Oh, she's my mom's partner." One girl was like, "Oooooh." When my daughter told us about that we asked her, "What was that Oooooh about?" She said the little girl called us disgusting. We asked her, "What is it that we do that is disgusting? We're not dirty, we're not doing anything wrong, we do our private things in private places, like other decent people. We have a house, we have a dog, what is it that they all have that we don't?" That little girl, she's in some kind of church I don't know anything about, but that's probably where she got that attitude. What kind of lesson is that about all God's children?

I would marry Gabriela right now. We both want to get married, of course. We are in a marriage, really. We've been together two years and we have a good life together, we're a family. I believe that we can be in a long, committed relationship. If we could get legally married, then I could get citizenship, I could—well, I guess I can't wait around hoping for that.

I don't think things for gays will change here very soon. We're not going to be able to legally get married, not soon enough for me. If there's no amnesty within a year or two, I really have to get this immigration business fixed. I know a couple guys who may be willing to marry me, but I hate this idea. It's only an idea for my last possible chance. It's funny, I could legally marry any kind of guy, even a gay guy, but I can't marry the person I love.

I had been keeping my hopes high about immigration reform; when that didn't happen I was very disappointed. I would have qualified for a lot of the programs they were planning to offer. I have a good record, paid all my taxes, I've been here a long time. But that dream faded away so fast I've almost forgotten about it.

The idea of deportation is very real for me now, more than ever. It scares me because it could stop my life in a minute. Excuse my French, but you're very fucked up if you get officially deported. They cut you into pieces. If they catch you back in the United States within ten years of deportation, it gets way worse. If you try to come back, now you've broken the law twice. Now they have your name and your fingerprints; it's much harder to hide. And ten years is a long time. If I was deported to Mexico, my daughter would be twenty before I could try to come back to the United States. That's why I try not to take risks.

MY GOLDEN BUBBLE

I hate to say it, but I even try not to look totally Mexican. Our Latina friends think I'm a coconut—white on the inside. It's not because I think there's anything wrong with being Mexican, but there's racial profiling. Here I can look like a lesbian, but I can't look like a Mexican. In Mexico I just can't look like a lesbian. I couldn't take this kind of family—a lesbian family—back to Mexico. That would be too hard, too dangerous. Mexico is not a good place for gay people. I've been open here, I'm open and I'm out. I walk down the street with my family. We are what we are. In Mexico, I'd have to go back in, into the closet, back into fear.

If they ever do deport me, we have a plan. Gabriela knows where all my information is, and she will take care of my daughter for the time it takes me to get married to a United States citizen right away. I don't know if it would work, but that's the plan.

I've talked to my daughter about it a little, the idea of having to leave and go to Mexico. I try not to scare her, but I have to warn her. She says that she would go with me. Of course she says that, she's only nine years old. She barely speaks Spanish anymore, and you've never seen a more American kid. She's a California girl, a born citizen of the United States. She doesn't realize what being Mexican is at all.

Gabriela calls Berkeley my "golden bubble." I feel kind of protected here, but to be able to move around freely, to go other places, that would be amazing. Maybe I could even go visit Mexico. I'm ready to go and talk to the people I think should know, from my lips, what's going on, how it's been for me up here.

Last Sunday night after dinner, I was watching TV with Gabriela. My daughter was getting ready to go to bed when she came down and stood up in front of the TV and started dancing for us. There was Nemo, our dog, and Gabriela on the couch laughing, and my daughter dancing. I got all these kinds of emotions, like happy and sad, all at the same time. And anxious inside that something could ruin it at any moment. I can't believe I finally met someone I want to spend my life with, who happens to be a U.S. citizen, and because she's another woman I still have to live in fear every day, fear that I could lose my daughter, fear that I could lose everything I've worked for all these years, fear that I could be deported.

I have to work something out soon. Very soon.

FARID

AGE: *62*
COUNTRY OF ORIGIN: *Iran*
OCCUPATION: *Entrepreneur*
HOME: *Los Angeles, California*

ALL MY EMPLOYEES
ARE AMERICAN

Farid grew up in Tehran under the oppressive regime of Shah Mohammed Reza Pahlavi. He fled after the Iranian revolution of 1979. Now a youthful sixty-two-year-old businessman, he lives and works in the Los Angeles area, where we met with him and his attorney in Farid's cluttered office. Above his desk hangs a New York Times *front page featuring a photograph of the remains of the Twin Towers the day after 9/11, which he hangs to remember the human lives lost that day. It was extremely hot, but Farid remained crisp and cool in his white open-collared dress shirt. He told us his story in English, detailing both his life in Iran, and his current fight against a pending deportation order.*

I left Iran with nothing, with no money at all. I built ten factories, at least two thousand people worked there, and many of those factories still belonged to me when I left. The government just waits for people like me to leave and then they take over whatever we leave behind. They say, "If you're leaving Iran, then leave, but you can't take your assets with you." But I had to go, I felt I had no choice. I finally decided to leave when too many bad things happened. I haven't talked to many people about these things; some things are too hard to talk about. I was one of those who lived well in Iran. Money was not my problem at all, but I didn't have freedom, I couldn't talk, not even with my family. The atmosphere was so bad that everybody was scared of everybody else.

I was born in Iran in 1945 in the city of Rasht, but I was raised in Tehran and so were all of my brothers and sisters. All of my very first memories are there. We were a working-class family. My father was working for the Ministry of Culture, as a worker, as a driver. At the time it was quite a good job, but we were a big family—six children, four boys, two girls. I was second from the eldest, not the popular one. Always the first born is popular and the last one is popular; children in the middle are just… lost. I was raised by a stepmother and half of my brothers and sisters were stepbrothers and sisters. The first three shared my same mother. At the time—even now in Iran—you could marry several women. But my mom didn't want that. When she realized my dad was having an affair with somebody else, she filed for divorce. I stayed with my father and stepmother.

As a child I went to school and I worked, too. I never had to work to help the family, but just for myself. After I was six or seven years old I worked all the summers to make money for supplies for school, and for clothes. I became very independent.

At the time of my childhood it was the Shah's regime, the second Shah.[1] It was a fifty-five-year regime, total, through the father and the son. One time, there was fighting in the streets. I was a child then, only seven years old, but I remember. They shot statues down in the public places. It was summertime and I was on holiday. We saw the broken statues, heard the guns. My family was not political, but we weren't happy with the regime either. And even though we didn't talk

---

[1] Shah Mohammed Reza Pahlavi ruled Iran as a military dictator from 1945 to 1979. His secular, authoritarian regime oversaw the modernization of the Iranian economy, but also the violent suppression of dissent through the use of secret police.

about such important things in our family, from childhood I did have this tendency to see. I could see the discrimination between people, the ones who have something and the ones who don't have anything. But what I learned, I learned from the street, not in my home.

It was actually forbidden to talk about politics at home, in every house, not just ours. After the coup d'état, the secret service, the SAVAK,[2] tried to spread their power. You were scared to talk in your own home because the neighbor might hear you and report you. People were afraid to speak to their own children or uncles and aunts— they didn't know who might be an informant. You never knew. If somebody needed something from a government official, some help, they might trade information to get it, bring in information about you perhaps. Everybody was scared of the government. Even now, here in the United States, nobody from Iran wants to talk about politics. If you get involved, if you go public, the Iranian government knows all about you.

I had a neighbor in Tehran when I was eleven or twelve years old. He was a master's student at the university, and I learned a lot from him. I would go to his house for tea, and he would talk to me about things that we couldn't discuss in my home. He was against the Shah's regime. He was very religious too, he was praying all the time, but he also loved to listen to music. There was a singer in Iran, her name was Marzieh. My neighbor would be praying to God, but when he heard Marzieh, he would stop praying and just listen to her sing. My neighbor was an artist, a painter. He was a good, loving person, but they kicked him out of the university because of his free thinking and his opinions, and he was never allowed to graduate. That affected me, especially because I was so young. I learned from him to open my eyes. I wondered, Why? Why is my friend not allowed to continue in

---

[2] *Sazemane Ettela at va Amniat-e Keshvar.* Dismantled in 1979, SAVAK was the secret police force of the Shah's regime.

the university? I really did understand that I couldn't do anything, I could only watch. Like a million other people, I just watched and did nothing, but that was the beginning of my understanding.

I finished high school in 1967. My goal was to study at the university. Nobody in my working-class family was educated at the time, but my father was always pushing us to study. He said, "I didn't have the chance to go to school, but you do." In Iran if you're not a very good student you cannot enter the university and if you don't have a relationship with the parties at the top you can't go either. My only choice was to study abroad, but to do that you had to finish your military service first or they didn't let you out of the country. In the military, I was serving the Shah's government, but I had no choice, I had to stay there for those eighteen months. This was not a time of any combat, thankfully, because I hate wars and fighting.

Shortly before I left to go to university in Germany, the student movement became very strong in Iran, burning buses, stuff like that. Two different groups were going up against the Shah's government, one related to the communist ideology and the other to Islam. But their aims were the same, to overthrow the Shah. Their plans were to move toward a more democratic society, with many different groups represented in a real democracy.

I didn't speak German before I went there, and English had been my worst subject in high school; I'm not good at foreign languages. But I went to a German-language university, and I even learned to correct my Farsi grammar through German. I mean, of course I spoke Farsi, but I didn't know where the verbs and the adjectives and objects were supposed to go. In my classes in Germany I met some Iranian students. That didn't help me much with learning German, but I did meet some political people, and I began learning more. Later I joined a student organization that was against the Shah's regime.

PLAY DUMB

When I went back to visit my family in Iran in the summer of 1973, I was stopped in the Tehran airport. They had me write down all my travel information: where I lived, what my contact address and phone number would be in Tehran. Later the SAVAK called my mom's house and said they wanted to talk to me, that I must go in, answer questions. I went to this very old house—from the outside you couldn't tell at all that it was a cell of the SAVAK—a place where they interviewed people. The windows were covered with cardboard. It looked like an abandoned house, but when you went inside you saw that everything was modern. But it was very dark, to scare you. I had been active in Germany and the secret service knew everything. They wanted to ask me about my political activities. The SAVAK were people who had not been successful in their education; people who are educated don't need to do dirty jobs like that. And they all had plenty of complexes; they wanted to show that they were somebody. They had power and money and they controlled everybody. They got money from people's blood.

I had spoken with some activists about what to say and what not to say to SAVAK. They told me, "Play dumb. It's the best way." If you talk, they just try to get more from you, but if you play dumb they say, "Okay, he's stupid, let him go." I think I did a good job. When I first got there the SAVAK had me sign a letter that said I was not going to join any party. So I signed that. I signed it so they would release me. After that, later in the interview, they asked me to join their party, the only official party there was. I said, "I can't join your party. Just a half an hour ago, I signed a paper that said I would not join any party." Then the guy slapped me. He said some bad words, too.

They let me leave the building that day, but I couldn't leave the country. I only had a thirty-day break from the university, but it took a hundred days for me to get out of Iran that time. They asked me for extra fees and they wouldn't give me a visa in time. They had taken my passport and I was waiting to get it back—that's what took a hundred days. They finally gave it back, but everything had expired by then and now they wanted me to pay fees to renew everything. In the end, the only way for me to get to Germany was through another country. I went through the south of Iran, on a small merchant boat, because from there you didn't need a visa to enter into Kuwait. I traveled through Kuwait and Jordan. From there I could go to Germany, no problem, because in Germany I was registered as a student. The problem was in leaving Iran.

I was in Germany seven years, from 1970 to 1977. I got my master's degree, too, in industrial management, and I met my wife there. She was not German, she was Persian also. My wife and I graduated at the same time. I got some job offers in Germany, and so did my wife. She was a textile designer. But at the time we didn't want to stay in Germany. My belief then was that if you learn something you must use it to go serve your own country. That's why we went back to Iran.

IS THERE ANYWHERE ELSE TO GO?

In 1977, I was happy to be back home. Even if it was under the Shah's regime, it was still my country. Shahs come and go, but the country stays. We lived in Tehran and I started my business there and began to establish my life, never really thinking the revolution would happen. I had studied business, industrial management, in Germany, so when I first came, I started working for a company that had several building-material factories. But I always knew that I wanted to work for myself, so in less than a year, I built my first building-material factory for myself.

In the ten years I was home, I built ten factories. To build a factory from scratch and run it, to make it work and make it profitable, that was my job. As I said, money was not a problem for me in Iran, but I still couldn't speak freely. I couldn't even talk within my family. My wife and I had a daughter, and we spoke only of family matters, not politics. My wife worked at first, but later the Islamic Republic made it too difficult. They didn't say women absolutely couldn't work, but they made it so hard that she said, "Okay, I give up."

Six months before the revolution,[3] the Shah had gotten wind of what was happening. He thought it would be a smart move to release all the intellectuals from the prisons and give people the freedom of speech. That way it would seem like things were changing, even though it was really too late. So for the first time in my life I saw the intellectual people in Iran—the poets and writers and artists. They came out of the jails for the first time in many years. I went to some of the seminars and speeches during that time. I remember the first time I saw a poet sitting in front of me reading poetry. That was a very emotional time for me. Unfortunately, after the revolution, the Islamic Republic started to identify everybody who had been against the Shah's regime.

When the revolution did happen—eighteen months after we came back—there were mass demonstrations. Most of the fighting was not with guns. The army had guns, but the people's weapons were stronger; we had human power. The streets were so full of people that the soldiers could not really use their weapons. They'd kill one person, maybe two, three, ten, but what about the rest? In the beginning, I was part of that, out on the streets, but soon I realized that it was the very religious people who influenced most of the demonstrations, and I had to back away from all of that. I have never been

---

[3] Widespread discontent with the Shah culminated in the Iranian Revolution of 1979. Massive religiously inspired protests eventually led to the expulsion of the Shah from Iran, and the return of exiled religious leader Ayatollah Ruhollah Khomeini. Under the Ayatollah's new Islamic regime, thousands of political moderates and non-Islamics were executed.

religious, not one day of my life. So I stopped going to the demonstrations. I saw the religious people taking over, taking power away from the Shah, but I was against the religious powers, too.

So all of these intellectual people had finally come out of jail, but a year later they disappeared, one by one, not just back to jail, but killed by the mullahs.[4] They had mass executions of intellectuals who had spoken during the Shah's regime about freedom or about Gandhi or Mandela or Martin Luther King or socialist ideas—painters and writers and professors and teachers and students. These people were thinking and asking questions and talking about change, so the mullahs were threatened by them, too. They had spoken about freedom for the people, but that's not what the mullahs had in mind either. The Shah had been pulling individuals up on their own, but the Islamic Republic took whole families up by their roots, their whole ancestral ties came up with them. There were mass trials. In one day they would try hundreds of people and by midday they would all be convicted. Their sentences were execution. They were hung and they were shot en masse, against the wall, the wives and the children, too.

I remember that time so well. I listened to the poet Seyyed Soltanpour read at a cultural center. There were a lot of people there and he had a very powerful mind. A few months later they killed him. They took him on the night of his wedding, right out of his marriage bed. The papers said it was because he had sent some money out of the country.

My dad passed away a couple of months before the revolution. My two brothers who had followed me to Germany and also gone to the university—they both stayed there. My sisters all went away right after the revolution. I was the only one left in Iran. My wife wanted to leave, too, but I didn't want to go anywhere. This was my country.

---

[4] Islamic clerics with political posts.

Besides, there was a revolution, and I wanted to see a change in the regime. I didn't like the new regime, but the change from a dictatorship had been my wish and I wanted to be a part of the future.

The Shah's secret service had twenty-five years of collecting information about people, so after the revolution, the new government, the Islamic Republic took all of that information. They knew exactly who you were, what your background was, where you lived, what you did. And those were just the people against the Shah's regime. Now they added to the list all the people who had been a part of the Shah's regime, too. They killed as many of the Shah's regime as they could and then, one by one, they went after many others, including me and many people in my family. A lot of people got killed, and a lot of people ran away from the country. The mullah's regime killed one of my cousins. They shot him. They tortured another cousin of mine who had been in jail under the Shah. He still lives in Iran, but since he was tortured, he never talks about that, ever. He only speaks about routine things, necessities—"What's for dinner?"

I was still in Iran in 1980 when the war began between Iran and Iraq. Bombs dropped two kilometers from our house. War gave the government another reason to silence people's voices in Iran. This was the first time that an enemy had attacked us, so everything was focused on that—this was the only important thing—and the people's rights were again forgotten. Back in the Shah's regime, they'd slap you once and it was over, but this new Islamic Republic; they were a serious enemy. That's why there are so many suicide bombers—they believe in the law of God, of Islam, and they strap explosives onto their bodies and go kill other people.

Not long before I finally decided to leave Iran, I went with my wife and daughter for a hike. We liked to climb high into the mountains. At about six thousand feet up, a *basseegee,* one of these young guys with a machine gun on his shoulder, asked us, "Where are you going?" We were hiking up this very steep mountain, and there was only one way to go and there was nothing but a mountain there.

I said, "We're going hiking. Is there anywhere else to go up here?"

He asked me, "Who is this woman?" He pointed to my wife who was wearing all the correct clothing, everything they want—everything up to code. I said, "She's my wife." He said, "Show me your marriage certificate." I started yelling, "What kind of idiot goes hiking with their marriage certificate?" We turned around and started walking back down the mountain and he did not follow us, but he could have. He worked for the Islamic Republic, a fourteen- or fifteen-year-old boy with a machine gun. They are supposed to uphold the code of God, but they don't even know what that means. They put a gun in the hands of a child and then he gets to determine what is the conduct of God, on the spot.

In my business, I always wore a tie and I was always clean-shaven. I've never had a beard and in Iran this shows you are an outsider, that you are not religious. From the very first look people see that you are not one of us. If the Iranian government knows you have no religion, the law is that they have the right to kill you. Not just that you're not practicing religion—you have to practice—but if they realize that you don't believe, then your punishment could be death. That is supposedly the law of God, the law of Islam. It was a difficult and dangerous way to live, without a beard, but I never thought about growing one. My father didn't wear a beard; he was not a religious person at all. Religion is something that sticks to your identity, though. If you were born Muslim, it doesn't matter if you believe or practice or not, it's always there. I don't believe in any religion, not just Islam, but any religion.

My opinion is that before you choose your religion you are born as a person, a human. That's enough. You don't need to follow a religion to do right. So I took my chances in Iran. Every day I'd go to the offices of the Ministry of Industry; I had to deal with them for everything. For all the business I did, I needed permits and signatures. The authorities would not cooperate with me, and it got harder and harder. To this country I'd given my expertise, my whole life, but in the end I felt I had to choose to protect my family. Freedom was missing from my life. I didn't have freedom of speech, freedom of opinion. Iran was a place where you had no right to say anything. I wanted to scream but there was no place to scream. If you put your head under water you can scream as much as you want, but you drown. They actually did that, that's one of the ways they would torture you in Iran, by putting your head under water.

WATCHING US STILL

I first left Iran by myself, to find work and a house, planning to later bring my family to join me. I went to Sweden. When I arrived I told the Swedish government why I was there and they immediately accepted me as a refugee, for asylum. It was very fast, even though I didn't tell them my personal stories, just the general situation for me and my family after the revolution. Unfortunately, during that time my wife had an affair. That was another personal result of the revolution for me. When you leave your family you have to expect that something will happen. The man she had the affair with was my best friend. We had been friends since childhood.

After my divorce, I decided to visit my mom, two brothers, and one sister, who were already all living in California. They were worried about my situation and my feelings, and they called and asked me to come over for a visit. That's how I came to stay here. Soon I saw that this was a place where there was freedom. It was relative, but it was more freedom than I had ever had before. My visitor's visa expired, but I continued to stay here. I talked to some attorneys, but they said that if I went to apply for a work permit or residency that

I would be denied, and I always hesitated to apply for asylum because I thought a lot of people had been more politically active than me, in more danger, and I didn't want to take their place.

In the beginning I didn't feel I could speak out about Iran in the United States, because a lot of Iranians here have different political opinions, and I didn't know anybody. Even now there are Iranian people defending the Islamic Regime here on radio and TV stations. Do you know what that means? It means they are here and watching us still.

I didn't have a permit to work in the United States, but I learned that legally you can work for yourself. I had money that I'd made in Sweden, so I immediately invested it and established work for myself here. I started a small business and I always paid taxes, and I still have all that paperwork. I have all the taxes and checks, everything, and when I first came here I got a Social Security number, bank account, driver's license. Everything was done legally, except for the expired visa.

I met a lady the first week I came to America. We went out with my brother, two girls and two guys—a double date—that was how it began. I couldn't speak much English then, but she was good to me. She was a teacher, a very nice lady. She and I started dating, and I was with her for six or seven years. She was a U.S. citizen, originally from Bolivia, but she had lived in Los Angeles for a long time. She wanted me to marry her to get my papers, fix my immigration status, but I didn't want that. I said I would never get married for that reason.

To make the story short, seven years later we did marry each other, but not for papers. I wanted to make sure it was true love before I married anyone, because if you marry for a reason besides love, when you take that reason away, there's no other reason to stay together. We'd known each other for a long time and we were adults, so the decision was made and we knew it was for the right reasons.

After I got married and applied for residency, I finally had a base here. I felt more confident, more safe, and that's when I became more politically active. A lot of the Iranian opposition is based here in the Los Angeles area, and pretty soon I saw that there was an opportunity to speak out openly. I was interested in meeting people to talk about what was going on in Iran, so I went to a place called the Center of Dialogue, where I heard different ideologies and opinions. This was my heaven—compared to the Islamic heaven.

Also, I was reunited with my daughter when she came to this country to study. She's twenty-four now, in college in Los Angeles. She isn't a U.S. resident or a citizen, she came here as a foreign student.

So things were going well—I was married. My daughter was near me. But at that time I didn't know what was going to happen.

TOO LATE TO LEAVE THIS COUNTRY

Maybe I was wrong, maybe my wife and I should have gotten married earlier, all those many years before, because our life together was short. She passed away after only eighteen months of marriage. She had a very sudden illness, a liver problem. The doctor told me that she would live for two weeks, at most, and then she would pass away. This was the best hospital in Los Angeles and they were not joking. I got a letter from the doctor to get a visitor's visa for my wife's mother to come here from Bolivia. In three days she arrived, and my wife only lived one more week. I had intended to live out my life with this woman.

My wife had asked me to take her ashes to Bolivia, but I didn't have a valid passport. I went to Immigration to get a U.S. passport, and they charged me some money, and just put a big stamp on the application: Denied. After you marry a citizen, you're granted a conditional-status green card, and after two years of marriage they lift the conditional status. The reason they do that is to weed out fake marriages. If I hadn't applied for that passport I would have

automatically gotten my residency in just a few months. I made the
mistake of telling them that the reason I needed a passport was because my wife passed away. They looked that up and they said, "Wait
a minute, you've only been married eighteen months, and you need
to be married two years to be granted residency." My wife's death
meant that my petition for residency was dead too.

My wife owned a house and I inherited it. The thing is, I didn't
even want it! Nothing had value for me anymore. The only thing
I wanted now—my papers—they didn't give me. I had the rights of
marriage, but not any rights to what I really needed. By then I was
openly involved in politics, an active member of MEHR.[5] I thought
I could safely be active, that it was no problem because I was married
and would become a resident and out of danger. It was known that
I was part of this group.

In the meantime I had bought a hotel, and I already had an ATM
machine business and another business which is involved with the
internet. I've had these businesses since 1993. Right now I employ
six people in this office, four in the internet business, and when I had
my hotel and my payphone business, I had about twenty-five people
working for me. All my employees are American—except myself.
I put up all my assets to establish these businesses. I created jobs, and
have paid my taxes.

U.S. Immigration says if you have a million dollars to invest
in the United States and employ X number of U.S. citizens, they'll
grant you a green card.[6] So, I had that. I have businesses, I had seven
hundred thousand dollars here in the U.S., and I had another three
hundred thousand in Sweden. I got a new attorney and we tried to
show that I had made a one-million-dollar investment here. I had

---

[5] Mission for the Establishment of Human Rights in Iran, a nonprofit organization based
in California.

[6] See Appendix F for more information on immigration through investment.

made the investment, but Immigration wanted to know where this money came from. They wanted to know if even one of the dollars that I had in Sweden came first from Iran. I had a receipt from Europe for three hundred thousand dollars, but they said, "No, you have to show how the money came from Iran to Europe." You can't send money out of Iran! They found the poet Seyyed Soltanpour guilty and executed him because he was sending money outside of the country. At the time I left Iran you could take, I think, something like fifty, maybe one hundred dollars with you. You could not even take a taxi from the airport for that amount. So how did Immigration expect me to show proof that I took three hundred thousand dollars from Iran to Europe?

I believe it is lack of knowledge on the part of the officers, the Immigration people. They just don't know. They are doing their job, but they don't understand, they don't know any of the political background. In my opinion it seemed that they didn't understand that Iran and America don't have a relationship with each other and that there is no money exchange, no business at all. They absolutely did not know.

After my wife died and then the business visa possibility fell through, I realized my only chance left was asylum. I had always hesitated to apply for political asylum, but finally I told my attorney I wanted to apply and he said, "No way, they will not give you asylum. There are just three thousand cases granted a year, for the whole world." But I thought I had the background of recent political activity. And it is the truth: I face danger in my country. But the lawyer said it wouldn't work, that I shouldn't even try. At this point I wasn't worried about deportation yet, but I wanted to fix my status, because after my wife passed away I became mixed up and worried. My activities after I got married became much more public, so everything was different now.

It seemed very late to try to leave this country—too late. After

9/11 my main concern was that I had been too public about my political ideas and that with no legal status my life would be at risk. That's why I applied for political asylum myself in December of 2001. My attorney would not support my idea for asylum, so I said, "Just give me the paperwork, I'll do it myself." I filled it all out myself and I sent it to Immigration.

VERSACE SUIT, TIE, HANDCUFFS

Right after that, it became mandatory for people from twenty-four Muslim countries to register in the United States.[7] Even if you had never been Muslim one day in your life, if you were born in a Muslim country, you had to register. My attorney, he said I definitely had to register. He said, "Here in Los Angeles it will be very crowded, so let's go to San Diego." So I drove down to San Diego in my Mercedes. I was wearing my Versace suit, a tie. The officer asked me a few questions and then he said, "My computer is not working, I'll go upstairs to print this out and I'll be right back." He came back with two other officers with handcuffs. They took my tie and suit and belt and shoes and they handcuffed me. They put me in a small cage, in an Immigration jail. That was almost the end of December—two days before Christmas. I spent the holidays in the jail and I stayed there, I think, about eleven days. Nobody knew what happened to me, not my daughter, nobody. I was in San Diego and I didn't know anybody. I had never been to a police station in my life, not even in Iran. My lawyer went on his New Year's vacation and left me down there. Nobody asked me any questions.

Right after they let me out of jail, I had to go before the judge in San Diego without an attorney to defend me. And the judge just stamped over my name one simple word: Deport. I told them that

---

[7] See Appendix G for more information on Special Registration.

my attorney had requested that the case be sent to Los Angeles, and the judge asked me why I had registered in San Diego. I explained that my other attorney had said, "Los Angeles is too crowded, let's go to San Diego." It was all just bad luck. Here I was in San Diego with nobody to protect me. More bad luck, like my wife passing away. One-in-a-million chance happenings—my wife was twelve years younger than me. There's no guarantee of anything, whatsoever. Ever since that deportation order, I've been fighting to get that word removed. Remove the stamp.

Here's a funny thing, though—right after I got out of that jail in San Diego, I got home and there was a letter from Immigration. They'd approved my political asylum request. I got my asylum approved without even an attorney, just by myself. I went there for a final interview and I answered all their questions entirely truthfully. They only give political asylum to three thousand people a year and I was one of them. They said, "You should be okay now, but we have one problem here—because you've been to jail, the judge has to release you first, then you can come back and finish up the process. If the judge approves it, then come back here and it'll be done, you'll have asylum." But when I went to the judge, he said, "The problem here is that you entered the United States on December 19, 1990, and you've exceeded your visa." He didn't see anything but that—not what I've done here, not my background, my businesses, my marriage, my tax-paying, nothing. He didn't see anything but that I'd exceeded the time of my visa, that's it.

They see only the papers. They don't know what's happening in Iran, or maybe they don't want to know. I didn't feel racism from the judge, but this society has a hatred of the fanatical, of people like bin Laden. And this is how bin Laden has damaged people like me. You see this photograph on my wall? I got that photograph from the *New York Times* the day after 9/11. I copied it and hung it on my wall. There was human life there before the fanatics did this. Do you know how long it will take to build this again? Years. How many lives were lost there?

I'm scared about my future. I keep saying I'm definitely going to stay here, but it's hard, I'm going to have to fight for it. If they sent me someplace other than Iran, I would start again, but where to go? This is my home now. I have my businesses here, I have several pieces of land, a house, my life, my family, my daughter. There's no way I will go to Iran though, that's guaranteed. I believe they would take my life in Iran. I cannot take that risk. Can American Immigration force me to go home to be executed?

ROSE, 43
Galesburg, Illinois

Rose was born in Beijing, China in 1965 to working-class parents. She married a laborer and graduated from nursing school in 1989. She remembers attending many of the student lectures in Tiananmen Square. In 1990, she gave birth to a son and named him "Sunrise." After divorcing her husband, Rose found an opportunity to come to the United States and make a better life for her child, then nine years old. By way of San Francisco, she went to Chicago to stay with a friend who got her a job waiting tables at a Chinese restaurant. There she met her boyfriend, a cook, whom she would later follow downstate. Surrounded by corn and soy, Galesburg, Illinois lies between the Mississippi and Spoon Rivers.

When I arrived in Chicago, I wandered the streets of Chinatown, which didn't seem strange to me. It was clean and prosperous, just like Beijing. Lots of merchandise in the windows. I thought I would learn English and then apply for nursing school, but I had debts to repay. So I changed my mind and went to work at a restaurant in Chicago. Working in a restaurant is simple physical labor. Although the restaurant was owned by Chinese, these Chinese were from a different region, with different customs and dialect, which made things hard. I missed my family and friends and often wanted to cry, but didn't dare in public. One time a cook found me crying during a break. When he saw me, he tried to console me. He took care of me and we became close. We started to date and have been together for eight years. Before, we laughed together more. Now, we are silent more.

Now that we live in Galesburg, I work in a different restaurant but it is all the same. The pressures and monotonies of work and lack of social activities in this town make me feel like I will go stir-crazy. I love to watch television when I'm not working. I cry with the people on TV and sometimes my eyes swell up from the crying.

The tears on my cheeks feel warm and I think it's relaxing. It doesn't seem normal.

I wonder what I will be like eight years from now. Will I be insane? I worry. Did I do the right thing? I left my son and everything I love back in China. My parents are more than seventy years old and every day they hope for my return. Whenever I think about them, I think I couldn't face them. When I was little they went to work every day, came home, cooked, and did laundry. My mother did physical labor, loading and unloading crates. Every day she came home stressed and tired and still tended to our needs. During the New Year, she bought cloth and made clothes for us under a single light bulb. She sewed one stitch at a time and it took her a month. I didn't understand and complained that the clothes were ugly. When I think of this, I feel embarrassed and full of regret.

My son is growing older and getting more and more distant with me. On the morning he was born in 1990, the sun rose bright in the east so we named him "Sunrise." I had great ambitions for him. I wanted him to be like a dragon! I wanted him to be outstanding. I tried to teach him to be virtuous, like my father. He was bright and remembered all the stories and fairy tales that I read to him. But before he was big enough to understand, I had already gone.

ADELA

AGE: *45*
COUNTRY OF ORIGIN: *Mexico*
OCCUPATION: *Homemaker, activist*
HOME: *Modesto, California*

HOW DO YOU HAVE
THE GUTS TO DO THIS?

Adela and her seventeen-year-old daughter, Estrella, opened the door of their apartment in Modesto, California just as we were walking up the concrete path. They are accustomed to watching for visitors, especially since raids in their town have increased over the last year. The two came here as EWIs seventeen years ago, when Estrella was six weeks old, and both have remained undocumented. As Estrella has started to realize the consequences of her status, her mother has become increasingly vocal in struggling for undocumented persons' rights. Adela and Estrella spoke with us at the large, round table in their kitchen while Adela's younger daughters watched a movie in the next room. Adela spoke to us primarily in Spanish, while her daughter spoke English.

I never minded working in the tomato harvest. You're under the hot sun for hours, you get pains in your back and your waist from being doubled over, and your hands cramp because you have to take care not to damage the fruit. But the color of the fruit is beautiful, and, even though you're under the sun all day, you get time to think. And it was nice to be with other people—you get to talk with them, laugh. When I was out there working I would even sing. I've had to work at night before, cleaning the warehouses where they store the harvested plants, or working on the line to clean the leaves and stalks from the fruit. You encounter every type of animal there at night. One night I was cleaning the warehouse and a rattlesnake came out of the corner! I was so scared. So the tomato harvest was beautiful compared to other jobs.

My husband usually doesn't like me to work, but I helped with the tomato harvest when we needed money. I would sometimes substitute for my friend Dolores when she was ill. She was one of the first friends I made when I came to California with my husband and six-week-old baby and no one else. I left everyone else in Mexico.

THE LEAST TERRIBLE PATH

I come from a small town called Arroyo Seco in the state of Michoacán. There were ten of us in my family: ten children, and my parents make twelve. It was difficult, with so many children, to feed us all, keep shoes on our feet. I went to a school where we had to wear skirts and white blouses for a uniform. Those little black shoes. My papa could give me the uniform, but only one shirt, only one pair of shoes, only one of everything. And they would get dirty so quickly! I was embarrassed that the other children would see that I only had one shirt, one pair of shoes, so I would come home every day and wash my blouse, scrubbing it to make it white again. I would take off my shoes and clean them every day. I'd walk around barefoot the rest of the day just to save my shoes from getting worn.

Since there were so many of us, we had to work to help Papa with money. So when I was twelve or thirteen I started to work as a servant. I would do the cleaning and cooking for families that were better off than we were. I felt bad sometimes when I worked at my friends' houses—they knew then how much we needed money. And to work as a servant in others' homes was to be vulnerable. Once

I was cleaning one of the bedrooms, and one of the master's sons came in and shut the door. He threw me on the bed and held me down, trying to take my clothes off—I thought he was going to rape me. I screamed so loudly that he let me go and I ran out of the house to escape. I ran all the way home. After that, I was too scared to go back. I found out that an older woman with no sons at home needed help, so I started working for her instead.

I kept working as a house servant until I finished middle school, and then I went to secretarial school. I thought I might be able to get a better job if I had better skills. I didn't finish school, though. I met Miguel at that time. He was also from Arroyo Seco, and was home visiting from the United States. We met through his cousin in the small plaza where, every Sunday, all the young boys and girls would gather. We took a walk around the plaza—that's what everyone does at that age—and then slowly we started to see each other. We kept up our long-distance love, as he liked to call it, when he went back to California. And when he came back to Arroyo Seco after several months, we got married. Miguel stayed in town for four months after we got married, and by the time he left I was pregnant.

I called Miguel after I gave birth to say, "Now you have your daughter. Come see her if you want to."

He arrived eight days after I gave birth to Estrella. He was very happy to see her, but he said he needed to get back to his job in California. I said, "How can you leave us here, your wife and new baby?" And I remember he said, "Well, you and Estrella should come back with me."

And at the time I thought, No! I had heard so many things about newborns who die making the trip from Mexico to the United States because when Immigration is close the mothers cover their babies' mouths to keep silent. They don't want the baby to make a sound for fear of getting caught, but the babies can't breathe. They suffocate. And my mama, too, she said, "But the baby is not going to make it.

What are you going to do with her? You can't take her." It was such a difficult situation to be in. I didn't want to endanger Estrella, but I also knew how terrible I would feel alone in Arroyo Seco without my husband. Finally, when my husband was getting ready to return, I decided to take Estrella and risk the journey with him. It seemed like the least terrible path to take.

LOS TRES

Just a few days after the *cuarentena,*[1] I said goodbye to my family and I left with my newborn baby and my husband—*los tres.* We stayed a week in Tijuana, searching for a guide, trying to decide when to go. We waited until midnight, while the Border Patrol was changing guard, and then crossed.

We walked for two nights in the mountains. It was just our guide and the three of us. At one point in the night, as we were walking in a canyon just below one of the Border Patrol trucks, Estrella started to cry. It was so quiet otherwise that, even though she was covered with a blanket, everyone else who was making the crossing around us heard her. They started whispering for me to quiet her, and getting worried. I tried to move her into different positions, and then I tried to feed her because I thought she might be hungry, but she just kept crying. I thought, Oh my God, what should I do? My husband said we should take the blanket from her head, let her breathe—and that was the trick. The moment Estrella saw the night sky, and the mountains and trees we were walking through, she stopped crying. After that she stayed silent the rest of the trip, even when I slipped in mud while I was holding her, and even when we crossed the freeway. Silent.

When we came out of the hills by San Clemente, we were tired,

---

[1] The traditional forty-day rest period after giving birth.

scratched up from the thorns, muddy. The guide told us to wait in a tree grove. There were hundreds of us migrants gathered there. They told us not to talk, scream, not even whisper, because the Border Patrol station was right on the other side of the trees. I was scared the entire time.

We finally made it to Concord, in northern California, where my husband was working as a window washer. So we got here but, as they say, we arrived struggling.

EXPOSED

Though we still needed money, last spring I decided to stop working in the fields. The truth is I was afraid. Immigration stepped up their raids at the fields. Agents with their vans would show up in the fields where we were harvesting. They would stand out at the exits at the end of the day and wait for us. We'd have to go through them just to get home. We heard of others trying to leave after their shifts and Immigration stopping them right there and demanding, "Your papers, your papers!" Those who didn't have papers, Immigration took them away right then. Not even a chance to go home first to tell their families.

Even if you have warning that Immigration is coming or already outside, there's no place to hide when you're in the fields. Working construction is safer because you can hide in a closet or beneath the roof if you don't make noise, or you can hide behind the seats of cars or trucks parked nearby. But in the fields you are exposed.

So we decided not to show up for the harvests. So many workers didn't show up that the field owners had to throw out the grapes, the strawberries. All of the fruit was lost.

Those raids—the more intense ones—started around April 2006. I think it did have something to do with our being more vocal, after we had organized the marches to be legalized. Things started getting harder for us after that. But that's why we need to be struggling more than ever now—because everything is getting more difficult.

A DIFFERENT KIND OF JOB

When my daughters started going to school I began to get involved in the issue of immigrant rights. I have five girls, five little flowers. I was twenty-six when I had Estrella. Then I was pregnant every year after that for five years. Estrella is seventeen, then comes Adriana, then Mirreya, then the little ones, Paula and Mirabel.

In the beginning, my kids went to schools where the teachers and some of the administrators were bilingual. You could always find a teacher who could speak Spanish, so I didn't have to worry about how my English sounded. But then they closed the Spanish-speaking schools around here. The kids were funneled into schools farther away, where they didn't have bilingual programs. Even the adults who were taking English classes in the elementary schools at night had nowhere to go. My girls had to transfer to a school farther away from here— about a forty-five-minute drive—where they speak only English.

When they first began there, I felt I couldn't talk to their teachers. At the parent-teacher conferences I would sit there as they would tell me, in English, "Estrella's talking too much in class, she's playing games, she's not doing well in math." Then they would stop and ask, "Do you understand me?" And I would turn to Estrella and say in Spanish, "Why are you talking in class, Estrella? Why are you playing games in class, Estrella? Why aren't you paying attention to your mathematics, Estrella?" And she would answer in English to both of us. I could understand some of what the teacher was telling me, I just couldn't respond.

I started taking classes in English so I could talk to the teachers and understand more about the girls' education. Now I can go to the teacher directly and ask, "How is she doing in class? Is she behaving well? Is she talking too much? Is she doing well in math?" These things, they're little details, but day by day I am losing the fear of speaking.

I began to go to my daughters' schools more often. I wanted to be more involved in their lives here in America. I would find out what was going on in the school and then come back and tell the parents around here in our neighborhood so they weren't kept in the dark. The parents would tell me other problems they were having: how they weren't able to make it to the school for meetings because they had to work two jobs, or they couldn't take their children to the new, more distant school when they closed the others because they didn't have a car, or were afraid of driving without a license. They told me so I could go back to the district and tell them about our concerns. After I'd been volunteering within the schools for a while, I was made head of the Latino Parents' Committee. It was a simple election— I was one of the only Latinas present the night the parent-teacher association called for nominations. My cousin had come with me, and one of the teachers knew me, so I think I won with just three votes.

As my other daughters started at primary school, middle school, I became the leader of those committees, too. It was still unpaid work, but that was okay: I understood it was a different kind of job.

BIRDS, DOGS, GOLDFISH

During this time my husband held various jobs. For a while he worked in *la uva,* the grape harvest. He worked in different areas around here. They worked for a season in the fields—June, July, August, toward the end of September—to cut the grapes, and then their work was over. He would have made more money following the harvests to the north, but since his family was here, he stayed. At the end of the harvest my husband would have to find other work. He worked in restaurants—sometimes as a cook or a busser, or, in the beginning, as a dishwasher. But when he was a dishwasher his feet would always get wet, and stay wet. He would come home soaking wet, head to toe. He got sick. In the fields he would almost never get sick. The pollen was bad for his allergies, but it was nothing like what happened when he was dishwashing. He was sick once for eight days, his throat swollen, his lungs… He still didn't have his Social Security at that point so he couldn't go to the doctor. I tried to take care of him, but he couldn't work for those eight days. Eight days not getting paid.

Sometimes it has been difficult between us, too. My husband worries that all of the housework won't be done if I'm always volunteering and working with the schools. There are a lot of things to take care of here: our place is small but there are many of us. Each day I get up, I make breakfast for my husband first, then the girls. Everyone eats breakfast before going to work and school. While they're eating, I clean up the kitchen, I pick up the living room, and I clean out the birds' cages and the puppies' box in the bathroom. After they've all left, I'm home alone, alone with the birds and the dogs and the goldfish. Then I try to finish cleaning, clean the bathroom, the bedrooms, maybe start dinner. The beans take many hours. The *pozole,* too, that takes a while on the stove. Sometimes I make chicken stew, with orange juice and a little Coca-Cola—Estrella loves that. There is always something to do here. The work is never finished… Especially since now my husband doesn't eat leftovers. In the beginning he was more tolerant of it, but later, as I got more involved, he has liked it less and less.

PARENTS' COMMITTEE

After I became head of the Latino Parents' Committee, I started working with the district's English Learners Advisory Committee. I would go to the meetings and the workshops they had for Latino families and I would come back and report to the parents in my church or in the neighborhood. I even began attending the County Board of Supervisors meetings to talk about other concerns. If the county was planning to close another school, or make more cuts to English classes for the parents or kids, or was going to close a medical center that served us, I would tell them why those medical centers are so important, that they help those of us who have no other way to get care.

Many of us don't have health insurance. Many of us can't get Medi-Cal: there are too many requirements to qualify. And without insurance the hospitals are not very kind. I remember when I started to go into labor with Mirreya, I came to the hospital in so much pain. Before I could even start speaking they said, "Wait here until we can get an interpreter." Or, "Fill out these forms first to see if you can be treated." When we're just waiting, in pain, waiting for someone who speaks Spanish, or to prove we have insurance, I think, This is discrimination against us for being immigrants.

So when they were talking about closing one of the medical centers that serves us immigrants, everyone was concerned. The doctors at those centers will see us even if we don't have insurance; the staff speaks Spanish, and they understand our particular problems. It's difficult to discuss your problems with doctors when you're always scared you might reveal you're not legal here. We live with this fear because a lot of times we just don't know what our rights are or whom we can talk to.

HE'LL TAKE CARE OF EVERYTHING

A few years ago a friend of mine gave me the name of a lawyer. She said, "Look, he'll help you get legal. He'll take care of everything." So a lawyer came to our apartment. This man said he knew my sister who lives in Los Angeles and said he would help me like he was going to help her. He charged us fifteen hundred dollars, and he said that in five months he would arrange our situation and we'd have papers and be legal.

Well, he might have been this one man I heard they ran out of Los Angeles for tricking so many people, or he might have been a different swindler. But after we gave him money, we never heard anything. We received nothing from him or the government. Nothing happened. We tried talking to him, but he was never there.

We were left with the fear that lawyers aren't going to help us, only rob us. So we never sought out another one. Other people, people we trust, told us that in our situation the best thing to do, maybe the only thing to do, is wait for amnesty. So now we just wait.

A MAN SHOULD NOT HAVE TO EAT LEFTOVERS

My husband was more tolerant of my involvement with the schools and with our community in the beginning. He would understand, or at least he would tolerate, when I would leave after dinner and go to meetings, or that I would sometimes not have dinner ready right when he got home. But at one point he changed. He started spending more time with friends after work. He started drinking more with them, and they started influencing his thoughts.

They gave him the idea that a wife should always cook fresh meals for her husband, that a man should not have to eat leftovers. So, from that point on, I had to start cooking all the meals each day from scratch, not using any leftovers for him. It made it difficult with all the other things I wanted to do, with the church, my work with the schools and the parents. He never used to before, but now he would come home from work and demand things. He would say what a woman should do for her husband and what a working man deserves and all. He would come home and drink. He drank a lot. And sometimes, yes, he would get angry. I guess I wouldn't think that much of it, except when he would get angry at the girls. And then I didn't like it—we would fight because I wouldn't like for him to yell at the girls.

I think about Latino machismo, that it is at the root of all this. It is something very strong in our culture. There is a lot of alcoholism, a lot of abuse—violence in our homes is very, very common. And it's not just in men; it's in women sometimes, too. Especially the alcoholism. At the migrant education conferences held near the airport in Los Angeles, I've seen some men stand up in the middle of room of a hundred people and say, "I was raised to be a man in this particular way. I was raised to be the master of the home. I used to come home to my wife and feel that I had to be the master in order to really be a man. We work in jobs where we don't feel like men. So we go home and have to be men at home." These men would talk about getting drunk, hitting their wives, hitting their children. We all are taught these things from our childhood, from what our parents have done and what we've seen. I had so much respect for those men because they stood up and talked. I could see they were trying to better themselves, to change.

The woman, too, she is taught that to be a woman is to be submissive. To do anything for her husband because he is the master. And this causes problems as well.

For a little while, things between us got better. My husband didn't drink as much after work. He wasn't as angry. But last year, when Adriana thought she was pregnant, he became very upset again.

What happened was, when she was fourteen, she missed her period. Her menstruation stopped for almost three months in a row. She was having pains in her stomach, she couldn't sleep. I think she really was pregnant—at fourteen years old! I was worried. Well, after the third month, it passed. Maybe she was under too much stress. Maybe drugs. But it passed. She lost a lot of blood, and then her period came regularly.

But then last year, as she was turning fifteen years old, she missed her period again. Twice. Two months, and I thought, Oh my God, again! This is it. But she wasn't—it turns out she was just having irregular menstruation.

My husband was angry at me. He thought it was my fault for not being home, for doing all of these other things. That's when things started turning bad again. They were bad for a while.

But my daughters and I try our best to talk to my husband about the things I do. Especially Estrella—Estrella and I try to tell him that these other things are important to us, that they could mean a better life in the future. But my husband tells me that I have changed. That I used to be happy doing my work at home, helping the girls here, not getting involved in everything outside the home. I used to be how I was raised—submissive. But as my daughters grew, I realized I didn't want to be weak around them. I shouldn't be scared because I'm a woman or an immigrant or anything. I think to myself, Well, I can change, too. I can be different than what I was taught. I can be stronger for my daughters. You know, the truth is, it has been difficult being a woman. But I don't want my daughters to think that because they were a born a certain way, they have to be weak.

JURY SUMMONS

Last month I was called for jury duty. It was the third time I had received a summons in the mail, delivered right to my home. The first time I received a summons, three years ago, I had to read the notice over and over again, and talk to my daughters, to make sure that's what it was. Estrella told me that immigrants can't vote. But here they were sending me a jury summons. At first I wanted to go because I thought any kind of civic involvement might help Estrella in the future since she's undocumented. But I was too scared.

So the first two times they sent me the summons, I didn't go. This year, though, I saw on the notice: "If you don't appear, you'll be fined a thousand dollars!" And I thought, Oh my goodness, what should I do? I sent back the notice right away saying I couldn't come and trying to explain that I didn't speak English well enough to serve as a juror. Then later they sent me another notice in Spanish explaining how it was mandatory that I attend. But I had the same fear as before—what if they deport me when I show up? So I sent back the notice and explained again that I wouldn't be able to attend. In the end, I was confused: if I can't vote, how can I sit on a jury?

This was the kind of thing that made me want to struggle more for our rights: the fact that we live in fear all the time. I didn't want my daughter, Estrella, to have to live her whole life with that fear because she is also undocumented. I wanted to make sure my children had the same opportunities as other American children.

KEEP MARCHING

For weeks, the Parents' Committee met and we talked about having a rights march so we could go public and show the community who we were. It wasn't easy, but we agreed that it was something that needed to be done. We organized our first march for April 10, 2006. We had planned to gather at three-thirty in the afternoon at the high school and march from there to the city park and back. That morning my daughter was worried. She said to me, "Mommy, are you really going to go?" And I said, "Yes, I think so." And she said, "But Mommy, doesn't it make you scared?" And I knew why she was asking—she and I still don't have our papers. If we go out there, we will put ourselves at risk of being caught by Immigration and deported. But I thought, Well, this march is just because of that fear. I want to give her a better future, without so much fear, with the opportunities that other children have here. I thought about this and then I said, "Yes, I'm going."

When I arrived, though, there were only twenty parents there—no more than twenty! I imagined just the twenty of us marching out on the streets like that, so vulnerable, and I wanted to run and hide. Oh my God, what do I do? I thought. Four of us coordinators from the district had decided to organize the march, and they were there, along with the handful of parents, sitting and waiting in their cars. When I arrived they got out of their cars and just looked at me. I looked around and on one side of the school parking lot there were four patrol cars. Well, I have some friends who are police officers. They know me from my work with the schools, they know the situation a lot of us are in, and they understand. Police officers won't bother you if you're not doing anything bad. They aren't Immigration agents.

I had told some of the officers I am friends with, "I'm organizing a march." They said, "How do you have the guts to do this?" because they know who I am and what my status is. "I don't know," I told them. "I really don't know. But I want you all to be there with me so that there's order. I want you to send three or four patrol cars that will accompany us because I want it to turn out well. If there's no order, no peace, there will be no amnesty—it'll be a failure." So they had sent patrol cars there. And the police approached our group.

"Who's in charge?" the police asked.

"She is!" they said, and they pointed to me.

I said, "No, you all are."

They said, "No, she's the leader!"

"Okay, I'm the leader," I said finally, "We're going to do it. We're going to leave from this end of the school, go out in order, and march."

We went out. There were not many parents, and it was difficult for me. I'm not going to tell you it wasn't. Because I thought, Ay, no more than twenty parents? That's all? It seemed like too small of a group to make any difference.

We marched until we reached the police department and from

there we were going to turn and double back. But when we reached the turning point, I knew the parents didn't want to keep going. They didn't want to double back because they thought, What might be following us at this point? Now that we had been marching for a while, we were scared that Immigration agents might be following behind us, waiting to arrest us. People didn't want to risk it. They wanted to leave at that halfway point. I said, "No. Let them arrest us. We're going to risk it. We're going to keep marching."

So we followed our route: we crossed the park and went to double back. And all of a sudden I looked behind me as we made the turn, and there were so many parents! I don't know where they came from; I think they were hiding before because they were scared, too. But they came out, and when we turned to double back on the route, they continued behind us, marching, a huge group of I don't know how many hundreds of parents. That's what gave me the most courage to keep marching and not be afraid.

At that point, with so many people now in the march, reporters and photographers started gathering. I could see a bunch of them on the hill above the park taking pictures of us. We were now a big group, calling a lot of attention to ourselves. The parents had their flags. Some had Mexican flags, some had American flags. I had my own flag. I was worried about the people that had Mexican flags, because I didn't want to start any trouble. It's difficult because you are split in two: on one side you are Mexican—it's your childhood, your family, your traditions. On the other side, you're American: your kids were born here, your years are spent here, your job is here, your house is here. But I think ultimately, I am an American.

Well, after we made the turn and were marching back, one of the reporters came down from the hill and started asking me questions. "What does the flag mean?" was her first question. The flag that I carried was a white flag.

"It means peace," I said.

"And what does peace mean? What are you doing here?"

"I am here to work and to get a better future for my daughters."

"And how did you arrive?" and so on. It had begun. I don't know where I found so many words to speak, but suddenly I was saying everything about our struggle here, about wanting better lives for our children—I gave a big speech that day of the march. I thought after the reporter left, it probably won't even be printed anywhere.

The next day, my daughter Estrella calls me from school. She says, "Mommy, can you believe it?"

"What?"

"You were in the paper!"

"Huh? How can it be?"

"On the front page!"

No! I thought. And when she got home and showed me the newspaper I saw a big picture of me at the front of the march, and it had my name and the speech I had given the day before. "Immigrant Adela, who isn't a criminal, who is here with her family," and so on. Estrella said, "Mommy, aren't you scared? There's all your information there." I thought, Well, I can't do anything about it now. Things are already out of my hands.

TOO LONG WITHOUT FAMILY

I have been in California for eighteen years. It's been eighteen years since I saw my mother and father, my sisters and brothers. It's too long to go without seeing your family. I've thought many times about going down to visit them, and then trying to return on foot through the mountains again. No, I tell myself, I wouldn't make it back across. No, there are too many that have died in the desert, too many who have drowned. And what if Immigration grabs me, what happens then? Then they'll have my fingerprints, they'll have me with a record, they'll deport me. What will happen to my children then? No, I tell myself, better to stay here and try to someday get a visa to see them.

Now I no longer what my parents are like. They must be older, slower, grayer. If one day I have the opportunity to see them, I'll run to them! If I'm still young enough to run. I hope to be able to visit them soon. A few years ago my brother died, but I couldn't be there, I couldn't go to his funeral because I don't have papers to let me come back. I hope that, God willing, there is amnesty. I hope they do something before the rest of my family is no longer there.

BOYFRIENDS AFTERWARD

Now, yes, I guess I am quite involved in the whole thing. The schools, the church, now marching for our rights. For a chance for amnesty. It comes from wanting something better for my children.

Estrella has always wanted to be in biogenetics, or is it bioengineering? And Mirreya, since she was little, has wanted to be a police officer. I tell the girls they have to get their careers in order before they get married. I tell them they have to get a job, so that they're never depending on a man. Because some of the boys will just grab them by the hair, as they say, with one fist, and carry them off. I say no. If you want to study biology, fine. If you want to be a police officer, fine. Boyfriends afterward. "No, right now!" they say. "Mommy! I want to get married now." I say, "No, wait! There's still time. You want kids? What's gonna happen? If you want kids just to give them to me to care for, no."

If you have your education you can come out and earn yourself a better life. A life where you don't have to be working in the fields, working in hard jobs, labor jobs, arriving all dirty, with clothes full of dust. If you don't have your education, you'll do everything that those without papers are doing now.

You're not going to be the same as me, I tell them. You can be a good doctor, a good lawyer. You can do the jobs we can't do. Because we don't have the language, we don't have the papers. You already have years living here. Speak English, become educated, do the jobs I can't do, *m'ijas.*[2]

TURNING INTO THEIR LEADER

More than three thousand people showed up for the second march, on May 1. They came from towns all around Modesto. I placed an announcement on the local television station. I said I didn't want to give my name, I only wanted to give the hours and the date and the route of the march.

There were more of us coordinators this time and I thought, I don't want to be in front this time. But what happens? When we got part way through the route one of the coordinators tells me to get out front. I said, "I am fine right here, you all are leaders, you can go up front."

They were very serious. They said, "No, look, everybody has come, all of the kids and youngsters, and it's only you who they respect."

Well, they finally pushed me and pushed me and I went up front. All the kids were running around, in front of the police department and out in front of the march in a big group.

I said, "You know what? Why don't you get yourself in a line and, just like we came, we can walk in order?" All of the kids quieted down and got in line! And the coordinators said, "See? Look what you do when you're out in front. We're already seeing you turn into the leader."

There were so many people! Everybody was there, even my husband. My man said to me, "You're not scared?" I said, "Well, if something happens here, they're going to have to take all of us."

---

[2] Colloquial pronunciation of *mi hijas,* my daughters.

And when we got to the park we stopped and raised all of the flags we had above our heads. This time, I didn't want to give my name to the reporters. I stayed quiet that day.

It's been over a year since the marches and so far nothing's happened. Estrella still asks me if I'm scared and I say no. And she says, "They're going to record you and maybe it will get to the government. Mom! It scares me that you just tell everyone that we're immigrants. Me, because I wanna go to college. Everyone knows that you don't have papers, and since they ask questions they know that I don't have papers either. I'm nervous all the time," she says. "Please Mommy, no more—I'm scared now. I don't want something to happen to you 'cause we're really close. We're the closest of all, we've been through everything together. I gotta keep my mommy with me."

I understand her. I feel the same. "But I'm not scared," I say. "Because," I tell her, "there's a chance that the people that you talk to will be able to help you. You talk to them and maybe they can help you with your papers, help you fix your situation. My daughter, with luck maybe they'll be able to fix things for you."

She says, "Yes mommy, I know, but I don't want to stay here alone."

But I say, "These are opportunities. Maybe talking about these things will change them. In case this is an opportunity that they'll offer us, you have to take advantage of it. You must, as they say, come out of the darkness. Come out and say, 'Here I am! See me.'"

ESTRELLA

AGE: *17*
COUNTRY OF ORIGIN: *Mexico*
OCCUPATION: *High school student*
HOME: *Modesto, California*

I LOVE DEALING WITH DNA

Estrella is the eldest daughter of Adela, whose story is featured in the previous chapter of this book. Carried by her mother across mountainous terrain into Southern California when she was only six weeks old, Estrella has no memory of Mexico. She is seventeen now, the oldest of five girls, the rest of whom were all born in the U.S. and are therefore U.S. citizens. This interview took place after school in the kitchen of Estrella's apartment. Her mother and sisters, along with some visiting teenage friends, sat in the adjacent living room watching television. Estrella spoke to us in English.

I'm a senior. I don't have a first period, so I only have five periods. I like school, but I'm not very good at it. I'm not a straight-A person, but I do the average. So far I'm going to graduate. I'm taking econ, which is one of the required courses to graduate. I'm taking English. And I'm a TA for second period. I'm taking human anatomy, too, where we've been able to dissect different animals—a frog, a shark, and a cat. It was difficult to work on the frog, because the organs are so much smaller. With the shark, it's really hard to get the skin off, because it's really stuck to the muscles. But the cat was the hardest, because it has more organs, more muscles.

The cats still had their fur on them. They already had a hole where they were injected with something to dye the veins and arteries. It dyes the arteries pink and the veins a dark, navy blue. To skin the cat, we put our fingers through the hole, separating the fur from the little piece of skin that holds the muscles and organs together. We skinned them completely from head to tail. After skinning them, we removed the superficial muscle, the top layer, and then we moved down to the deep muscle, toward the organs, and examined them. Then we moved onto all the tendons, and then onto the bones. And finally we moved on to the organs, the stomach, the liver, the heart. We cut open the stomach, the intestines, to see how they're shaped. Then we cut open the mouth and checked inside the esophagus.

When we were dissecting the cat, I was able to feel inside where the stomach was. When I got home, I felt around on my dog to see if I could feel where the stomach was connected. It was a little weird. I ended up wondering what it would be like if I dissected my dog.

I'm taking orchestra, and I play the violin. That started in fifth grade. My friends and I saw it as a way to get out of class. I stayed with it through eighth grade, and then, when freshman year came around, the counselors tried to get me out of it. They said, "You won't have room to take these certain classes. You have to take two years of this, two years of that." But I ended up figuring it out, because I could go to summer school and make up some of those classes. In high school, I started out in the intermediate orchestra. At the end of last year, I entered the full orchestra.

Last year, the orchestra went to Hawaii, for tour, and I couldn't go because of my status. You have to show ID at the airport. I wanted to go, but I understood why I can't, so it wasn't that big of a deal. I guess I felt left out, because all my friends were going. Most of my close friends know I'm undocumented. Just the ones I don't really hang out with a lot don't know.

I did the biotech program at my high school last year. It was an ROP class,[1] so it gave me some sort of college credit. We went on field trips to community colleges and checked out their biotech program, and we went to some biotech firms. That's exactly why I want to become a biotechnician. I loved dealing with DNA, the cells and everything. I find it so fascinating, how you can make gel out of certain things, and make cells grow.

I'm focusing on going to college next, and majoring in biotech research. I've never really wanted to go to a four-year university right after high school, because it would be complete chaos. I don't have the money. It's not impossible. I might qualify for grants, but still, it just wouldn't work.[2]

My plan is to go to a community college and then transfer to UC Davis, because UC Davis has a great biotechnology program. And hopefully I can get an internship at a biotech company to help pay for my education.

FIVE SISTERS, THREE BIRDS, THIRTEEN FISHES, TWO DOGS

I'm the oldest of five girls. My sisters were all born here, so they're citizens. I'm seventeen years old. Adriana is sixteen. Mirreya's fourteen. Paula just turned thirteen. And Mirabel just turned eight. And then there's my mom and my dad, so seven members total in my family.

My mom says I cried a lot when we were crossing the border. They walked across, and I would cry every time a migration guy, or whatever, I don't know what they call them in English, but when they would drive by, I would start crying. I was less than two months old.

After we crossed, we went to San Diego, where we stayed in a house with a bunch of people that had crossed at the same time.

---

[1] A Regional Occupational Program, or technical education course.

[2] Access to financial aid for undocumented students is limited in most states.

And then eventually, we went to where my auntie was staying. I believe it was San Fernando. And we stayed there till I was about two years old. And then we came here, to Modesto, where my dad was before he'd gone back to get my mom and me. I've pretty much lived my whole life in Modesto. We've lived in a few different places in town, and now we've been in our current apartment for ten years.

When we first moved to the place we live now, the apartments were really trashy. There was vandalism all over, and drugs and stuff. The apartment's paint job was a mess. The cabinets weren't fixed. But as the years have gone by, we've gotten everything fixed. People that were drug dealers moved out, and it was pretty calm for a while. But then a couple families moved in that caused a lot of problems. We had helicopters and canines out here in the apartments, looking for people. That went on for about two or three years. Then it calmed down, and now it's doing it again. There are some drug activities going on, as well as gang activities.

Our apartment is a three-bedroom, one-bathroom. The kitchen isn't big, but it's not tiny. And the living room's a pretty normal size. The middle bedroom is the biggest, and the two side ones are pretty normal size.

Two of my sisters sleep in my room with me. It was my room, but one by one, they migrated into it. For some weird reason, everyone else sleeps in the living room. My mom, my dad, and my little sister. And Adriana, the one that's sixteen, because they don't trust her. The two other rooms are not being used. There's stuff in them, but nobody sleeps in them.

For a while, my dad's sister, her husband, their son, and her husband's brother were staying in the last room, because they were getting their house remodeled. We have three birds, and thirteen fishes. We have two dogs. Before, we had two hamsters. And we've had cats before. My dog stays with me. She sleeps with me like she's a baby.

She lays right next to me on my arm. She also pees in the bathroom where she's supposed to. But the other dog does not. She pees and does everything everywhere.

I get to sleep in, so I get ready when they're all gone, and I get the bathroom to myself. I don't have a first period, but when I did, it was bad. Because we were all coming in, one getting out, one pushing in, one getting out. And two or three at the same time in there, brushing our teeth, doing our makeup, doing our hair. So my dad ended up adding mirrors to the house. We have one big mirror next to the bathroom, and there's a long one that's on the hallway. That's pretty much where we do our hair and makeup. It's been easier after my dad added the mirrors.

When I was in elementary school, it was weird, because I didn't know I wasn't the only one without documents. I wouldn't say anything to anybody. My parents always told me, "Don't tell anybody, not even your friends." My friends would talk about going to Mexico and stuff like that, and I wouldn't say anything. I was so terrified.

And my parents would always tell me how it was so hard for them to cross the border. My mom had a messed-up leg at the time, so her feet were just bad when they finally crossed. My parents didn't speak English when they got here, no English whatsoever. So they had to start from scratch. So far my mom's learned a lot. My dad's been really closed-minded, though.

My dad is really strict. Old-fashioned Mexican dad. He was telling me I couldn't get married, I couldn't have babies, even if I was thirty. We only go to the movies about once a week. And if I go out, even though I'm the oldest, I have to bring all my sisters wherever I go. If I go anywhere, I have to bring every single one of them. My mom, she's somewhat strict. She still has some Mexican traditions in her, but she knows how to bend them, because we're not in Mexico anymore. Things are not the same.

THAT'S JUST ONE OF THE THINGS I DO

I box with the Modesto PAL[3] program, and I love boxing. A couple of years ago, my mom said, "It's time for you guys to do some sort of sports, so you're not home all the time." She told us to choose from the sports they had at the Modesto PAL—soccer, basketball, stuff like that. But they were really far, and my mom doesn't know how to drive. Boxing was close by, so it was more of a convenience thing than anything.

The third day I was there, they tried to get me to spar, but I said, "I'm not going to fight somebody, I'm not getting in the ring." But a couple months later, I tried it.

The first time it was scary. I didn't know how to move around the ring. It wasn't against a girl, it was against a guy. The first time I got hit in the face, it was like a reality check. You get hit, and it's not a little tag. You get popped. I shook my head. It made me open my eyes. I realized then that I had to do what I learned how to do. I put my guard up and hit back. The first couple of punches I threw, I thought, Oh my God, am I hitting him hard? Is it hurting him? Is it going to make a difference? Eventually I got used to it.

Then, after about two months of sparring, I got hit in the face by one of the older guys, and it left a bump on the right side of my nose. After that, I boxed with another big kid, and he hooked my left shoulder and dislocated it. Then my mom said, "I don't want you doing that, it's not a girl's thing, it's more of a guy thing." I'm still boxing, but I don't spar anymore.

I taught catechism for two years, from 2002 to 2004. I was also in the choir, seventh and eighth grade, and half of freshman year. And both things, I ended up getting out because my dad told me it was a waste of time. I was also involved in the youth group, on Fridays.

I was doing hip-hop for about a year, too. I took classes at DeeDee's

---

[3] Police Activities League, an organization offering extracurricular youth activities.

Step Class, but that was too expensive, so I joined the Modesto PAL program. So, after boxing on Mondays from seven to eight, I would go to hip-hop. I love dancing. That's just one of the things I do, in addition to makeup and hair. But then my dad said it was a waste of time.

My dad and I don't have that daughter-and-father connection. He's never really been there. When I first started playing an instrument, he never went to my concerts. When I graduated from sixth grade, he didn't go to my graduation. When I did my first communion and confirmation, his brother, *mi tio* Pepe, had to force him to go. For my *quinceañera,* he didn't want to show. He acts different toward me than to my sisters. There are days where it seems like we get along, but really, inside, I have no connection toward my dad. And sometimes the things he says make it even worse. He might say he doesn't mean them later, but really, at the moment, they hurt a lot. I love him, but we've never had that actual good connection.

Sometimes my dad gets really ugly toward me. He doesn't understand how things here are different. In Mexico, you party every day. Like they say, if you can reach the bar, you can pretty much buy a beer. Here it's completely different. When you get older and you're able to do all this, it means a lot. Here there's prom and stuff like that. It means a lot to some people when they graduate. That's a once-in-a-lifetime thing. But to my dad, that's just stupid. If any party happens in Mexico, anybody gets to go. We're two different places. Things are different.

WHERE YOU CAME FROM

On May 1, 2006, because of the march,[4] we walked off campus. And teachers and principals were taking pictures to see who walked off.

---

[4] Hundreds of thousands of immigrants and immigrants' rights supporters walked out of jobs and schools as part of a national demonstration called "Day Without an Immigrant." The walkouts took place on May 1, 2006, in cities all across the U.S.

Everybody in Sacramento and San Francisco made their marches the same day. It was to show that we wanted equal rights for immigrants.

I was scared because of Immigration and everything. A lot of my white friends didn't know about my status. I'm friends with a lot of white people. Most of the people that walked off didn't have papers. I was scared of the way people might look at me afterward, and I didn't know if I wanted to take the risk. But seeing my friends and my mom encouraged me, and I ended up walking off.

Pretty much all the Hispanics left school that day. So it was pretty big, around two hundred people, not including the elementary and junior high schools that walked off that day, too.

When we were leaving campus, some of the other students, mostly the guys, were flicking us off, saying things like, "You beaners shouldn't be coming over here."

We walked toward downtown until we ended up at City Hall. As we marched through town, there were people driving by, flicking us off, and some had posters on the cars that said, "Go back to where you came from," and stuff like that.

When we came back, we were given detention or Saturday school. But if we wanted to get out of it, we could write an essay about why we decided to walk off campus. So I wrote my essay on what I wanted for my future and why my parents came here in the first place.

I gave it personally to Mr. Santiago, our vice principal. A week later, I got called into the office. I had no idea why. When you get the blue pass, you know you're in trouble.

I walked in, and Mr. Santiago said, "We're going to suspend you."

And I said, "What for?"

And he said, "No, I'm just playing." He said, "After reading your essay, I think you really made a point, and it was great writing. We just need to know if we have your permission to publish it in the newspaper."

I said, "Sure." They published it the following week.

We marched again this year, but not as many people came, because they were scared. Everything going on around town, the whole immigration thing. The raids of people's houses and workplaces. People were afraid of exposing themselves to being caught by Immigration out in the open. We didn't do it during school hours this year. It just didn't have the same energy as it did last year.

STAYING ON TRACK

I don't really get along with my sisters, because none of them are like me. Every other word out of their mouth is the F-word. And Adriana and Mirreya are somewhat involved in gangs.

Adriana got suspended once, and the school was calling our house for three weeks straight. That's never happened to me. There was a time period where I got in trouble at school, but it wasn't to the point where I got suspended or the school had to call my house.

I was fourteen. I had a big mouth. That was pretty much it. I wasn't a fighter or anything. I was more of a big mouth. I didn't like people saying anything to me. I wouldn't shut up.

What changed me, I think, was that I was growing up. I was the oldest, which made me want to focus on doing good. And having certain teachers helped a lot. Like Ms. Barnes, my biotech teacher. She was a great teacher. She encouraged me a lot. She wouldn't let me give up. Ms. Sanchez is another great teacher. And Mr. Bloom is a great teacher, too.

My sister became a freshman last year, and she had problems with *Sureños*.[5] She and this girl did not like each other. And then somehow my name got involved in it. The girl started talking smack about me, and it got to a point where I was like, either she shuts up or I'll have to do something about it. I confronted her, and it made this big

---

[5] A primarily Mexican-American street gang originating in Southern California.

thing. Then my mom got tired of it and came to the school. They got us all together, and we talked.

Then Officer Rodriguez, the gang-prevention officer, called me in. I explained to him that I wasn't involved in gangs. I told him, "I'm not this kind of person. Nobody tells me what to wear or what I can't wear. If somebody doesn't like the color I'm wearing, then they don't need to talk to me." And he said, "Well, I really appreciate the fact that you're not involved." That's how we started talking.

He started helping me. I asked him to help to keep my sisters out of gangs. And I help with teaching him about gangs from a teenager's point of view, so he looks at everything differently from what they teach up there, wherever they go to. I don't know where they go to learn about gangs. I tell him what I know, what I see. And if I know something about a certain person, I help.

He started out by asking questions like, "Do you know what this means? Do you know what this means?" Certain signs and symbols of gangs. It went from there to me going with him to conferences. I go with him, and parents get to ask me questions about gangs from a teenager's point of view. I was never involved in them, but I have a lot of friends who are, and my sisters are still kind of involved in it.

Right now, one of my cousins is locked up. Officer Rodriguez has actually dealt with him personally. And he's dealt with friends of mine. All of them are *Norteños*. Or, they bang red. X4 and all that stuff.[6]

If your kid is in trouble, you have to go to these classes for parents to learn about gangs. I go with Officer Rodriguez to these. First he gives his Powerpoint, his information about gangs, and explains what his job is, how they detect gangs and everything. After that, he gives the parents time to ask me questions.

---

[6] Traditional rivals of the *Sureños, Norteños* are a largely Mexican-American gang with roots in Northern California. Gang members make heavy use of the number fourteen—N is the fourteenth letter of the alphabet—and the color red in tattoos and attire. The number fourteen is often written as X4, a distortion of the Roman numeral XIV.

Their main questions are, "How can you say no? How do you avoid everything, and how is it that you can get away with being friends with both of them and not being harassed or attacked by one of the gangs?"

I tell them it depends on the person. If you stand up, they don't do anything. Because they never come up to you in a big gang. Usually, it's one or two people. And if you say, "No, I don't bang," then they pretty much leave you alone. But if you just keep your head down, and they keep bullying you around, then they'll try to pull you in.

It's also based on the parents. The cops can only do so much. Like Officer Rodriguez, he's doing as much as he can, trying to get as many kids as he can out of gangs. But like, one of the actual gang members told him a while ago, you can't save anybody that doesn't want to be saved. And there's no stopping it if the parents don't put their feet down and say, "Look, you're not going to do this," instead of, "Oh, he doesn't listen to me, what am I supposed to do?" He will listen to you. You just have to be hard. I tell the parents it's pretty much their job to make sure their kids are not out there doing what they're not supposed to.

That's pretty much how it all started for me, all by a problem. I'm trying to become somebody in life and not just get pulled into either one of these gangs. So Officer Rodriguez has been helping me stay on track.

BIG TROUBLE

Officer Rodriguez knows about my status. Around January of 2006, I mentioned to him that I needed a job. So we were thinking of places we could apply. He said, "Just give me your general information and I'm pretty sure I could find you a job." That's when I told him I don't have a good Social. And he said, "Oh, so you weren't born here?" I said, "No, I wasn't." After that, he was really nice. He's helped me even more after that. Thanks to him, I received a five-hundred-dollar scholarship from the police department.

My mom got me a Social during that time when you were able to get them. They just put on it: Not Valid for Working. But when my mom filled out the papers, somehow it ended up saying that I was born in 1986. And really, my birthday is in 1989. Somehow, it got messed up. The point is that right now, according to the data on my Social, I'm twenty-one. But I can't go back and fix it, because there's the possibility they could take it away. And it's what I've been using to go to school, the PAL program, everything.

I'm afraid, because when you apply for a job, there's places where they'll do a background check, to see if you've ever been convicted or anything like that. So if that happened, and they checked my date of birth that I put down on the application compared to the birth on the Social, I could end up in big trouble.

Something like that happened when I filled out the FAFSA.[7] I was waiting for my PIN number to come through email, and they sent me a letter, saying, "The information you gave us does not correlate with the information on your Social. Please check the material and reapply." So now I don't know what to do.

I can't become independent if I don't get a job. If I can't get some kind of scholarship or financial aid, my parents will have to pay for my education, and that's a lot of money. Especially for a seven-member family.

I've thought of applying at stores, as well as fast food places, but they all ask for Socials. I have noticed that on some applications it's not required, because there's some law I guess, where you don't have to give your Social out, because it's personal. So, at Chuck E. Cheese, for example, if you apply, in the box that says Social Security number, it says, "Optional." And then it explains why.

---

[7] Free Application for Federal Student Aid.

My mom and I are thinking maybe I should just apply somewhere. And if I get the job, and everything works out, just make sure I do well, so there's no reason for them to fire me.

My dad's been working pretty much in the same thing his whole life. He paints houses. He almost always has good jobs. He's so good at it that they usually make him a foreman. So he's not just a painter, but he actually has keys to the things.

The last company he worked for, he was in for five or six years. But then he had an accident, and they fired him. He had a couple of accidents. One time, he was cleaning the paint gun out, and he forgot to put something on it, and the water cut through his skin. And it still had paint in it.

Another time he got a piece of wood in his finger, and it got really bad. The piece of wood was stuck in his pinky finger, and it swelled his whole hand up. He had some sort of infection. He had to go to the doctor, and they injected him with so many things. The doctor asked him, "What happened? Where'd this happen?" My dad told him it was at his job, and the doctor was actually the one that encouraged my dad to get his job to pay for what happened. But as soon as the job found out, they fired him. So my dad ended up getting a lawyer, and he got some money out of it. He didn't get much because he's not documented. But he was able to get something.

The company he works for now is not a very good company. He doesn't work as much as he used to. But for now, it's what's been bringing the food to the table.

I even paint now. I know how to do pretty much everything when I paint houses. My dad gets side jobs. People will want him to paint their house, and if he can't find somebody else to help him, then he'll take me. Sometimes I'll do it just for the fun of it, but sometimes he pays me.

I started around eighth grade. At first it was just covering up windows, making sure the paint wouldn't get on the windows, on the carpet, stuff like that. And then finally, when I was a freshman, I asked him to teach me how to paint, and he did.

JUST GO STRAIGHT

I know how to drive. I learned the hard way. My dad's an alcoholic. The very first time I ever even touched the wheel of a car, we were coming back from Stockton, and my dad was completely drunk. He was swerving all over the road. He tried to get my mom to drive, but she was too scared. So I had to take the car.

I was thirteen. I sat on my dad's lap. He controlled the gas, and I controlled the wheel, made sure we went straight. That late at night, on the freeway, that's pretty easy. You just go straight. No turning, no stopping.

The second time, the same thing happened. Eventually, I got the hang of it, and if my dad was too drunk, I'd say, "You know what, I'm driving." The last time I drove when he was really drunk was from Sacramento. And then for the last year and half, I've been driving. I have a permit now. But I can't get my license.

Right now the van's kind of messed up. We don't know what's wrong with it. But before that, every Friday, I was the taxi. I drove everyone everywhere. I like driving. Gas is just really expensive.

THE IMMIGRATION THING

They've been doing the Immigration thing, going out door to door.[8] And it's getting closer and closer every time we hear it on the news. We heard about how they did it in Oakland. And then my uncle heard they did it in Stockton. Every time we hear about it, it's getting closer and closer to Modesto, and it terrifies us. Because my sisters

---

[8] See Appendices H and I for more information on recent immigration raids.

are not old enough to be left alone. We've seen on the news how a lot of parents are being separated from their children, because kids are citizens and the parents aren't. If anything like that happened to us, it would mean that all my sisters would stay, and my parents and I would get deported.

I speak English better than most of the other Mexicans that are undocumented, so I'm not really worried about being seen in the streets or anything. I'm more worried about them coming to my house and my mom and my dad being here because they still have an accent.

If I had any problems with Immigration, I have Officer Rodriguez and plenty of teachers that I could go to as references. I'm not a criminal.

I agree with some of the arguments people make about immigration. Sure, we came here illegally. But people that were born here are able to go to other countries. What if Mexico did the same thing as the U.S.? What if Mexico closed all the doors on people that weren't born there? Just as Mexico needs things from the U.S., the U.S. needs stuff from every other country in the world.

If it wasn't for most of the Hispanic workers that work in the fields, nobody else would do those jobs. And in Mexico, if you go to college and study, it doesn't mean anything if you come over here. You could be the greatest lawyer in Mexico, and it wouldn't matter here. Your diploma or your master's degree from over there doesn't mean anything here.

Most people don't come here just to trash the United States or commit crimes. Most of the Hispanics here are here to become somebody in life, to give their children a better life than they could have in another country. Sure, sometimes the children are the ones who screw it up for everybody, because the gang activity and vandalism are pretty much done by teenagers. But why not just deal with them, instead of blaming everyone for what one does?

So many of those people that work out in the fields, if you look at them, people that are really old are still out there working. In the heat, picking tomatoes, picking whatever. And if you ask anybody else, they're not willing to do it. Black people aren't going to do it. They'll say, "I'm not your slave."

I had night school last trimester, and the teacher was Caucasian, and she said it herself: "There is no Caucasian person that would do that job. Even the homeless Caucasians wouldn't do it." She said that. And I think that if the U.S. wants to give just temporary visas to people, just so they can work, that's pointless.

That's the way that all Hispanics are looking at it. We still have to pay rent wherever we're staying while we're here. There's no point in you keeping us here just to work, and we produce your resources to make your products, and then you just kick us back out. I don't think that's fair.

I've been here pretty much all of my life. I can't really say I'm from Mexico, or that I'm Mexican. But I wouldn't consider myself Mexican-American. I speak English better than I speak Spanish. I got my first shots here. When I started walking, my first few steps, I took them here, in the United States. It wasn't in Mexico. It was here. Everything I have is from here.

ENRIQUE, 60
Chicago, Illinois

Originally from Emiliano Zapata, Michoacán, Enrique works as a day laborer in Chicago and finds it difficult because he is consistently one of the oldest men on the street. He came to the U.S. recently in the hopes of sending money back home to his wife and seven children.

I've been here for twelve months and there are days when I don't make enough even to eat. There are days I work for one, two, three hours. When I work eight hours, I'm a king, but sometimes a week passes without getting anything. I leave home at five a.m. everyday to come here, to wait here on this corner. Sometimes the other men say, "The old guy, don't take him because he's too old." I have seven children to support at home and I must pay rent here; you can't imagine. It has been eight days since I've worked and we've been standing here since seven in the morning. At night when we go to bed our feet are all swollen.

EDITOR'S NOTE FOR THE AFTERWORD

In America, we often speak of heroes, those women and men whose bravery inspires us to reach for something comparable in ourselves. Let me tell me you about a hero of mine. Her name is Lorena, and she's been with the *Underground America* project since the beginning. One of our interviewers, David Hill, made contact with her in 2007, and she immediately agreed to share her story with the public (see page 183). On first reading the transcript of her interview, I remember being struck by Lorena's candor and great storytelling ability, as well as her obvious love of life, learning, and justice.

For me, Lorena is truly an American hero, the sort of person who stands up for what she believes in and who helps those who are less fortunate—even when she's in a precarious position herself. Of all the many striking details in this book, one that has stuck in my mind all these years is Lorena's description of how, as a six-year-old, she endured crossing the desert with her mother and brothers by practicing her math tables. As she says, "One of the coyotes was holding my hand, and he asked me if I was tired, if I wanted him to carry me. And I said, 'Oh, no, I can do this. This is easy.' I said, 'This is as easy as the three-times tables. Three times one, three times two, three times three.' I remember they were making fun of me because I said that." It's such an incredibly human moment. As the father of a four year-old myself, I stand in awe of her strength of character, as a child, and as a young woman, recounting a harrowing story with such warmth and humor. When she made the grueling trek into this country, Lorena was a frightened but tough kid, with hopes and dreams and a love for math. She was an individual. But how often we forget this. Why is it that, when we talk about immigration, we so often speak in terms of numbers, not people, not families? Let Lorena's story, and the others in this book, stand as a reminder that immigration policy is, above all, about individuals—sisters, brothers, sons, daughters.

Time and time again, since the publication of *Underground America*, Lorena has agreed to speak on behalf of the book at public forums, on the radio, and at universities. When I heard we were going to re-issue Underground America, I asked Lorena to write the afterword because I wanted her—as a so-called DREAMer—to have the last word. Now, I'm proud to introduce, once again, to readers in the U.S. and abroad, one of the most articulate, humane, and courageous people I have the honor of knowing: Lorena.

—Peter Orner,
July, 2013

Afterword

AMERICAN DREAMER

by Lorena

When I decided to share my story with Voice of Witness, I set out to change people's perspectives on undocumented immigrants. It turned out, however, that the biggest change of perspective happened to me. Publishing my life story with Voice of Witness gave me exactly that—a voice. Sharing my story made me visible. It made me a real person. I was finally "documented" and accounted for, if only in a book. The book's success is something I am now able to tell my son I was a part of.

My parents brought me to the U.S. when I was six years old. Since that day, I knew I had to be invisible. *Don't make waves, don't bring attention to yourself, make yourself as undetectable as you can.* That's what I told myself every day. Yet I had a voice, a powerful voice that I wanted others to hear, and that I wanted to use to do good. So why couldn't I use it? As afraid as I was for all those years to speak up about my life and struggles, my desire to finally let others hear my voice was greater.

I began fighting for passage of the DREAM Act when I was a freshman in high school. I remember being so hopeful. I was convinced that, because I was personally involved, the DREAM Act would pass. It didn't. And it didn't the next time either, or the time after that. But when President Obama finally did sign deferred action in the summer of 2012 (which is not the DREAM Act, but does allow us to come out of the shadows for the first time), I considered it a personal accomplishment.[1] After the announcement of deferred action, my two brothers and I immediately hired an attorney and filled out our paperwork.

Then just one day before I received my approval letter in November, my youngest brother Julio passed away. Julio was an amazing person. He was unbelievably bright, generous, funny, and driven. He was only two-and-a-half years old when our parents brought us to this country. We were very close. All of us siblings were close—our mom made sure of it. She would say, "Your siblings are all you have in this country. Cherish them." Julio was the first and only one in our family to go to preschool, something my older brother and I envied. Schoolwork came easy to him. He was so intelligent he didn't even have to try at school. In high school he enrolled in advanced classes because college prep courses were "too easy." Although he was my youngest brother, he was someone I admired and felt proud of. While in college, he worked in a restaurant to pay for tuition, and he made friends with all his coworkers. But restaurant work was not for

---

1 In June 2012, the Obama administration established the Deferred Action for Childhood Arrivals program under the auspices of DHS. DACA provides temporary legal status for qualified applicants who entered the U.S. as children.

him. He wanted to use his love of fitness and knowledge of psychology to be a P.E. teacher or a personal trainer. That is what fueled his desire to legalize his status. And at the first opportunity he got, he started the process. But he never got the chance to see it through. On November 11, 2012, he passed away unexpectedly. One day later, he would have celebrated his six month wedding anniversary, the same day I received my own documentation letter. Julio is a citizen of God's Heaven now. He doesn't need documentation there.

I waited twenty-one years for the day that I would receive an approval letter from USCIS. For twenty-one years I imagined the joy, excitement, and relief I would feel when I received this letter. Little did I know what I would have to give up before I got it. However, as a good friend told me, I should be used to playing the hand that has been dealt to me. We cannot go back to the past where things were easier and happier, but I can make a happy future for the sake of Julio's memory. I must continue with my dream of doing good in this country, especially now that I can be here legally.

In the first edition of this book, I purposely chose not to include details about the ways my legal status affected my marriage. I made the decision to tell my future husband about my legal status a month after we started dating. I wanted him to know my one and only secret, and if he chose to stay, he'd know exactly who I was. I was hesitant to tell him. I was embarrassed. I was afraid he would be insulted that someone with "no papers" would want to date him. But he just laughed, hugged me, and said, "I still love you." A month later, he proposed.

My husband is an amazing man who has helped me get through the most difficult moments of my life, and I wanted him to never doubt the reason why I chose him as my life companion. So when we married, I purposefully did not pursue legalization. My status bothered me more than it did him. I think I overdid it trying to prove that I didn't marry him for citizenship, due to my own lack of self-confidence that arose from being an undocumented immigrant. Of course, this tendency affected my relationship and was exhausting. I always felt the need to prove I was self-sufficient, intelligent, and not afraid to work. Five years of marriage later, I have learned to trust him with my one weakness. I've learned to tear down the wall I built long ago to protect myself from being hurt by the insensitive or hateful remarks of others toward undocumented immigrants. Rather than being embarrassed by who I am, my husband makes me feel proud of my accomplishments and determination. With his support, I hope to one day achieve my dream of becoming a neurosurgeon. When I become a doctor, I will not only be saving lives—this DREAMer kid will be the personification of the American Dream.

As a country, I think we have remained at a standstill with our immigration issues. Despite the publications of books like *Underground America*, hundreds of pro-immigration rallies, and proposed immigration reform bills, some of the public still live under the impression that creating a pathway to citizenship will make America vulnerable to terrorism and is the equivalent of "rewarding criminals." I must adamantly disagree. Immigrants such as myself love this country as their own. I have lived here since I was six. My own child was born here. I buried my little brother here. Yes, I am proud of my heritage and culture; however, the United States is my home. This is the country I love for so many reasons.

Many of us undocumented immigrants would proudly defend this country. When I was eighteen years old, a recruiter tried to enlist me in the armed forces, but my legal status prevented him from doing so. When I asked if there was anything he could do, his helpless response became engraved in my brain. He said, "Fighting with the INS is like fighting with the IRS. You'll never win." I was ready, willing, and able to serve my country but was turned down because I didn't have a social security number. So often I asked myself, *How does this make sense to anybody?* Yes, my parents crossed the border "without proper inspection" so that made me "illegal." But everything I did from the moment I set foot on this soil was to guarantee I wouldn't be a waste of space. And so far, I believe I've accomplished that.

I recently read an article that stated children of immigrants have lower IQs, and therefore would not be an asset to this country if the latest immigration reform bill was passed. Additionally, it went on to state that government benefits awarded to the parents of immigrants far outweigh the positive impact immigrant children make on the economy. The article went on to claim that undocumented Mexican immigrants do poorly in school, have high dropout rates, and high teen pregnancy rates.

I can only argue that the author's claims are contradicted by my own experience. I disagree with the author because of who I have become, what my family has become, and what the children of immigrants that I know have become. Our IQs are just fine, thank you. My youngest brother and I are both college graduates. My oldest brother is in college now. My parents never allowed us to get anything lower than Bs in school. I was salutatorian of my high school class. I didn't get pregnant in my teenage years, and my brothers didn't impregnate anyone in their teenage years either. Nothing about the author's studies applies to my family and the immigrant families we know. My mom worked two full-time jobs and still found the time to go to school and learn English. She writes essays in English with better vocabulary and grammar than most adults born in this country. My father prides himself on having learned English immediately after arriving here, and he continues to expand his vocabulary to this day.

There were days when we had very little money for food, but rather than ask for food stamps or WIC or welfare, we made do with what we had. The children of undocumented immigrants have witnessed the struggles, abuse, and humiliation their parents had to endure in order for them to go to school. My mom always told me, "You don't want my life. Earn a better one." And I did.

As I write this, a sweeping immigration reform bill is working its way through the Senate. The public comments and blogs on this topic are, for the most part, shameful. It's unfortunate that there are still people in this country who live such hateful lives and spread their ignorant views wherever possible. Regardless of what these people's perceptions of immigrants are, we—and I speak for myself, my family, and countless other undocumented people I know personally—don't want a free ride. Far from it. If our parents risked their lives and our lives to come to this country, doesn't that show we are willing to work for what we want?

Some may be shocked to learn that many of us "illegal" immigrants actually support a more secure border, including a more prominent border agent presence at all borders as well as giving them the tools they need to properly do their jobs. We want the good people in this country and the bad people out. We want to make this country better.

When I become a doctor, I will save lives without discriminating based on patients' backgrounds or birthplaces. I won't ask them first what their thoughts on immigration are. I live by this golden rule: treat others as you want to be treated. And I fantasize that everyone else does too. Unfortunately, as soon as the phrase "immigration reform" is brought up, the focus tends to be on policy, not people. But this policy directly affects human beings. It affects their lives and their family's lives. Whether laws change or stay the same, there will be drastic consequences for mothers, fathers, and children. Sometimes, the consequences are life altering or life ending.

As I was about to finalize this piece, I was notified that my brother Julio's deferred action application had been approved. I never knew the true meaning of "bitter-sweet" until this moment. As joyous as I was, I couldn't help but feel as though fate forced my family to make a trade-off. We finally received what we wanted after twenty-one years of trying. However, my brother wasn't here to celebrate with us. And as my tears started flowing, my phone's music app turned on by itself and started playing a song by the Black Eyed Peas. "Pea" in Spanish translates to *chicharo*. Chicharito was Julio's nickname as a toddler. His favorite soccer player's nickname was also Chicharito. The soccer player's jersey number is fourteen. My brothers both received their DACA approval letters on the 14th of the month. So I know Julio is taking care of us. He makes his presence known every chance he gets.

My older brother and I now have double the responsibility to do great things with our new opportunity. We have to make the positive changes we originally set out to make and the ones Julio wanted to make. I have no doubt we will accomplish this and more.

APPENDICES

APPENDIX A: IMMIGRANT LABOR AND POST-KATRINA RECONSTRUCTION

The rebuilding process following Hurricane Katrina brought an influx of workers into the Gulf Coast. A large number of those workers were undocumented Latino laborers, who were vulnerable to exploitation at the hands of contractors. Reports of poor working conditions, harassment, and wage theft were widespread.

An estimated **25 percent** of construction workers in post-Katrina New Orleans were Latino.[†]

100,000 Latino workers relocated to the Gulf Coast after Katrina.[†]

28 percent of undocumented reconstruction workers reported having difficulty obtaining payment for their work.[†]

19 percent of workers reported not being equipped with proper protective gear when working with hazardous substances or in dangerous conditions.[†]

In September 2005, Immigration and Customs Enforcement dispatched **725 officers** to the Gulf for detention and removal of undocumented workers.[‡]

In 2006, a report issued by the Advancement Project, National Immigration Law Center, and New Orleans Worker Justice Coalition concluded that:

New Orleans is being rebuilt on the backs of underpaid and unpaid workers perpetuating cycles of poverty that existed pre-Katrina, and ensuring their existence in the newly rebuilt city. Exploitation and exclusion are deeply immoral grounds upon which to reconstruct and repopulate the city. The racial fault lines that were revealed during Hurricane Katrina are being drawn even deeper by the continued actions and inactions of government and private institutions that disadvantage communities of color. The structural racism that shapes New Orleans today is the result of a series of policies and practices (public and private) that create, maintain, and worsen inequities faced by survivors and other workers of color.

Hurricane Katrina has created a situation where there is no government or private accountability for the creation and maintenance of these inequities. Displaced voters have no voice back home, while reconstruction workers are either nonresidents or noncitizens. As a result, contractors have free reign to exploit workers, and the government has felt no pressure to ensure that survivor and migrant workers are protected and able to access basic human needs. Progressive reform will occur only when advocates band together—

across race, ethnicity, and legal status lines—for the advancement of all workers in New Orleans.

Sources:

[†] "Rebuilding After Katrina: A Population-Based Study of Labor and Human Rights in New Orleans," International Human Rights Law Clinic, University of California, Berkeley/Human Rights Center, UC Berkeley/Payson Center for International Development and Technology Transfer, Tulane University, June 2006.

[‡] "ICE Law Enforcement Support Proves Critical to Hurricane Katrina Rescue and Security Efforts," United States Immigration and Customs Enforcement Press Release, September 8, 2005.

"And Injustice for All: Workers' Lives in the Reconstruction of New Orleans," Advancement Project/National Immigration Law Center/New Orleans Worker Justice Coalition, July 2006.

"One Year After Katrina: The State of New Orleans and the Gulf Coast," Gulf Coast Reconstruction Watch, Institute for Southern Studies/Southern Exposure, August 2006.

APPENDIX B: CHINESE HUMAN SMUGGLING

Excerpts from "Why Do They Leave Their Homes?" an essay published by the U.S. State Department about the motivations of Chinese immigrants, specifically those from the Fuzhou region of China.

The search for economic opportunity and social pressure are the top two reasons why some Chinese chose to leave their homeland, according to immigration scholars.

International immigration theory describes "push" and "pull" factors: Greater economic opportunity "pulls" immigrants to the United States, while lower wages and unemployment "push" emigrants from China.

Immigrants believe they can become wealthy in the United States, known as "the Golden Mountain," because wages in the United States are high relative to wages in China. The majority of illegal aliens originate in small villages around China's coastal cities, especially Fuzhou, in Fujian Province. Workers in China earn twice as much in the average city as in rural areas, and seven or eight times more in large coastal cities, such as Shanghai and Guangzhou, than in rural areas.

* * *

It is important to note that workers who leave China tend to come from developed areas that have the infrastructures to provide communication with and transportation to the West. Chinese who choose to enter the United States illegally must have access to significant funds. Smuggling fees run as high as $60,000 and are usually paid with loans from family members and friends. In contrast, most of the 300 million people living in poverty in China have less exposure to the lures of the West and cannot afford to travel—legally or otherwise.

Around the Fuzhou area, emigration abroad is commonly seen as the only possible way for an individual to succeed. In some villages, no industries have developed because the majority of workers between the ages of 18 and 45 have left China. Families will loan money to pay smuggling fees, but will not invest in a relative trying to start a business in China, both because of the difficulties of running a business in China and because of the attitude that more opportunity exists in the United States.

The faith that some communities have in the "American success story" causes them to generate a great deal of social pressure on their members to emigrate abroad. Fuzhounese have a long tradition of sending at least one family member "to make a living abroad." More recently, having a family member in the United States has become a status symbol. "When people get together they always talk about how their sons or daughters or relatives or husbands or brothers are doing in the United States," according to Ko-lin Chin, an expert on Fuzhounese immigrants.

* * *

Not only do some Chinese feel that they must go to the United States to be successful, they also feel the need to appear successful after they do. Although they often find themselves crushed by long work hours and financial demands, Chinese illegal immigrants may be embarrassed to admit their condition to family and friends at home. If immigrants do try to talk about their hardships, their families may choose to believe that the immigrants are lazy or "whiners."

If a husband is unwilling to venture abroad, his wife may threaten to leave him and make the trip herself. Because of the loneliness such separations cause, many illegal immigrants will attempt to help other family members to come to the United States. In addition, the money illegal immigrants send home inspires others to risk being smuggled into the United States.

In addition to pressures from family and friends, Chinese are also encouraged to move abroad by smugglers or "snakeheads." Sometimes, smugglers advertise work overseas, but most find their customers through connections and by word-of-mouth. Smugglers operating within Chinese communities add to the phenomenon of small areas generating large numbers of illegal emigrants. Snakeheads—much more than the emigrants themselves—profit from illegally sending their clients abroad. Some scholars estimate that human smuggling generates an estimated $8 billion a year worldwide for criminal enterprises.

APPENDIX C: TRAGEDY AT A NEW BEDFORD
FISH PROCESSING PLANT

In his narrative, Abel refers to the death of one of his friends, a fellow fish-processing-plant worker. The story to which he is referring is that of Antonio Ajqui. A native of the Quiche region of Guatemala, Ajqui died in a tragic accident at a fish-processing plant in New Bedford, Massachusetts in 1998. At the age of forty, he was crushed to death by a machine that steams and grinds fish into meal, as his nineteen-year-old son, Francisco, watched helplessly.

The two men worked at Atlantic Coast Fisheries, which employed two hundred people at the time of Ajqui's death. On the morning of his death, Ajqui was cleaning inside a ten-by-twenty-foot vat, when the hose he was using caught on the power switch. Ajqui fell into the machine's rotating blades and was killed.

Coworkers report that they were never instructed to "lock out" the machine's power. Safety signs in the factory were written in English, despite the fact that a majority of the company's employees did not speak English as a primary language.

APPENDIX D: TEMPORARY AGRICULTURAL WORK VISAS

The following are excerpts from the U.S. Department of Labor's H-2A (temporary or seasonal agricultural work) guidelines for employers.

H-2A Certification for Temporary or Seasonal Agricultural Work

The H-2A temporary agricultural program establishes a means for agricultural employers who anticipate a shortage of domestic workers to bring nonimmigrant foreign workers to the U.S. to perform agricultural labor or services of a temporary or seasonal nature. Before the U.S. Citizenship and Immigration Services (USCIS) can approve an employer's petition for such workers, the employer must file an application with the Department stating that there are not sufficient workers who are able, willing, qualified, and available, and that the employment of aliens will not adversely affect the wages and working conditions of similarly employed U.S. workers. The statute and Departmental regulations provide for numerous worker protections and employer requirements with respect to wages and working conditions that do not apply to nonagricultural programs. The Department's Wage and Hour Division, Employment Standards Administration (ESA) has responsibility for enforcing provisions of worker contracts.

"Temporary or seasonal nature" means employment performed at certain seasons of the year, usually in relation to the production and/or harvesting of a crop, or for a limited time period of less than one year when an employer can show that the need for the foreign worker(s) is truly temporary.

Qualifying Criteria

The following general categories of individuals or organizations may file an application:

* An agricultural employer who anticipates a shortage of U.S. workers needed to perform agricultural labor or services of a temporary or seasonal nature, may file an application requesting temporary foreign agricultural labor certification.

* An authorized agent, whether an individual (e.g., an attorney) or an entity (e.g., an association), may file an application on behalf of an employer. Associations may file master applications on behalf of their members.

An employer who files an application for temporary foreign labor certification pursuant to H-2A regulations must meet the following specific conditions:

Recruitment: The employer must agree to engage in independent positive recruitment of U.S. workers. This means an active effort, including newspaper and radio advertising in areas of expected labor supply. Such recruitment must be at least equivalent to that conducted by non-H-2A agricultural employers in the same or similar crops and area to secure U.S. workers. This must be an effort independent of and in addition to the efforts of the SWA (State Workforce Agency). In establishing worker qualifications and/or job specifications, the employer must designate only those qualifications and specifications which are essential to carrying out the job and which are normally required by other employers who do not hire foreign workers.

Wages: The wage or rate of pay must be the same for U.S. workers and H-2A workers. The hourly rate must also be at least as high as the applicable Adverse Effect Wage Rate (AEWR), federal or state minimum wage, or the applicable prevailing hourly wage rate, whichever is higher. The AEWR is established every year by the Department of Labor for every state except Alaska.

If a worker will be paid on a piece rate basis, the worker must be paid the prevailing piece as determined by the SWA. If the piece rate does not result in average hourly piece rate earnings during the pay period at least equal to the amount the worker would have earned had the worker been paid at the hourly rate, then the worker's pay must be supplemented to the equivalent hourly level. The piece rate offered must be no less than what is prevailing in the area for the same crop and/or activity.

Housing: The employer must provide free housing to all workers who are not reasonably able to return to their residences the same day. Such housing must be inspected and approved according to appropriate standards. Housing provided by the employer shall meet the full set of DOL (Department of Labor) Occupational Safety and Health Administration (OSHA) standards set forth at 29 CFR 1910.142 or the full set of standards at 654.404-645.417. Rental housing which meets local or state health and safety standards also may be provided.

Meals: The employer must provide either three meals a day to each worker or furnish free and convenient cooking and kitchen facilities for workers to prepare their own meals. If meals are provided, then the employer may charge each worker a certain amount per day for the three meals.

Transportation: The amount of transportation payment shall be no less (and shall not be required to be more) than the most economical and reasonable similar common carrier transportation charges for the distances involved. The employer is responsible for the following different types of transportation of workers: 1. After a worker has completed fifty percent of the work contract period, the employer must reimburse the worker for the cost of transportation and subsistence from the place of recruitment to the place of work if such costs were borne by the worker. 2. The employer must provide free transportation between the employer's housing and the worksite for any worker who is provided housing. 3. Upon completion of the work contract, the employer must pay economic costs of a worker's subsistence and return transportation to the place of recruitment.

Workers' Compensation Insurance: The employer must provide workers' compensation insurance where it is required by state law. Where state law does not require it, the employer must provide equivalent insurance for all workers.

Tools and Supplies: The employer must furnish at no cost to the worker all tools and supplies necessary to carry out the work, unless it is common practice in the area and occupation for the worker to provide certain items.

Three-Fourths Guarantee: The employer must guarantee to offer each worker employment for at least three-fourths of the workdays in the work contract period and any extensions. If the employer affords less employment, then the employer must pay the amount which the worker would have earned had the worker been employed the guaranteed number of days.

Other Conditions: The employer must keep accurate records with respect to a worker's earnings. The worker must be provided with a complete statement of hours worked and related earnings on each payday. The employer must pay the worker at least twice monthly or more frequently if it is the prevailing practice to do so. The employer must provide a copy of a work contract or the job order to each worker.

Violations, Penalties, and Sanctions

The Wage and Hour Division of the Employment Standards Administration (ESA) of the U.S. Department of Labor has a primary role in investigating and enforcing the terms and conditions of employment. ESA is responsible for enforcing the contractual obligations employers have toward employees, and may assess civil money penalties and recover unpaid wages. Administrative proceedings and/or injunctive actions through federal courts may be instituted to compel compliance with an employer's contractual obligations to employees.

The Employment and Training Administration (ETA) enforces other aspects of the laws and regulations. ETA is be responsible for administering sanctions relating to substantial violations of the regulations (denial of certification for up to three years) and less than substantial violations of the regulations (reductions of one-fourth of job opportunities certified).

APPENDIX E: SHORTCOMINGS OF H-2A TEMPORARY VISAS

Despite the existence of the H-2A temporary agricultural worker program, farmers continue to hire undocumented workers in large numbers. The reasons vary: from the expense of providing housing, food, and fair wages to H-2 workers; to sporadic enforcement of labor laws; to the difficulty of filing for H-2 visas. Comments from farmers and agricultural organizations—like those from the Idaho Farm Bureau Federation excerpted below— shed some light on the persistent presence of undocumented workers in the field.

August 10, 2007
Immigration Situation Worsens
By Frank Priestley, President

Two federal agencies announced plans this week to crack down on the hiring of illegal immigrants. With consideration of the current bureaucratic-laden guest worker program (H2-A) coupled with a rapidly approaching harvest season, this news is troubling for Idaho agriculture.

Currently there are 40,000 fewer farm workers on U.S. farms and ranches than there were at this same time last year. In addition, there are 175,000 fewer workers on farms and ranches than there were at this same time five years ago. But it's not because there are fewer jobs. The U.S. agricultural sector produced 15 percent more crops and 17 percent more livestock products during 2006 with five percent less total labor, according to the National Agricultural Statistics Service.

As U.S. farmers continue to call for an adequate workforce, a recent American Farm Bureau economic analysis showed $9 billion of U.S. agricultural production could be lost to foreign competitors who have lower labor and production costs. In a nutshell, that means this problem needs a solution—quickly, or more of the food Americans consume will come from foreign countries. This problem highlights some of the social costs attached to U.S. food production. Consumers need to understand clearly that many of our global competitors enjoy significant competitive advantages in the marketplace. Many of these competitors don't police illegal immigrants, nor do they require a minimum wage, workers compensation programs, face steep insurance costs, require guest worker housing programs and many other regulations unique to the U.S.

Federal authorities announced tough new rules this week requiring employers to background check and fire workers who use false Social Security numbers. In addition, there will be stepped-up raids on workplaces across the country that employ immigrant workers. These announcements could grind Idaho's potato harvest and the shipping of the crop to a halt. Several other sectors of Idaho agriculture, including sugarbeets, dairy, and a variety of other field crops could feel the effects of this federal crackdown. It's tough to predict an outcome, but we know with certainty that harvest season can be a short window. Every day of lost or lowered production brings us closer to cold weather that can ruin crops and the resulting losses could be staggering.

The Idaho Farm Bureau Federation does not advocate the hiring of illegal workers. However, we are also aware of the fact that documenting every worker's status is a daunting task. What's needed is a streamlined federal program that helps farmers, ranchers, and the operators of food packing and processing facilities find a legal workforce. It's a shame that Congress missed an opportunity in June to reform immigration policies. Some states are now taking on that responsibility and some tough new laws have been passed in Arizona and Florida. Immigrant workers play a crucial role in providing safe, reliable, affordable, American-grown food.

Family farmers and ranchers recognize the need for improved border security. We seek a plan that improves security and also allows people who want to enter the country to work, to do so legally. Despite repeated attempts, farmers and ranchers cannot find enough people within the U.S. who are willing or able to take the farm jobs that need to be filled.

June 8, 2007
Comprehensive Immigration Reform Needed
By Frank Priestley, President

American farmers and ranchers face a "Catch 22," when it comes to hiring and verifying the status of their workforce. It is illegal to knowingly hire someone who is not authorized to work, but the employer is limited in what he or she may ask to determine who is authorized.

If an employer requests more or different documents when the originals appear reasonable, the employer could be subject to a Justice Department investigation, or employment discrimination lawsuits. On the other hand, if the employer accepts documents but is later notified by the Social Security Administration that information contained in the documents does not match agency records, then the employer may not be safe from prosecution for knowingly hiring an illegal worker.

What's needed is a workable program to allow for recruitment of temporary agriculture workers from abroad, and provide an opportunity for some current workers to apply for permanent U.S. residency.

Currently, the only alternative to a program that works, is called the H-2a temporary guest worker program. But H-2a is expensive because it requires prospective users to offer free housing and transportation as well as a minimum of the adverse effect wage rate (AEWG), which is an average wage derived from all field and livestock workers in a region. Moreover, the program is excessively bureaucratic, requiring subsequent approval from four different government agencies including Labor, Homeland Security and State, as well as the state government employment agency in the given state. This program has been a magnet for litigation in the past, forcing growers to spend large sums in court or accept the demands of taxpayer funded attorneys. Most year-round livestock operations are not eligible for H2-a, even though labor difficulties are no less of a problem for these than for other livestock operations.

APPENDIX F: IMMIGRATION THROUGH INVESTMENT

Under section 203(b)(5) of the Immigration and Nationality Act (INA), 8 U.S.C. § 1153(b)(5), ten thousand immigrant visas per year are available to qualified individuals seeking permanent resident status on the basis of their engagement in a new commercial enterprise.

Of the 10,000 investor visas (i.e., EB-5 visas) available annually, 5,000 are set aside for those who apply under a pilot program involving a CIS-designated "Regional Center."

A "Regional Center:"

* Focuses on a specific geographic area within the United States; and,
* Seeks to promote economic growth through increased export sales, improved regional productivity, creation of new jobs, and increased domestic capital investment.

"Alien investors" must:

* Demonstrate that a "qualified investment" (see below) is being made in a new commercial enterprise located within an approved Regional Center; and,

* Show, using reasonable methodologies, that 10 or more jobs are actually created either directly or indirectly by the new commercial enterprise through revenues generated from increased exports, improved regional productivity, job creation, or increased domestic capital investment resulting from the pilot program.

Eligibility

Permanent resident status based on EB-5 eligibility is available to investors, either alone or coming with their spouse and unmarried children. Eligible aliens are those who have invested—or are actively in the process of investing—the required amount of capital into a new commercial enterprise that they have established. They must further demonstrate that this investment will benefit the United States economy and create the requisite number of full-time jobs for qualified persons within the United States.

In general, "eligible individuals" include those

1. Who establish a new commercial enterprise by:

* creating an original business;
* purchasing an existing business and simultaneously or subsequently restructuring or reorganizing the business such that a new commercial enterprise results; or
* expanding an existing business by 140 percent of the pre-investment number of jobs or net worth, or retaining all existing jobs in a troubled business that has lost 20 percent of its net worth over the past 12 to 24 months; and

2. Who have invested—or who are actively in the process of investing—in a new commercial enterprise:

* at least $1,000,000, or
* at least $500,000 where the investment is being made in a "targeted employment area," which is an area that has experienced unemployment of at least 150 percent of the national average rate or a rural area as designated by OMB; and

3. Whose engagement in a new commercial enterprise will benefit the United States economy and:

* create full-time employment for not fewer than 10 qualified individuals; or
* maintain the number of existing employees at no less than the pre-investment level for a period of at least two years, where the capital investment is being made in a "troubled business," which is a business that has been in existence for at least two years and that has lost 20 percent of its net worth over the past 12 to 24 months.

APPENDIX G: SPECIAL REGISTRATION

Now replaced by the Department of Homeland Security's US-VISIT Enrollment, Immigration and Customs Enforcement's National Security Entry-Exit Registration System— Special Registration—was implemented on September 11, 2002 to track the thirty-five million nonimmigrant visitors in the United States. Male citizens of twenty-five countries were required to report to a designated INS facility to be photographed, fingerprinted, and interviewed. The twenty-five countries designated—divided into four "call-in groups"— are as follows:

Call-in group 1:
Iran, Iraq, Libya, Sudan, or Syria

Call-in group 2:
Afghanistan, Algeria, Bahrain, Eritrea, Lebanon, Morocco, North Korea, Oman, Qatar, Somalia, Tunisia, United Arab Emirates, or Yemen

Call-in group 3:
Pakistan or Saudi Arabia

Call-in group 4:
Bangladesh, Egypt, Indonesia, Jordan, or Kuwait

Below is an extension notice and instructions for citizens in call-in group 1.

REOPENING OF REGISTRATION PERIOD
FOR CERTAIN NONIMMIGRANTS
(January 27–February 7, 2003)
(Call-In Group 1 Grace Period, Federal Register Notice–January 16, 2003)

IF YOU ARE A CITIZEN OR NATIONAL OF IRAN, IRAQ, LIBYA, SUDAN, OR SYRIA

- And you were last admitted to the United States as a nonimmigrant on or before September 10, 2002; and
- If you are a male, born on or before November 15, 1986; and
- If you did not apply for asylum on or before November 6, 2002, or if you are not otherwise exempt as described in the attached questions and answers; and
- If you remained in the United States at least until December 16, 2002: and
- You were required to register with INS between November 15, 2002 and December 16, 2002 and you did not register during that time frame.

WHAT YOU NEED TO DO

1. You must come to a designated INS office to be registered (photographed, fingerprinted, and interviewed under oath) between January 27 and February 7, 2003.

2. If you remain in the United States for more than 1 additional year, you must report back to a designated INS office within 10 days of the anniversary of the date on which you first registered. For example, if you were registered November 20, 2002, you would report back between November 10 and November 30, 2003.

3. If you change your address, employment, or educational institution, you must notify INS in writing within 10 days of the change, using Form AR-11 SR.

4. If you leave the United States, you must appear in person before an INS inspecting officer at one of the designated ports of departure and leave the United States from that port on the same day.

IT IS VITAL THAT YOU COMPLY

If you do not follow these procedures, you may be considered to be out of status and deportable. You may be subject to arrest, detention, fines and/or removal from the United States. Any future application for an immigration benefit from the United States may be adversely impacted. If you do not properly exit through a designated port, any future attempts to reenter the United States may be impacted. Decisions will be made on an individual basis, depending on the circumstances of each case.

APPENDIX H: OPERATION RETURN TO SENDER

The following is a press release issued by Immigration and Customs Enforcement (ICE) Public Affairs office on June 6, 2006, approximately ten days after the start of Operation Return to Sender.

ICE Apprehends More Than 2,100 Criminal Aliens, Gang Members, Fugitives and Other Immigration Violators in Nationwide Interior Enforcement Operation

Houston, Texas—Julie L. Myers, Assistant Secretary for U.S. Immigration and Customs Enforcement (ICE), today announced that ICE agents and officers have apprehended approximately 2,179 criminal aliens, illegal alien gang members, fugitive aliens, and other immigration status violators as part of a nationwide interior immigration enforcement operation that began last month.

Dubbed "Operation Return to Sender," the initiative began on May 26, 2006 and concluded yesterday. Virtually every field office in the nation from ICE's Office of Investigations and ICE's Office of Detention and Removal Operations carried out the enforcement operation in conjunction with numerous state and local law enforcement agencies.

Among the roughly 2,179 individuals arrested in the operation, roughly half had criminal records for crimes that ranged from sexual assault of a minor, to assault with a deadly weapon, to abduction. For example, approximately 146 of those arrested had convictions for sexual offenses involving minors. In addition, roughly 367 of the arrested aliens were members or associates of violent street gangs, including Mara Salvatrucha (MS-13). Finally, roughly 640 of those arrested were fugitive aliens who had been issued final orders of removal by an Immigration judge but failed to comply.

ICE officers arrested the majority of these individuals on administrative immigration violations and have placed them into deportation proceedings. Roughly 829 of those apprehended on administrative violations have already been repatriated to their home countries. ICE agents also apprehended 121 individuals on criminal charges that range from felony re-entry after deportation, to illegal alien in possession of a firearm. The latter individuals are being processed in federal criminal courts.

"Operation Return to Sender is another example of a new and tough interior enforcement strategy that seeks to catch and deport criminal aliens, increase worksite enforcement, and crack down hard on the criminal infrastructure that perpetuates illegal immigration," said Homeland Security Secretary Michael Chertoff. "The fugitives captured in this operation threatened public safety in hundreds of neighborhoods and communities around the country. This department has no tolerance for their criminal behavior and we are using every authority at our disposal to bring focus to fugitive operations and rid communities of this criminality."

ICE Assistant Secretary Myers said, "America's welcome does not extend to immigrants who come here to commit crimes. ICE will leave no stone unturned in hunting down and deporting aliens who victimize our communities. Interior enforcement initiatives like Operation Return to Sender are a critical and necessary complement to our nation's border security measures."

Some of those arrested in Operation Return to Sender included:

* Franklin Ademir Rodriguez, a 25-year-old Salvadoran national and member of the street gang Mara Salvatrucha (MS-13). Rodriguez, also known as "Hollywood," boasts a lengthy criminal history that includes an assault and battery conviction for helping other MS-13 gang members permanently paralyze a 13-year-old boy by stabbing him in the spine with a sharpened stake. The victim is now confined to a wheelchair for life. ICE officers arrested Rodriguez earlier this month at his place of employment at Budget Rental Car at Boston Logan Airport after he failed to appear for his removal hearing.

* Jose Garcia Rios, a Mexican national whose criminal history extends from 1985 to present. Garcia has been arrested roughly 13 times, has been removed from the country several times, and has past convictions for crimes ranging from aggravated robbery to drug dealing, drug possession, terroristic threats, and evading arrest.

* Wilber Kuk, a 24-year-old Mexican national and member of the 18th Street gang in Washington, D.C. who has convictions for abduction, malicious wounding, robbery and use of a firearm.

* Samuel Gil Martinez, a 24-year-old Salvadoran national and member of the MS-13 gang. Martinez has twice been convicted in Boston of assault and battery with a dangerous weapon. In one case, he beat an individual with a baseball bat. In another, he attacked an individual at a bus stop with a "Club" automobile lock. Martinez was arrested with other MS-13 members during the commission of these crimes.

* Angel Lira-Alvarez, a 26-year-old Mexican national and member of "East Side Homeboys," a major street gang in Dallas, Texas. Lira has previous convictions for manufacture and delivery of a controlled substance, theft, and burglary. He had previously been deported from the

country, but re-entered the United States and was arrested again for marijuana possession. He was the subject of a local arrest warrant for parole violations when ICE arrested him.

Those arrested in the operation came from nations around the globe, including Angola, Bangladesh, Brazil, Cape Verde, China, Colombia, Dominican Republic, Ecuador, El Salvador, Egypt, Gambia, Georgia, Ghana, Guatemala, Honduras, Indonesia, Iraq, Italy, Ivory Coast, Jamaica, Kenya, Liberia, Libya, Mexico, Nicaragua, Nigeria, Pakistan, Peru, Poland, Portugal, Senegal, Thailand, Uganda, United Kingdom, and Uzbekistan.

The arrests are the latest enforcement actions under the interior immigration enforcement strategy that was announced on April 20, 2006 by Homeland Security Secretary Chertoff and Assistant Secretary Myers. A critical element of this interior enforcement strategy is to identify and remove criminal aliens, fugitives, and other immigration violators from the United States.

The interior enforcement strategy is part of the Secure Border Initiative (SBI), which is the Department of Homeland Security's comprehensive, multi-year plan to secure America's borders and reduce illegal migration. SBI's border security efforts are focused on gaining operational control of the nation's borders through additional personnel and technology, while re-engineering the detention and removal system to ensure that illegal aliens are removed from the country quickly.

The interior enforcement strategy complements the Department's border security efforts by expanding existing efforts to target immigration violators inside this country, employers of illegal aliens, as well as the many criminal networks that support these activities. The primary objectives are to reverse the tolerance of illegal employment and illegal immigration in the United States.

APPENDIX I: FALLOUT OF
OPERATION RETURN TO SENDER

Seven-year-old Kebin Reyes was one of the more than twenty-three thousand people caught in the fallout of Operation Return to Sender, an Immigration and Customs Enforcement initiative aimed at arresting and deporting undocumented workers around the country. Below are excerpts from a complaint filed by the attorneys from the American Civil Liberties Union Foundation of Northern California; the Lawyers' Committee for Civil Rights; and Cohlentz, Patch, Duffy, and Bass LLP on behalf of Reyes against the San Francisco ICE Field Office.

FACTS GIVING RISE TO THE CLAIMS

8. On March 6, 2007, Defendants seized Kebin, a United States citizen, and took him into their custody, without lawful cause and without a warrant for his arrest, at his residence in San Rafael, California.

9. Defendants arrived at Kebin's residence in the early morning hours of March 6, 2007. Armed and wearing clothes bearing the word "police," Defendants entered the residence and demanded the immigration papers and passports of Kebin and his father. Upon information and belief, Defendants did not have lawful authorization or a valid warrant for entering the home. Kebin's father provided Defendants with Kebin's U.S. passport, identifying Kebin as a United States citizen. Kebin's father truthfully answered the questions asked of him.

10. Defendants informed Kebin's father that they were taking him into custody. Despite being placed on notice that Kebin is a United States citizen, Defendants instructed his father to waken Kebin because they were going to seize him as well. Kebin's father requested repeatedly that Defendants permit him to make a phone call to a family member living nearby who could care for Kebin so that he would not be taken into forced custody. But Defendants refused to permit Kebin's father to make a phone call. Defendants seized Kebin and his father. Defendants took Kebin and his father to an ICE office in San Francisco and held them there against their will.

11. At the ICE office, Kebin's father requested to make a phone call to arrange for Kebin's care, but Defendants did not allow him to make a phone call. Defendants told Kebin that he would only need to stay at the ICE office for an hour or two. Instead, they held him in a locked room all day against his will. Kebin thought he was in jail. Defendants refused to give Kebin any food, other than bread and water. Kebin was hungry and crying. He did not know when he would be free to leave.

12. That afternoon, a family member and family friend who had learned about the incident from others in the neighborhood, came to the ICE office to seek Kebin's release and to bring Kebin home. Defendants forced Kebin to remain in custody, without cause, for several more hours, until evening, before they released him.

FIRST CLAIM FOR RELIEF

16. The Fourth Amendment to the United States Constitution provides that each person has the right to be secure in his or her person, houses, papers, and effects, against unreasonable searches and seizures.

17. By committing the above-described acts, Defendants violated Plaintiff's rights under the Fourth Amendment to the United States Constitution.

18. The conduct of Defendants violated clearly established constitutional or other rights of which Defendants knew, or of which a reasonable public official should have known. Defendants exceeded their authority to make detentions, seizures and arrests, including the limitations set forth in Title 8 United States Code Section 1357.

19. Plaintiff has no effective administrative mechanism or other remedy at law by which to seek the proper measure of damages for these constitutional wrongs.

APPENDIX J: TREATMENT OF IMMIGRANT
DETAINEES WITH HIV/AIDS

In December 2007, Human Rights Watch released Chronic Indifference, *a report on the inadequacy of HIV/AIDS services for detained immigrants. Victoria Arellano, whose story is told in this book by her mother Olga, is featured in the excerpts below.*

I. Executive Summary

Victoria's condition steadily worsened during the month of July, and she began to vomit blood, and blood appeared in her urine. The detainees in Pod 3 at San Pedro became increasingly concerned for her welfare as she became too weak to sit up in her bunk. Victoria was seen in the medical clinic, but she was told only to take Tylenol and drink large amounts of water... she died a week later.

—excerpt from a cellmate's account of the death in immigration detention of Victoria Arellano, a 23-year-old transgender detainee with HIV/AIDS

The death of Victoria Arellano in federal immigration custody is an extreme, but not surprising, example of the suffering experienced by immigration detainees with HIV/AIDS. The US Department of Homeland Security (DHS) fails to collect basic information to monitor immigrant detainees with HIV/AIDS, has sub-standard policies and procedures for ensuring appropriate HIV/AIDS care and services, and inadequately supervises the care that is provided. The consequence of this willful indifference is poor care, untreated infection, increased risk of resistance to HIV medications, and even death.

Human Rights Watch's investigation of HIV/AIDS care for detained immigrants, which included interviews with current and former detainees, DHS and detention facility officials, and an independent medical review of treatment provided, found that ICE-supervised facilities:

- Failed to deliver complete anti-retroviral regimens in a consistent manner. This practice creates a risk of drug resistance that endangers the health of the detainee and can impact public health.

- Failed to conduct the necessary monitoring of detainees' clinical condition, including CD4 and viral load testing as well as resistance testing. These tests are fundamental to effective treatment of HIV and AIDS.

- Failed to prescribe prophylactic medications when medically indicated to prevent opportunistic infections.

- Failed to ensure continuity of care as detainees are transferred between facilities, including failure to ensure access to necessary specialty care.

- Failed to ensure confidentiality of medical care, exposing detainees to discrimination and harassment.

With inadequate monitoring and unenforceable standards, it is not surprising that Human Rights Watch found that medical care for HIV positive detainees in ICE custody was delayed, interrupted, and inconsistent to an extent that endangered the health and lives of the detainees.

DHS fails to collect basic information concerning HIV/AIDS cases in the hundreds of detention facilities contracting with Immigration and Customs Enforcement (ICE) to incarcerate immigrants. Human Rights Watch requested, through the Freedom of Information Act, data as fundamental as the number of immigration detainees with HIV/AIDS—only to discover that this information is "not tracked." Failure to collect this vital information, as well as information about the treatment and services provided to detainees with HIV/AIDS, prevents DHS from improving its programs to meet the needs of this vulnerable population.

The DHS policies and procedures for HIV/AIDS should describe appropriate treatment protocols for people living with HIV/AIDS to be followed in its own facilities as well as those it utilizes to provide care. DHS policies and procedures, however, are conflicting, confusing, and incomplete, and fail to conform to national and international guidelines for HIV/AIDS care in correctional settings. Further, DHS has failed to adopt the detention standards as formal administrative regulations, making the standards largely unenforceable. Although ICE "outsources" much of its immigration detention to local jails and facilities across the United States, its responsibility for adequate standards of care may not be delegated or evaded by contracting with third parties.

The current ICE inspection system is limited to one brief visit per year to each jail or detention center. These visits fail to provide the oversight necessary to identify and resolve the deficiencies in medical care. The Government Accountability Office (GAO) recently found serious flaws in ICE's mechanisms for ensuring that detainee complaints, including those pertaining to medical care, are properly monitored and resolved. Further, ICE has no policies designed to protect HIV-positive detainees from harassment and discrimination by staff or other prisoners.

Without improved standards for medical care, strengthened external and internal oversight, and meaningful accountability to the public, immigrant detainees with HIV/AIDS will continue to needlessly suffer, and in some cases, die in US immigration detention.

II. Recommendations

To the U.S. Department of Homeland Security

- Protect vulnerable populations from abuse and harassment by revising the Detention Standards to include a non-discrimination policy with education, training, and enforcement provisions for the protection of lesbian, gay, bisexual, and transgender detainees and detainees with HIV/AIDS.

- Promote alternatives to detention for immigrants with HIV/AIDS and other chronic medical conditions. Ensure implementation of existing policies permitting prosecutorial discretion in such cases.

To the Division of Immigration Health Services

- Ensure the adequacy of care for detainees by gathering information from all detention facilities holding immigrants about the number of detainees with HIV/AIDS and the treatment and services provided to them. This information should inform the development of evidence-based policies and programs designed to address the needs of this vulnerable population.

- Ensure the adequacy of care for detainees by revising the HIV/AIDS provisions of the Medical Care Detention Standard to ensure access to voluntary testing and counseling. These provisions should ensure informed consent, confidentiality, and counseling and should conform to national and international recommended standards for HIV/AIDS testing in a correctional setting.

To Immigration and Customs Enforcement

- Incorporate and require compliance with Medical Care Detention Standards (as revised above) as an express condition of contracts with private, local, or county facilities. Provide training to each facility designed to ensure compliance with the standards.

- Improve the current system for tracking complaints from detainees. Ensure that complaints relating to medical care can be monitored and serious or systematic violations of the medical care standards can be identified and redressed. Ensure that detainees who complain are protected from retaliation. Ensure that all immigrants detained by ICE receive notification of complaint procedures in their native languages.

- Ensure that all detainees receive medical services free of charge.

To the U.S. Government Accountability Office

- Increase executive and legislative branch oversight of conditions of detention for immigrants by ensuring that ICE has taken appropriate action in response to the recommendations in its recent report.

To the U.S. Congress

- Ensure that all immigrants detained in federal custody are subject to comparable standards of medical care. These standards should comply with national and international correctional health care standards by requiring medical care equivalent to that afforded in the community.

- Establish a monitoring body independent of the Department of Homeland Security with the responsibility and the expertise to ensure that each facility housing immigration detainees complies with national and international correctional health care standards by providing medical care equivalent to that afforded in the community.

Victoria Arellano: Death in Detention

Victoria[1] Arellano, a 23-year-old transgendered woman from Mexico with HIV/AIDS, died in ICE custody on July 20, 2007. She had been detained at the San Pedro Service Processing Center (SPSPC) for 8 weeks. According to her cellmates,[2] her health began to deteriorate when medical staff refused to continue her regular prescriptions.

Victoria's condition steadily worsened during the month of July, and she began to vomit blood, and blood appeared in her urine. The detainees in Pod 3 at San Pedro became increasingly concerned for her welfare as she became too weak to sit up in her bunk. Victoria was seen in the medical clinic, but she was told only to take Tylenol and drink large amounts of water.

On the night of July 12, 2007, her condition appeared critical to her cellmates, who were cleaning her and disposing of her bodily fluids. The "leader" of Pod 3 asked for an ICE representative to come to the pod. An ICE Captain responded to this request. He walked over to Victoria's bunk, placed his shoe on her pillow, and asked rudely, "What's wrong with you?" The detainees were shocked. "They were treating her like a dog."

The detainees began chanting "Hospital! Hospital!" A nurse came down and said "Oh it's Victoria! There's nothing we can do. She just needs Tylenol and water." Later that night, Victoria was taken to the hospital, but returned the next day. She was very weak and told her cellmates that the medical and security staff had put her in a holding cell and taunted her. Victoria told her cellmates that "it was a nightmare." The following morning she was taken to the hospital again, where she died a week later of meningitis, a condition often associated with advanced AIDS.

On August 9, 2007, an article about Victoria's death appeared in the *Los Angeles Daily Journal*. Three of Victoria's former cellmates were quoted by name in the article. Human Rights Watch attempted to interview these and other of Victoria's former cellmates at the SPSPC, only to find that more than twenty of Victoria's cellmates from Pod 3 had been transferred to other ICE facilities throughout the United States. Human Rights Watch and the ACLU of Southern California demanded that ICE conduct a prompt, comprehensive, and transparent investigation of Victoria's death, as well as the sudden transfer of more than 20 of her former cellmates from Pod 3. As of the date of publication of this report, ICE has failed to respond to Human Rights Watch's demand for a formal investigation.

The United States is a party to the Convention Against Torture (CAT), which requires that detainees must not be subjected to any form of torture or cruel, inhuman, or degrading treatment while in detention.[3] If true, the neglect of Victoria's suffering, the failure to provide medical care, and her subjection to taunting, harassment, and insults may constitute violations of the Torture Convention.

[1] Victoria Arellano's birth name was Victor.

[2] The information in this account is based upon testimony provided to Human Rights Watch and the ACLU of Southern California by Victoria Arellano's cellmates in July and August 2007.

[3] Convention Against Torture and Other Cruel Inhuman or Degrading Treatment or Punishment (CAT), adopted December 10, 1984, G.A. Res. 39/46, annex, 39 UN GAOR Supp. (no. 51) at 197, UN Doc. A/39/51 (1984) entered into force June 26, 1987, ratified by the U.S. on October 14, 1994, article 16 (1).

This full text of this report can be found on the Human Rights Watch website:
http://hrw.org/reports/2007/us1207/

GLOSSARY

alien—Any person not a citizen or national of the United States.

asylum—Asylum allows individuals who are in the United States to remain here, provided that they meet the definition of a refugee and are not barred from either applying for or being granted asylum. Each year, thousands of people who have been persecuted or fear they will be persecuted on account of their race, religion, nationality, membership in a particular social group, or political opinion apply for asylum. Those found eligible are permitted to remain in the United States. Unlike the U.S. Refugee Program, which provides protection to refugees by bringing them to the United States for resettlement, the U.S. Asylum Program provides protection to qualified refugees who are already in the United States, or are seeking entry into the United States at a port of entry. Asylum-seekers may apply for asylum in the United States regardless of their countries of origin. There are no quotas on the number of individuals who may be granted asylum each year (with the exception of individuals whose claims are based solely on persecution for resistance to coercive population control measures).

bolillo—Spanish slang for "white person."

cancellation of removal—A discretionary benefit adjusting an immigrant's status from that of deportable alien to one lawfully admitted for permanent residence. Application for cancellation of removal is made during the course of a hearing before an immigration judge. Created by the Illegal Immigration Reform and Immigrant Responsibility Act of 1996, cancellation of removal replaced the previous action, suspension of deportation, and introduced a more difficult standard of eligibility.

Day Without an Immigrant—A nationwide demonstration in which hundreds of thousands of people walked off from jobs and schools to advocate immigrants' rights. The demonstration took place on May 1, 2006.

deportation—The formal removal of an alien from the United States when the alien has been found removable for violating immigration laws. Deportation is ordered by an immigration judge. Now called "removal," this function is managed by U.S. Immigration and Customs Enforcement.

detention—Immigration and Customs Enforcement holds undocumented immigrants it alleges are deportable in hundreds of federal and local jails spread across various U.S. states and territories. Federal officials prefer to call these facilities detention centers. ICE also holds in detention a large number of those awaiting a decision as to whether they are deportable.

DREAM Act—Development, Relief, and Education for Alien Minors Act. A pending congressional bill that would provide certain undocumented students who wish to attend college with the opportunity to obtain permanent residency. The legislation has been introduced in Congress several times since 2003.

EWI(s)—Entry Without Inspection. A term referring to immigrants who cross into the U.S. by avoiding official scrutiny.

Fujian—A province in China from which a large number of Chinese immigrants originate.

green card—Lawful permanent residence card. Establishes official immigration status in the United States.

Golden Triangle—A nickname given to the three Kansas cities of Dodge City, Liberal, and Garden City, which contain the vast majority of the beef processing plants in the state.

H-2A—A classification of visa for temporary foreign agricultural workers. H-2A visas allow farmers to seek out undocumented workers when no American workers are available and a shortage of labor is expected. Employers must provide H-2 workers with housing, transportation, and fair wages. See Appendix E for more information.

Heat Illness Prevention Bill—A California health code order requiring farmers to provide adequate water, access to shade, and employee training to protect their workers from serious medical conditions resulting from heat exposure.

Hispanic—Generally refers to people from Spanish-speaking households, or with Spanish heritage.

Immigration and Customs Enforcement (ICE)—Created in March 2003, Immigration and Customs Enforcement (ICE) is the largest investigative branch of the Department of Homeland Security. The agency was created after 9/11 by combining the law enforcement arms of the former Immigration and Naturalization Service (INS) and the former U.S. Customs Service. ICE is charged with enforcing deportation orders, investigating employers of illegal workers, targeting smugglers of counterfeit products, and various counterterrorism responsibilties.

Immigration and Naturalization Service (INS)—Formerly the organization responsible for immigration and naturalization services. In 2003, the INS was split into ICE and USCIS.

Immigration Reform and Control Act of 1986—Signed into law by President Ronald Reagan, the IRCA made it illegal to knowingly hire undocumented workers, but also granted amnesty to certain illegal immigrants who had entered the U.S. prior to January 1, 1982.

immigration through investment—A provision of U.S. immigration law allowing immigrants who have sufficient assets invested in an American business and employ a set number of American citizens to apply for permanent residency.

Latino—The U.S. Census Bureau defines Latino—as well as Hispanic—as "a person of Cuban, Mexican, Puerto Rican, South or Central American, or other Spanish culture or origin regardless of race." The term is controversial as it encompasses a large number of ethnicities, and is often misused interchangeably with the term Hispanic.

la uva—Spanish name for the grape harvest.

mica—Spanish for "green card."

Minutemen—Members of one of two civilian-run operations intent on preventing unauthorized entry into the United States. Their activities include the patrolling of the U.S.-Mexico border and reporting would-be crossers.

mojado—Spanish for "wetback." A derogatory term for Latino immigrants, referring to people who cross through the Rio Grande into the U.S.

naturalization—The conferring of citizenship upon a foreign national.

Norteños—Traditional rivals of the *Sureños,* Norteños are a primarily Mexican-American gang originating in Northern California.

one-child policy—A Chinese government policy aimed at controlling population by limiting the number of children families are allowed to have.

Operation Return to Sender—An series of raids conducted by Immigration and Customs Enforcement on suspected employers of undocumented workers. ICE enacted the initiative on May 26, 2006, and it was carried out by almost every ICE field office in the U.S. By some estimates, the operation netted over 23,000 people, many of whom have been deported or are awaiting deportation in detention facilities.

OSHA—Occupational Safety and Health Administration. A division of the U.S. Department of Labor responsible for ensuring that proper safety regulations are upheld in American work environments.

OTM—Other than Mexican. A term used by the U.S. Border Patrol to designate immigrants of non-Mexican provenance.

permanent resident—Any person not a citizen of the United States who is residing in the U.S. under legally recognized and lawfully recorded permanent residence as an immigrant.

peso—The currency of Mexico.

poyero—Spanish slang for a human smuggler.

raitero—A driver responsible for transporting day laborers.

rand—The currency of South Africa.

refugee—1. Any person who is outside any country of their nationality and who is unable or unwilling to return to, and is unable or unwilling to avail himself or herself of the protection of, that country because of persecution or a well-founded fear of persecution on account of race, religion, nationality, membership in a particular social group, or political opinion, or; 2. in such circumstances as the President after appropriate consultation may specify, any person who is within the country of such person's nationality who is persecuted or who has a well-founded fear of persecution. The term "refugee" does not include any person who ordered, incited, assisted, or otherwise participated in the persecution of any person on account of race, religion, nationality, membership in a particular social group, or political opinion. A person who has been forced to abort a pregnancy or to undergo involuntary sterilization, or who has been persecuted for failure or refusal to undergo such a procedure or for other resistance to a coercive population control program, shall be deemed to have been persecuted on account of political opinion. And a person who has a well-founded fear that he or she will be forced to undergo such a procedure or subject shall be deemed to have a well-founded fear of persecution on account of political opinion.

RMB—Renminbi. The currency of the People's Republic of China.

SAVAK—*Sazemane Ettela at va Amniat-e Keshvar.* Formerly the secret police of the Shah's regime in Iran.

snakehead—Human smugglers, specifically those operating in China.

Special Registration—An initiative enacted by the U.S. Department of Justice following 9/11 requiring male immigrants from twenty-five countries to report to a designated INS center to be fingerprinted, photographed, and interviewed. See Appendix G for more information.

Sureños—A primarily Mexican-American gang originating in Southern California. See *Norteños.*

temporary protected status (TPS)—The Secretary of Homeland Security may designate nationals of a foreign state to be eligible for TPS with a finding that conditions in that country pose a danger to personal safety due to ongoing armed conflict or an environmental disaster. Grants of TPS are initially made for periods of six to eighteen months and may be extended depending on the situation. Removal proceedings are suspended against aliens while they are in Temporary Protected Status.

United States Citizenship and Immigration Services (USCIS)—Comprises the service and benefit functions of the former Immigration and Naturalization Service (INS). USCIS is responsible for the administration of immigration and naturalization adjudication functions and establishing immigration services policies and priorities. These functions include adjudication of immigrant visa petitions, naturalization petitions, asylum and refugee applications, adjudications performed at the service centers, and all other adjudications performed by the INS.

Violence Against Women Act (VAWA)—A section of the Violent Crime Control and Law Enforcement Act of 1994. VAWA includes numerous provisions pertaining to federal penalties for sex crimes and prosecution of violent crime against women. It also modifies federal immigration law to allow immigrant victims of domestic violence—at the hands of a U.S. citizen or permanent resident—to petition for relief in the form of permanent residency.

visa—A U.S. visa allows the bearer to apply for entry to the U.S. in a certain classification. A visa does not grant the bearer the right to enter the United States. The Department of State is responsible for visa adjudication at U.S. Embassies and Consulates outside of the U.S. The Department of Homeland Security, Bureau of Customs and Border Protection immigration inspectors determine admission into, length of stay, and conditions of stay in the U.S. at a port of entry. There are two categories of U.S. visas: immigrant and nonimmigrant. Immigrant visas are for people who intend to live permanently in the U.S. Nonimmigrant visas are for people with permanent residence outside the U.S., but who wish to be in the U.S. on a temporary basis—for tourism, medical treatment, business, temporary work, or study. Nonimmigrant visas are further broken down into categories based on reasons for traveling to the U.S. (ie. temporary visit for pleasure, temporary work, religious work, study, etc.)

About THE EDITORS

LUIS ALBERTO URREA was born in Tijuana, Mexico and is a member of the Latino Literature Hall of Fame. He is the author of numerous books, including *The Hummingbird's Daughter* and *The Devil's Highway*, a finalist for the Pulitzer Prize. His latest novel is *Into the Beautiful North*. Urrea is a professor at The University of Illinois–Chicago.

PETER ORNER is the author of two novels, *The Second Coming of Mavala Shikongo* and *Love and Shame and Love*, as well as two collections of stories, *Esther Stories* and *Last Car Over the Sagamore Bridge*. For the Voice of Witness series, Orner also co-edited *Hope Deferred: Narratives of Zimbabwean Lives* with Annie Holmes. He is currently at work, with Evan Lyon, on a new Voice of Witness book set in Port-au-Prince, Haiti. Orner has been awarded a Guggenheim Fellowship and holds a law degree from Northeastern University. He is currently a Professor of Creative Writing at San Francisco State University. He lives in Bolinas, California.

En las Sombras de Estados Unidos is the Spanish language edition of *Underground America*, edited by Sandra Hernandez and Peter Orner. SANDRA HERNANDEZ is a Los Angeles–based journalist who writes about immigration and criminal justice for the *Daily Journal*. Her work has appeared in the *Los Angeles Times*, *Miami Herald*, *Salon.com*, and on *National Public Radio*. She is a graduate of Columbia University's Graduate School of Journalism.

ACKNOWLEDGMENTS

A great many of the individuals we would like to thank have to remain anonymous. We are extremely grateful for your assistance. These are some of the people we can name and we appreciate their support:

Chris Abani, Sagal Abshir, Ellen Andes, Eugene Andes, Maxine Chernoff, Cindy Clark, Matt Donovan, Dennis Donohue, Michaela Freeman, Jim Freeman, "Gus," Eric Heiman, Tim Hoyt, Katsuhiro Iwashita, Ann Kalayil, Junse Kim, Ellen Levine, Jon Lezting, Kari Lydersen, Maria Marroquin, Eric Martin, Eric Orner, Steve Parks, Sarah Casman Perkins, Ashwin Philips, Dan Pierce, Rhoda Pierce, Johanna Povirk-Znoy, Chaz Reetz-Laiolo, Dan Schfrind, Paul Sherwin, Robin B. Simpson, Tim Soufiane, Robin Sukhadia, Miguel Trelles, Luis Alberto Urrea, Lori Waselchuk, Melinda Wiggins, and San Francisco State University.

The VOICE OF WITNESS SERIES

The Voice of Witness book series, published by Verso Books, empowers those most closely affected by contemporary social injustice. Using oral history as a foundation, the series depicts human rights crises in the United States and around the world. The other books in the series are:

SURVIVING JUSTICE
America's Wrongfully Convicted and Exonerated
Edited by Lola Vollen and Dave Eggers
Foreword by Scott Turow

These oral histories prove that the problem of wrongful conviction is far-reaching and very real. Through a series of all-too-common circumstances—eyewitness misidentification, inept defense lawyers, coercive interrogation—the lives of these men and women of all different backgrounds were irreversibly disrupted. In *Surviving Justice*, thirteen exonerees describe their experiences—the events that led to their convictions, their years in prison, and the process of adjusting to their new lives outside.

VOICES FROM THE STORM
The People of New Orleans on Hurricane Katrina and Its Aftermath
Edited by Chris Ying and Lola Vollen

Voices from the Storm is a chronological account of the worst natural disaster in modern American history. Thirteen New Orleanians describe the days leading up to Hurricane Katrina, the storm itself, and the harrowing confusion of the days and months afterward. Their stories weave and intersect, ultimately creating an eye-opening portrait of courage in the face of terror, and of hope amid nearly complete devastation.

OUT OF EXILE
The Abducted and Displaced People of Sudan
Edited by Craig Walzer
Additional interviews and an introduction by
Dave Eggers and Valentino Achak Deng

Millions of people have fled from conflicts and persecution in all parts of Sudan, and many thousands more have been enslaved as human spoils of war. In *Out of Exile*, refugees and abductees recount their escapes from the wars in Darfur and South Sudan, from political and religious persecution, and from abduction by militias. They tell of life before the war, and of the hope that they might someday find peace again.

HOPE DEFERRED
Narratives of Zimbabwean Lives
Edited by Peter Orner and Annie Holmes
Foreword by Brian Chikwava

The sixth volume in the Voice of Witness series presents the narratives of Zimbabweans whose lives have been affected by the country's political, economic, and human rights crises. This book asks the question: How did a country with so much promise—a stellar education system, a growing middle class of professionals, a sophisticated economic infrastructure, a liberal constitution, and an independent judiciary—go so wrong?

NOWHERE TO BE HOME
Narratives from Survivors of Burma's Military Regime
Edited by Maggie Lemere and Zoë West
Foreword by Mary Robinson

Decades of military oppression in Burma have led to the systematic destruction of thousands of ethnic-minority villages, a standing army with one of the world's highest numbers of child soldiers, and the displacement of millions of people. *Nowhere to Be Home* is an eye-opening collection of oral histories exposing the realities of life under military rule. In their own words, men and women from Burma describe their lives in the country that Human Rights Watch has called "the textbook example of a police state."

PATRIOT ACTS
Narratives of Post-9/11 Injustice
Compiled and edited by Alia Malek
Foreword by Karen Korematsu

Patriot Acts tells the stories of men and women who have been needlessly swept up in the War on Terror. In their own words, narrators recount personal experiences of the post-9/11 backlash that has deeply altered their lives and communities. *Patriot Acts* illuminates these experiences in a compelling collection of eighteen oral histories from men and women who have found themselves subject to a wide range of human and civil rights abuses—from rendition and torture, to workplace discrimination, bullying, FBI surveillance, and harassment.

INSIDE THIS PLACE, NOT OF IT
Narratives from Women's Prisons
Compiled and edited by Ayelet Waldman and Robin Levi
Foreword by Michelle Alexander

Inside This Place, Not of It reveals some of the most egregious human rights violations within women's prisons in the United States. In their own words, the thirteen narrators in this book recount their lives leading up to incarceration and their experiences inside—ranging from forced sterilization and shackling during childbirth, to physical and sexual abuse by prison staff. Together, their testimonies illustrate the harrowing struggles for survival that women in prison must endure.

THROWING STONES AT THE MOON
Narratives of Colombians Displaced by Violence
Compiled and edited by Sibylla Brodzinsky and Max Schoening
Foreword by Íngrid Betancourt

For nearly five decades, Colombia has been embroiled in internal armed conflict among guerrilla groups, paramilitary militias, and the country's own military. Civilians in Colombia face a range of abuses from all sides, including killings, disappearances, and rape—and more than four million have been forced to flee their homes. The oral histories in *Throwing Stones at the Moon* describe the most widespread of Colombia's human rights crises: forced displacement.

REFUGEE HOTEL
Compiled and edited by Juliet Linderman and Gabriele Stabile

Refugee Hotel is a groundbreaking collection of photography and interviews that documents the arrival of refugees in the United States. Evocative images are coupled with moving testimonies from people describing their first days in the U.S., the lives they've left behind, and the new communities they've since created.

HIGH RISE STORIES
Voices from Chicago Public Housing
Compiled and edited by Audrey Petty
Foreword by Alex Kotlowitz

In the gripping first-person accounts of *High Rise Stories*, former residents of Chicago's iconic public housing projects describe life in the now-demolished high rises. These stories of community, displacement, and poverty in the wake of gentrification give voice to those who have long been ignored, but whose hopes and struggles exist firmly at the heart of our national identity.

INVISIBLE HANDS
Voices from the Global Economy
Compiled and edited by Corinne Goria
Foreword by Kalpona Akter

In this oral history collection, electronics manufacturers in China, miners in Africa, garment workers in Mexico, and farmers in India—among many others—reveal the human rights crises occurring behind the scenes of the global economy.

PALESTINE SPEAKS
Voices from the Occupied Territories
Compiled and edited by Cate Malek and Mateo Hoke

The occupation of the West Bank and Gaza has been one of the world's most widely reported yet least understood human rights crises for over four decades. In this oral history collection, men and women from Palestine—including a fisherman, a settlement administrator, and a marathon runner—describe in their own words how their lives have been shaped by the historic crisis.

THE VOICE OF WITNESS READER
Ten Years of Amplifying Unheard Voices
Edited and with an Introduction by Dave Eggers

Founded by Dave Eggers, Lola Vollen, and Mimi Lok, Voice of Witness has amplified the stories of hundreds of people impacted by some of the most crucial human rights crises of our time, including men and women living under oppressive regimes in Burma, Colombia, Sudan, and Zimbabwe; public housing residents and undocumented workers in the United States; and exploited workers around the globe.

THE POWER OF THE STORY
The Voice of Witness Teacher's Guide to Oral History
Compiled and edited by Cliff Mayotte
Foreword by William and Richard Ayers

This comprehensive guide allows teachers and students to explore contemporary issues through oral history, and to develop the communication skills necessary for creating vital oral history projects in their own communities.

89665202R00251

Made in the USA
San Bernardino, CA
28 September 2018